LIE DETECTORS

LIE DETECTORS

A Social History

by Kerry Segrave

McFarland & Company, Inc., Publishers

Jefferson, North Carolina, and London

LIBRARY OF CONGRESS CATALOGUING-IN-PUBLICATION DATA

Segrave, Kerry, 1944–
    Lie detectors : a social history / by Kerry Segrave.
        p.   cm.
    Includes bibliographical references and index.

    ISBN 0-7864-1618-1 (softcover : 50# alkaline paper)

    1. Lie detectors and detection — United States — History.   I. Title.
    HV8078.S44   2004
    363.25'4 — dc22   2003021122

British Library cataloguing data are available

Manufactured in the United States of America

Cover illustration: ©2003 Getty Images

McFarland & Company, Inc., Publishers
  Box 611, Jefferson, North Carolina 28640
  www.mcfarlandpub.com

1/04

Contents

Introduction   1

1. Ancient Truth, the Years to 1869   3
2. The Black Box Takes Shape, 1870 to 1929   10
3. A Painless Third Degree, 1930 to 1941   21
4. The Polygraph Spreads in Cold War America, 1940s to 1950s   48
5. Government Use Increases, 1960s   73
6. The PSE: A New Truth Machine, 1970s   101
7. Business Embraces the Truth Machine, 1970s   111
8. The Government Blocks the Box, 1980s   134
9. The LD Survives; New Ideas Surface, 1990s to 2002   168
10. Conclusion   183

Notes   187
Bibliography   201
Index   213

Introduction

This book looks at the history of the lie detector, or polygraph as the machine is also known, from the experimental work of the late 1800s that led directly to the device's creation, until the present time. Initially the instrument was created and refined by academic people in mostly university settings, with some enthusiastic backing from a few early police agencies. In some cases law enforcement agencies embraced this new method of separating truth from lies because of its "scientific" background and because they were anxious to drop the various forms of physical harassment — the third degree — that had been used in the past and for which those agencies had come under increasing public scrutiny. Polygraphs held the hope for truth without torture or pain — truth through science.

As time passed the main proponents of the device became private companies in the security field, as the academics lost interest or moved on to other things. With courts always rejecting polygraph evidence, the focus switched to use of the device in both business and government. More and more it became apparent that although the device did not really work, it could exert powerful social control in certain situations. As a myth spread that the machine could coerce, intimidate and induce confessions, its infallibility aura was reinforced, which led to more confessions, and so forth.

More and more critics railed against the device and what it stood for. In time the polygraph industry had no supporters at all, except for its members and its users. Still, it took until 1988 before the use of the lie detector was curtailed, by a federal law, in most business applications. Even as that happened lie detector results were making slight inroads into the court system, despite the growing body of evidence that found the polygraph to be unacceptable in terms of accuracy.

Research for this book was carried out at the Vancouver Public Library, the University of British Columbia, and at Simon Fraser University using various databases, both in hard copy and online.

1

Ancient Truth, the Years to 1869

Everyone was accused ... and each man stuck to it that he knew nothing about it. We were ready to take red-hot iron in our hands — to walk through fire — to swear to the gods that we did not do the deed....
— Sophocles

Guilt carries fear always with it.... But take hold of his wrist and feel his pulse, there you will find guilt ... a sudden palpitation shall evidently confess he is the man....
— Daniel Defoe

Back in 1921, when the lie detector was making its appearance in American society, Raphael Demos, writing in *The Yale Review*, recalled the play about the man who started his day in the morning with the resolution to say nothing but the truth. By evening, as a result of putting his resolution into practice, he found himself deserted by all his friends and even his family. Demos believed that lies kept society from disintegrating; they were the oil that kept the wheels in working condition. In the sphere of industrial relations, Demos remarked, "Lying helps to smooth away the rough surface of motive and intention."[1]

Even if Demos was right, it has not deterred people from trying to separate the liar from the truth teller, Most of the methods used revolved around assessing the speaker's demeanor, or noting a physiological change in the person, or waiting for the intervention of a deity to reveal the true situation. At least these methods prevailed until early in the 1900s when the detection of deception was more and more given over to the deciphering of squiggly lines created by a machine.

Diogenes (412?–323 B.C.) belonged to the Cynic school of ancient

Greek philosophy, a sect that stressed stoic self-sufficiency and the rejection of luxury. According to legend he conducted his own famous search for an honest man by walking the streets of Athens in broad daylight while carrying a lighted lantern.[2]

Another famous search for truth came from the Bible. It was written there that when King Solomon had to decide which of two women was the true mother of a claimed infant, he based his decision on the observation of demeanor and emotion. When he threatened to cut the infant in half and divide it between the two women claiming the child, he decided in favor of the woman who was so upset over that possibility that she pleaded to let the other claimant have the infant. That other woman had —calmly agreed with Solomon's proposed division. Modern lie detection also relied on the reading of emotion, although in the opposite direction from Solomon. Overreaction meant truthfulness to King Solomon while it usually signaled deception to the lie detector.[3]

In one of the papyrus *Vedas* (oldest sacred books of Hinduism, started circa 1400 B.C.) written about 900 B.C. specific instructions were found for detecting poisoners by their demeanor. "A person who gives poison may be recognized. He does not answer questions, or they are evasive answers; he speaks nonsense, rubs the great toe along the ground, and shivers; his face is discolored; he rubs the roots of the hair with his fingers...." By the time of Erasistratus (300–250 B.C.), the well-known Greek physician and anatomist, very definite attempts to detect deception were found — attempts that appeared objective in nature and involved the assessing of physiological signs, that is, feeling the pulse. One such attempt concerned the love of Antiochus for his stepmother Stratonice and his efforts to conceal it from his father Seleucus I of Syria, surnamed Nicator. Sometime after the marriage, Antiochus began to lose weight and to languish with an unknown disease. Nicator called in Erasistratus, who discovered the truth by keeping tabs on Antiochus's pulse while he questioned the young man.[4]

From the time of Christ through the Middle Ages and beyond, accounts of the detection of deception were accounts of the ordeal, or torture. Mainly these accounts arose from superstition and religious faith. Water ordeals were mentioned in the *Code of Hamurabi* and in the ancient Hindu *Laws of Manu*. From Hincmar of Reims, 9th century, came the following, "Whoever, after the invocation of God, who is the Truth, seeks to hide the truth by a lie, cannot be submerged in the waters above which the voice of the Lord God has thundered; for the pure nature of the water recognizes as impure and therefore rejects as inconsistent with itself such human nature as has once been regenerated by the waters of baptism and is again infected by falsehood." During the witch trials of the 1600s in Europe and colonial America, a suspected witch was tied up and thrown into water. If she sank, she was considered innocent. However, if she floated, she was defined as a witch and executed. Again, it was the water accepting the pure and the truth teller and rejecting the impure and the liar.[5]

Boiling water was also used as a testing method world wide and used over a long period of time. Hincmar commended it as it combined the elements of water and fire — representing the deluge and the fiery doom of the future. A person tested had to plunge his hand or arm into boiling water, sometimes to retrieve a ring or something from the bottom of the pot. Sometimes the exposed arm was wrapped up for three days and then unwrapped to be inspected for damage. Those whose arms were not burned were declared innocent. Reportedly, the boiling water ordeal was used in modern Africa in the 1930s. Some calico cloth had been stolen from the supplies of an explorer. To find the thief, she allowed the natives to use a test previously outlawed along with local witchcraft. All 60 villagers, one by one, put an arm into a pot of cold water, then into a pot of boiling water up to the elbow. Apparently all took the test without a murmur of complaint, and all agreed it was a fair test. After the last person had finished the test the people were told to return to that spot the next day where the one who showed a blister or who had lost some skin would be revealed as the thief. On the following day only one person had any burn damage on his arm. He confessed to the theft. No other villager showed signs of a burn.[6]

Ordeals involving fire and hot irons were also plentiful. India's epic *Ramayana* told of Prince-God Rama's search for his wife Sita after her kidnapping. Rama found her and dispatched the villain but he then rejected Sita as soiled and dishonored. Sita's response was to have a pyre built. Walking into the flames, she called out to Agni, the god of fire to let the flames consume her if she had given any offense to her husband, but to protect her if she was chaste, as she claimed. Sita came out of the fire unharmed. Other Vedic and Hindu sources referred to the taking of fire, a hot iron, or a red-hot iron ball or spear head into the hand as a test of truthfulness.[7]

The red-hot iron ordeal was used by the hill tribes of Rasmahal in the north of Bengal where the accused was told to prove his innocence by applying his tongue to a red-hot iron nine times, unless he was burnt sooner. If he suffered burns he was put to death.

The *Avesta* of the ancient Iranians and legends relating to Zoroaster alluded to both fire ordeals and ordeals of boiling water. A medieval invocation connected with the red-hot iron trial went as follows, "If you are innocent of this charge ... you may confidently receive this iron in your hand and the Lord, the just judge, will free you." Sophocles work *Antigone* mentioned the practices of the Greeks. "Everyone was accused and no one was convicted, and each man stuck to it that he knew nothing about it. We were ready to take red-hot iron in our hands—to walk through fire—to swear by the gods that we did not do the deed and were not in the secret of whoever did it."[8]

The ordeal of the balance involved testing the veracity of the accused by placing him on one scale of a balance. It began in India where it was practiced as early as 600 B.C. A counterbalance was placed in the other scale of the device. Then, the accused stepped out of the scale and listened while a judge delivered an exhortation to the balance. When the judge was finished the accused got back on the scale. If he was found to be lighter than before, he was acquitted. Since the human body underwent a constant weight loss of about 12 grams per hour, a long exhortation by the judge could free the accused.[9]

Food ordeals also date back to Biblical times. When a rumor spread that Mary was pregnant, Joseph took an oath swearing he had never touched her. High priest Abiathar commanded him to drink water of the Lord's testing and then circle the altar seven times because "if a man at fault should drink and then circle the altar seven times, God will cause his sin to show in the man's face." Joseph drank, circled and passed. Then Mary drank, circled and "no fault was found in her." This test of "bitter waters" had been prescribed for cases of suspected adultery as far back as the book of Numbers in the Bible.[10]

The ancient Chinese made suspects chew dry rice and then spit it out. After a series of relevant questions were answered, grains of rice were placed in the suspects' mouths and the questions repeated. Then the rice was removed from the suspects' mouths. If it was dry, the suspects were declared to be liars. A variation of this test was used during the Inquisition wherein the suspect had to swallow a "trial slice" of bread and cheese; if it stuck in the suspect's throat or palate he was deceptive. Underlying such tests was the idea that lying produced reactions of fear and guilt which caused a decrease in the amount of saliva produced—dry mouth—and made swallowing difficult. Even at this early time it was often the psychological effect of the test that was more important than the actual working of the test. That is, if an accused believed the test was infallible and would brand him as a liar then it did. It was a concept that applied also to the modern lie detector. In Boccaccio's *Decameron* (circa 1351), Bruno and Buffalmacco stole Calandrino's pig and convinced the gullible owner they knew a variation of the trial by bread and cheese. On the following day they gathered together all possible suspects and were about to give them each a pill. Bruno told them, "What you have to realize straight away is that whoever's taken the pig will be unable to swallow his pill — he'll find that it tastes more bitter than gall and he'll spit it out. So maybe it would be better, before the culprit is shown up in the presence of so many people, if he goes and makes his confession to the priest, and I'll stay my hand." Just as with the modern lie detector, the first order of business was to try and establish a belief in the infallibility of the process to come.[11]

In the Chinese donkey tail test, the inquisitors constructed a replica of a donkey with a large frayed rope for the tail. The tail was saturated with powdered carbon and the entire replica placed inside a semi-dark cave. Suspects were sent alone into the cave to grab the donkey's tail. They were told that if they had been untruthful, the donkey would bray when they grabbed the tail, but if they had been truthful the animal would make no sound. Hands of suspects were checked when they emerged from the cave. Those with no carbon on their hands were declared to be liars. A variation of this test was used by Arabs, who put grease on the donkey's tail.[12]

Suspects in the fulcrum test were tied prone on a wooden beam perfectly balanced on a pyramid-shaped stone in several feet of water. When lying, so the theory went, blood tended to pool in the head. Therefore, if suspects lied while answering a series of questions, the beam tipped downward and plunged their heads under water.[13]

Many of the ordeals in use during the Spanish Inquisition, and throughout the Dark Ages by Europeans, were borrowed from India and China and adapted to suit local purposes. By around 1150 A.D. the Roman Catholic clergy had made full use of the practice of rice chewing. Consecrated rice was used as a test of veracity.

During the Middle Ages, it was related that a nobleman suspected his wife of infidelity and told his suspicions to one of his advisors, who agreed to run a test to determine the facts. At dinner the advisor sat next to the wife and casually laid his hand upon her wrist while conversing with her. He mentioned the name of another nobleman, suspected of being her lover, whereupon her pulse quickened. It was said that a confession was soon elicited. Galileo (1581) received credit for being the first to invent an objective way to count the human pulse and it was soon put to use in the quest to detect deception.[14]

By the 12th century, faith in the ordeal was starting to be undermined to some extent by the pious. God could intervene, it was felt, but, law professor Richard Underwood wrote, "It was the guaranteed nature of the result which was in question. It was increasingly viewed as impious to believe that a constructed human test — the ordeal —could 'force' God to show his hand. That was testing God." Professional people of the day like Peter the Chanter (the Cantor) expressed a scientific skepticism similar to that shown by modern day critics of the lie detector. He felt one of the worst things about ordeals was that they often "condemned the innocent and vindicated the guilty," since there was only a random correlation between innocence or guilt and the outcome of the ordeal. That was because the outcome depended on factors irrelevant to culpability — "the callousedness of the hand picking up the iron, the heat of the iron when grasped, and so on." Eventually a succession of Popes weighed in against the ordeal — Alexander II, Alexander III, Innocent III, Gregory IX, and Gregory XI.[15]

Also, it was suggested that many forms of the ordeal could have been fixed. Hands and arms could be coated with protective substances for the boiling water and hot iron ordeals, for example. A red-hot iron might have been a cold iron painted red. In one test, in which a blindfolded suspect was required to walk over red-hot ploughshares, the trick was to rehearse the suspect as to the positioning of the ploughshares, so they could be safely negotiated. However, if the inquisitor desired a guilty result all he had to do was to move the ploughshares so that the accused was likely to hit one. Just as the modern day operator of the lie detector could influence results, so could his counterpart of an earlier era.

For Richard Underwood, the trial by ordeal (and its near relative trial by combat, in which the disputing parties battled it out with the triumphant person winning the case) may have served a purpose even if it was not reliable in distinguishing lies from truths. "Frequently the primitive mind resorted to an ordeal not so much on the medieval theory that a deity would reveal the culprit as in the hope that the ordeal, however unjust would end a feud that might otherwise embroil the tribe for generations."[16]

Writing in 1730, celebrated author Daniel Defoe declared "Guilt carries Fear always with it; there is a Tremor in the Blood of a Thief ... but take hold of his Wrist and feel his Pulse, there you will find Guilt; ... a fluttering Heart, an unequal Pulse, a sudden Palpitation shall evidently confess he is the Man, in spite of a bold Countenance or a false Tongue."[17]

Sentiments such as those expressed by Defoe have continued to be held right up to the present time. Liars gave themselves away through aspects of their demeanor or behavior, such as averting their eyes, or blushing, or hesitating. Also, they gave themselves away through physiological changes in their breathing, pulse rate, and so on. While those latter signs were not necessarily visible to the eye, they were definitely there, or so it was believed. While a few attempts were made in olden times to use these signs to detect deception, science was just not up to the task. However, beginning near the end of the 1890s, a movement began to use an increasingly sophisticated body of scientific knowledge in the search for truth.

2

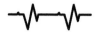

The Black Box Takes Shape, 1870 to 1929

No matter how accomplished at ordinary deception a man may be, he cannot hope to deceive Marston's apparatus....
— Boston Sunday Advertiser, 1921

[The lie detector] is almost infallible in its detection of whether or not a person is guilty of a crime.
— George K. Home, Los Angeles chief of detectives, 1924

During the years between 1870 and 1890, both Francis Galton and Wilhelm Wundt were very active in the development of "association" tests and made brief references to the possibility of their use in detecting emotions connected with deceit. This method enjoyed a brief period of attention in the early part of the 1900s. Anton Rose, writing in a 1914 issue of *Scientific American*, noted the difficulty in judging truth from falsehood but went on to state that "extraordinary and successful means for its detection" had been developed from studies in experimental psychology." The principal psychological factors employed in this method are the character and rapidity of the mental process known as association of ideas;" that is, word association. In criminal jurisprudence, explained Rose, a word was uttered and the suspect was required to say, instantly, what the word suggested to him. That process was repeated with a great number of words introduced in an apparently casual manner, some of which had a direct bearing on the crime in question. "If the suspect is really guilty he is pretty sure to betray himself unconsciously," declared Rose. "Even if he is cautious enough to modify the first response that occurs to him, he betrays himself by the slight delay thus caused, for the abnormally long interval between question and answer...."[1]

Prescott Leckey, a Columbia University psychology instructor, conducted a word association experiment in lie detection in front of 500 students in 1930 and apparently in front of the press. A reporter described the situation by saying, "It was a glorified third degree system, with stopwatches and scientific charts substituted for the rubber hose and fist of another day." Two students took part in the experiment, the hypothetical theft of money. Each student got a sealed envelope containing a set of instructions. One told the recipient to go and sit in front of a statue near the library. The other student was given directions to go and steal some money. Directions made the statue's nose a reference point several times. Then both subjects were recalled and given a word association test that consisted of 30 words—15 chosen at random and 15 related to the second note about stealing. Both students took about 1.5 seconds on average to respond to the neutral words by saying the first thing that came into their heads. While the first student maintained that average for the second group of 15 words, the other student took an average of over two seconds to respond to the second group. When the word "nose" was presented the first subject was expected to say something like "face" or "mouth." The second student was expected to say "statue" because of the recent association between the two which had just been established for him. However, explained Leckey, subconsciously the guilty student realized that would incriminate him and he looked for another word. "By this time difference, which, although slight, can be accurately measured by an electric stopwatch, we can determine whether or not a man has any knowledge of the details of a crime."[2]

A few years later Professor H. R. Crosland announced that he had devised a word association test that, like the others, did not reveal a lie, but instead showed a "very strong consciousness of guilt." Normal reaction time here was said to be 2.5 seconds. Anything longer was viewed as an indication that the subject was making a word selection, instead of saying the first thing that came to mind, or that there was an "emotional disturbance." Also, if a suspect made "strange or far-fetched" word associations, they were noted and held against the examinee. Reporter Henry Robinson stated that law courts were "inhospitable" to word association tests being admitted as evidence. Nevertheless, he presented it in his account as an accurate method of detecting deception.[3]

A. Mosso, an Italian physiologist of the era 1870s to 1890s, did studies in the field of emotions. Mosso was encouraged in those experiments by Italian criminologist Cesare Lombroso, his tutor and contemporary.

Especially relevant to deception were his studies of fear and its influence on the heart and respiration. Fear was considered to be an essential element of deception, that is, the fear of being detected. From records of pulsations, Mosso said he could distinguish the one who was afraid from the one who was tranquil. That is, from records presented to him for analysis.[4]

Lombroso was active in the period 1870s–1910s and became the first person to use a scientific instrument as an aid in detecting lies. In 1895 he claimed success by taking suspects' blood pressure while they were being questioned. He also claimed to have found a positive correlation, working with criminal suspects, between pulse rate and attempts to deceive on cross-examination. Several times he reportedly assisted the police in identifying criminal suspects through the use of blood pressure monitoring. In an 1895 book he discussed the application of a sphygmograph to the interrogation of criminals—an instrument for recording the rapidity, strength and uniformity of the arterial pulse. Lombroso was also convinced he could recognize a criminal by the shape of his skull.[5]

Probably the earliest suggestions for the application of psychogalvanic reactions to forensic problems came from B. Sticker in 1897. The galvanometer was named for the Italian physiologist Galvani. Electrodes were attached to the fingers and then a small electric current was passed through. Changes in the electrical conductivity of the skin due to sweating were measured and attributed to lying. Sticker was convinced that a person who was emotionally aroused by a picture, word, and so on, would react with a definite increase of the current while a person who was unmoved would have no skin excitation. One of the first to use word association tests in conjunction with a galvanometer (in contrast to the ones mentioned earlier, which involved no mechanical devices except a stopwatch) was S. Veraguth, around 1907. At the same time Hugo Munsterberg (who had been invited by William James to Harvard University to set up a psychology laboratory) was supporting the use of such tests in criminal cases.[6]

Munsterberg had many interests, one of which was the detection of deception. Also in the period from 1907–1908, Swiss psychiatrist C. G. Jung concluded it was possible to detect attempts at lying or evasion with the help of a psychogalvanometer. Jung also touted word association tests around 1900. Munsterberg also proposed that courts use the blood pressure test for gauging deception. Popular attention was first called to the desirability of utilizing scientific procedures and devices for the purpose of lie detection by Munsterberg in 1907 and 1908 when he wrote a series of magazine articles on the subject. He briefly described some experiments on word associations, on testimony and on emotional disturbances in breathing, circulation and involuntary movements. Even the galvanometer was mentioned in that connection.[7]

The first machine that was actually called a "polygraph" was invented by James Mackenzie, a famous London, England, heart specialist. He first described the device in an article "The ink polygraph," which appeared in the June 13, 1908, issue of the *British Medical Journal*. First exhibited at a meeting of the Medical Section of the British Medical Association in Toronto in 1906, Dr. Mackenzie described it as "a method of recording the movements of the circulation by means of an ink polygraph." This instrument had nothing to do with deception detection; Mackenzie developed it for use in medical examinations. The word meant "many graphs" and referred to any device that recorded two or more processes at the same time. Over the years, the polygraph was, and still is, used extensively in non-deception research work, mostly in academic settings. It was used, for example, with non verbal populations such as infants. As time passed, the instrument became much more sophisticated; by the early 1970s, it contained as many as 16 channels. "Polygraph" became the term of choice adopted by the deception detection industry for its instrument. It always fought hard, but unsuccessfully, to persuade the general media to not use the term "lie detector" (LD) but the preferred "polygraph." The industry argued accurately that the popular term of choice, lie detector, was a misnomer since the unit merely recorded changes in physiological processes; an operator decided if deception was involved. However, none of this had much effect on the media or the general public who continued to say "lie detector" more than they said "polygraph."[8]

Munsterberg also touted the use of word association tests in deception detection. He advocated, in 1908, the forensic application of the technique for diagnosing guilt. At that time, and for some years to come, word association tests were the only "scientific" methods of detecting guilt. Despite that, Munsterberg was definitely in a small minority of people who rated it highly. He was of the opinion that this new method "should be substituted for that crude and inhuman method of 'working on' suspected criminals, known as the 'third degree.'"[9]

Albert Schneider, dean of North Pacific College, Portland, Oregon, developed a word association test in 1924 to be used in conjunction with a galvanometer, or a "Capillary Electrometer," as he called his version of the device. No record of "normal" was made, as done with the lie detector, because "such standard is unnecessary...," said an account. When the examiner uttered a word, the subject was asked to say the first word that came to mind. No questions were asked. When a subject lied, said Schneider, "At the exact fraction of a second in which the subject thus checks his mind, looking for a word which shall not connect him with a crime, the current running to the capillary electrometer is checked, the rising column of mercury stops its climb, and we know that we have found in the man what the psychiatrists call a 'complex.'" At that stage, the operator checked back on the complex, knowing the suspect was concealing something and "further adroit questioning virtually always brings out the truth." Word association tests had only limited use through the early 1920s. Thereafter, they were mentioned very infrequently for a decade or so before apparently disappearing completely. The lie detector had won out.[10]

Experimental work that directly led to the development of the modern lie detector began in Graz, Austria with the work of psychologist Vittorio Benussi in 1914. He conceived of the use of a measure of respiration as an index of lying — the ratio of the duration of inspiration to the duration of expiration, the so-called I/E ratio, or "Benussi ratio," which had been suggested eight years earlier by the German psychologist, Storring. In Benussi's experiment, the subject was instructed to lie about the contents of a card, which contained a pattern of letters or numbers. A group of judges attempted to assess the credibility of responses by observation of subjects. Those judges reached 50 percent accuracy (the chance level) while Benussi's accuracy, using the pneumograph, which featured a coil around the examinee's chest to record respiration, was reported to be close to 100 percent for over 100 instances. Benussi found the ratio of inspiration to expiration was generally greater before truth telling than that before lying.[11]

While Anton Rose praised the word association test in his 1914 *Scientific American* article, he was even more enthusiastic about Benussi's work, which he called "simpler" and "more objective" than word association. Rose declared the Benussi test was "based on the intimate relation which has been proved to exist between mental processes and the pulse and respiration." It was a relationship that Benussi was said to have discovered for lying. Cards imprinted with various letters, figures and diagrams were distributed among a class of students. Each was required to give a truthful description of the card given to him, unless it had a red star in which case the recipient was required to describe it incorrectly. In either case he was watched by fellow students who tried to guess from his manner whether he was lying or telling the truth. Those observers made many mistakes, observed Rose, but "Respiratory tests, however, gave unerring and unequivocal results. The time occupied in inspiration and in expiration was measured immediately before and after each card test, and it was found that the utterance of a false statement always increased, and the utterance of a true statement diminished, the quotient obtained by dividing the time of inspiration by the time of expiration." Even if a clever liar tried to escape detection by breathing irregularly, said Rose, he would likely fail in the attempt as Benussi had investigated such cases and found that voluntary changes in respiration did not alter the results. To Rose, the importance of Benussi's discovery was obvious, "for it furnishes a certain and objective criterion between truth and falsehood."[12]

A few years later, researcher Harold Burtt further developed Benussi's method. While he did considerable experimental work on respiratory patterns in deception, he also found that systolic blood pressure had a greater diagnostic value than breathing. In one series of experiments involving simulated crimes, Burtt declared the detection of a lie was accurate 91 percent of the time when blood pressure was the criterion, but only 73 percent of the time when respiration was the criterion.[13]

A major figure in the development of the lie detector was American psychologist William Moulton Marston (1893–1947). Although he is not well-known today, he left behind two items of American popular culture. He was one of several people who could be given credit for inventing the infamous lie detector. In 1941, Marston created another icon in the search for truth and justice, the female superhero comic book character, Wonder Woman.[14]

Marston received an AB degree in 1915 from Harvard College. Then he went to Harvard Law School where he received an LL D degree in 1918, before returning to Harvard University for his Ph D, which he received in 1921. As a student of Munsterberg, Marston became interested in deception detection and began research in that area in 1913 in the psychological laboratory at Harvard. After experimental work, he became convinced that it was impossible for a normal person to lie without effort. He suggested using changes in the systolic blood pressure as the best physiological measure to detect lying and proposed using the sphygmomanometer— the medical doctor's familiar blood pressure apparatus—to chart such changes. In his 1917 experimental work Marston, using an increase in systolic blood pressure as his sole criterion, claimed he was accurate in detecting lies in 103 out of 107 instances. Again, a group of judges who relied only upon observation did no better than chance.[15]

During World War I, the National Research Council asked Marston and several other psychologists to investigate the various kinds of known deception tests and report on their possible usefulness in counterespionage work. War ended before the government could make any use of the report. Other tests evaluated included the psychogalvanometer and the word association methods. In an article in the popular media authored by Marston in 1938 the psychologist recalled that exercise and declared, in self-serving fashion, that all deception tests "were rejected except the Marston test," which he said "proved 97 percent reliable." Even the three percent error rate — due to human fallibility in administering the test — could be eliminated by retesting the subject anytime any doubt about the original judgment existed, he said.[16]

More publicity came Marston's way in May, 1921, when the *Boston Sunday Advertiser* reported on his accomplishments to that time. "William Moulton Marston, Boston lawyer, scientist and inventor of the psychological lie-detector, which he put forward in 1913, and has since greatly improved, has already sprinkled the way of the transgressor with thorns from Massachusetts to California." In keeping with the uncritical acceptance of the machine that was common in this period, the account added that "No matter how accomplished at ordinary deception a man may be, he cannot hope to deceive Marston's apparatus any more than a woman can humbug a weighing machine by lacing tightly and dressing in black." Some 20 years later Marston was still claiming credit for the invention of the device. Writing in the *Harvard Class of 1915 25th Anniversary Report,* Marston told his fellow students that he "had the luck to discover the so-called Deception Test, better known as the Lie Detector while researching the physical symptoms of deception." His entry in the *Encyclopedia of American Biography* (probably self-written, although in the third person) bragged in 1937, "But the remarkable thing is that he discovered his 'Lie Detector' while still an undergraduate, while all the big psychologists of the world had been trying to get a practical test for deception for the last fifty years."[17]

During the 1920s Marston devoted himself to developing his academic career. He conducted experimental work on the psychophysiology of emotion, wrote philosophical articles on such topics as consciousness, materialism and vitalism and taught psychology at various universities. In the 1930s he became a consulting psychologist, wrote articles on popular psychology for magazines such as *Ladies Home Journal* and *Esquire* and gave radio talks on psychology. Throughout his career he was a tireless self-promoter, prone to exaggeration and drifting back and forth between academic and popular psychology and between the serious and the silly. While he used the lie detector in the 1920s and 1930s, he did little or no research on the device with the torch for that task passing, about 1921, to John Larson. Mostly the uses Marston made of the lie detector were theatrical and in non deception situations. None of this would have done much to enhance the device as a truth verifier, but it did capture media interest, kept the machine in the public mind and perhaps helped in getting the device the public acceptance it did achieve in the 1920s and 1930s.

One example of Marston's theatricality occurred in 1928 when he used his LD apparatus to investigate the emotional responses of "blondes, brunettes and red heads." In a public demonstration at the Embassy Theatre in New York, he connected chorus girls from Broadway shows such as *Show Boat*, *Rio Rita* and *Rosalie* to his LD and then showed them emotional clips from films such as *Love* and *Flesh and the Devil*. After Marston studied the LD charts he declared his experiment "proved" brunettes enjoyed the thrill of pursuit, while blondes preferred the more passive enjoyment of being kissed. A decade later, Marston was still promoting his theory of the relationship between personality and hair color.[18]

Marston believed the act of deception was necessarily accompanied by specific bodily changes that could be accurately charted by his device. Belief in a specific "lie response" fell into disfavor fairly quickly, but the belief that the act of lying resulted in measurable bodily changes persisted. One of his failures established a legal precedent that would stand for half a century. He was called in to test a murder suspect who claimed innocence. The psychologist's reading on the test results led him to conclude the suspect was non deceptive in regard to the crime. However, in a celebrated case, *United States v Frye* (1923) a federal court refused to admit the LD results as evidence on the ground that the systolic blood pressure deception test lacked "general acceptance in the particular field in which it belongs." That is, it had no acceptance as a valid, reliable test among the scientific community of psychologists and physiologists. In the article he wrote in 1938, and in which he discussed the beginnings of the LD, Marston did not mention *Frye* at all, preferring to state that in 1924 the LD test "was first admitted in court in Indiana and is now admissible in 5 States." Occasionally a lower court did admit LD results but every time such a case was appealed, the higher court denied the admissibility of the LD results, citing *Frye*. It remained that way into the 1970s. The *Frye* decision took on even greater significance as it inadvertently established the legal criteria for the admissibility of all scientific evidence. In 1979 the Kansas Supreme Court declared, "The *Frye* test has been accepted as the standard in practically all of the courts of this country which have considered the question of the admissibility of new scientific evidence."[19]

Early in 1921 Dr. John A. Larson was a young medical student in the employ of August Vollmer, chief of the Berkeley, California Police Department. He read an article on deception tests by Marston in the spring of that year and then did some pioneer work in blood pressure testing. He modified the Erlanger sphygmomanometer so that heart activity could be recorded graphically on drums. Reportedly Larson used his device with success on hundreds of criminal suspects and with the enthusiastic support of Vollmer. In one celebrated case, he utilized the device to discover the source of losses in a girls' dormitory at the University of California. Larson assembled a polygraph apparatus in portable form so it could be taken into the field. Also he published more articles on the subject than any other researcher and assumed what was described as a "commanding position" in the field. Later Larson was joined on that police force by Leonarde Keeler (1903–1949). Soon thereafter both moved to Chicago with Larson becoming Assistant State Criminologist of Illinois while Keeler became part of Northwestern University in Evanston. The final evolution in the LD was the Keeler Polygraph, which was developed by Keeler beginning in 1926 as an improvement and enhancement of Larson's device. Keeler had known Vollmer since he was a child, and under his direction became something of an amateur criminologist. As he closely followed early work on the LD, he came to construct variations of the machine himself. He first made practical use of an LD in 1923 in Los Angeles where he acted as an assistant to Vollmer, who was then reorganizing the Los Angeles Police Department. Keeler's first case was larceny in a sorority house where money had been stolen on a number of occasions. As a result, a word association test was given to the residents. To the stimulus word "money" one female replied "bills." (The money stolen had been bills.) Reportedly, that was enough to make her the prime suspect. She was expelled from the sorority and was on the point of being expelled from the university when her parents appealed to the LAPD. Vollmer sent Keeler to give LD tests to all the sorority house residents. Supposedly he found the guilty female (not the original prime suspect, who had been the most unpopular woman in the sorority).[20]

Current Opinion ran a piece in 1924 that was full of uncritical praise for Larson's instrument. So successful was the device that it was being used in several cities. More than 2,500 tests had been made to that point and "Of those whom the instrument declared to be lying, approximately eighty-five percent have confirmed the findings by later confessions, either before or after conviction by juries," reported the account. The principle of the machine, it added, was based on the "fact" that "under the excitement of questioning, heartbeats and breathing cannot be controlled."[21]

In a 1925 article, Larson talked at length about the brutal police methods used to extract confessions at the time he was writing. Although he felt the public was aware of the existence of brutal methods employed in criminal investigations, "in some of our large cities especially such a condition is ignored and openly tolerated. With the improper type of administrative heads and officials it is difficult to prove the existence of the methods of beating prisoners." One of the things that made LDs attractive was the fact that they could replace existing brutal police methods—the third degree — which were often brought to the public's attention in the media in the first couple of decades of the 1900s. Such bad publicity obviously put a great deal of pressure on police departments. Factors favoring the polygraph were that it produced a "painless" third degree, and it had a "scientific" basis.[22]

According to Larson, George K. Home, chief of detectives in Los Angeles, wrote him a letter in 1924 to say he had been using the LD for the previous two months and "it is almost infallible in its detection of whether or not a person is guilty of a crime." One of the cases he cited concerned a man arrested for a bank holdup. An LD test given to this man showed nothing. After the officers "got the facts," the suspect took a second polygraph test, which determined he lied. Duluth, Minnesota, police chief Warren E. Pugh had been using the device since 1922. Pugh was more cautious in his assessment, believing it was a mistake to attempt to introduce LD records into courts. "It cannot prove guilt or innocence," explained Pugh. "Its function, from the police standpoint, is to aid detectives in determining whether or not they are working the right 'leads,' and in clearing innocent suspects." Larson concluded that a survey of the data accumulated to that point indicated that deception detection techniques "should be an indispensable part of all investigations." He believed that no person should ever be executed solely on the strength of a polygraph test although, on the other hand, he felt a man could safely be saved from the gallows on the strength of a test. "Every individual under suspicion in a criminal investigation could profitably be tested," he declared.[23]

Not everyone hailed the polygraph. In 1925 researcher Carney Landis used the blood pressure deception test but achieved an accuracy rate of 55 percent (not significantly different from the chance level). Later that same year Landis, paired with researcher L. E. Wiley, conducted an experiment on students at the University of Minnesota to test the idea that lying could be detected by observation of the blood pressure and the ratio of breathing in to breathing out. They achieved only 40 percent accuracy by means of blood pressure and pulse rate and 55 percent using the I/E ratio while an examiner assessing by observation only was 56 percent accurate. As a result of their findings Landis and Wiley concluded that "the method is unreliable."[24]

Keeler had gained first-hand experience as a high school student with the polygraph interrogations of Larson in the Berkeley Police Department and subsequently enlarged on the Larson device by adding a respiration-checking apparatus to the basic blood pressure checking instrument. Later still, he added a device to the unit for measuring changes in the electrical resistance of the skin (a galvanometer component). Although Keeler's machine was not the first polygraph to be devised, it was the first to be designed and marketed specifically for police use. For the following couple of decades it became the relatively standard instrument, often referred to as the Keeler Polygraph. The high cost of this apparatus reportedly thwarted further research in lie detection by academic psychologists.[25]

By the end of the 1920s the modern polygraph had been developed. Standard medical devices had been adopted and modified to suit. It would change very little over the coming decades. Some attention had been focused on the LD by the general media but not a significant amount. Its use was limited to a small number of police departments but it began to appear more often as its notoriety grew. Developed by academic researchers, it soon left their hands as first law enforcement, and later private industry, took control of the box. For law enforcement, the LD held hope that truths could be uncovered scientifically and painlessly, allowing them to abandon more brutal methods.

3

-\/\-\/\-

A Painless Third Degree, 1930 to 1941

Guilty by lie detector.
                                        — New York Times, 1930

Several Chicago banking institutions will not employ an applicant for a position unless he is tested on the lie-detector.
                                        — Fred Inbau, 1935

The lie detector is here to stay. It is slowly but surely worming its way into the cancerous and parasitical habits of deception which have been gnawing insidiously at the vitals of human society for untold centuries.
                                        — William Marston, 1938

It proved the lie detector not only could detect, as it does consistently in police work, but could reform.
                                        — J. P. McEvoy, 1941

In a 1932 book, *Lying and Its Detection*, John Larson devoted an entire chapter to the police method of interrogation, the third degree, with its harassing, browbeating, deprivation of sleep, food and lights, use of sweat boxes, and so on. These methods were all too common in America through the 1900s up to the time Larson was writing. He felt that as long as "ignorant officials" were employed in the district attorney's office or by the police, there would be cases in which a false confession was obtained by brutal methods. Again, he returned to the theme that while investigations of brutality were sometimes undertaken — usually in response to a public outcry — he remained convinced that such probes were never successful and that "it is difficult or impossible to secure sufficient evidence to warrant a conviction." Also, Larson devoted two chapters to human errors in

21

the justice system and outlined the great difficulty people had in sorting out lies from truth. "If the real facts could be ascertained, a survey of all the penitentiaries would doubtless reveal a varying number of inmates wrongly convicted and innocent of the charge for which they are serving time," he argued. His review of the current administration of justice led him to conclude that "the present judicial methods are inadequate in the determination of the innocence or guilt of the suspect...." It was sentiment and worries such as these that motivated some police agencies to turn to the LD.[1]

An example of a blending of the LD concept with the old third degree methodology could be seen in a couple of 1930s cases where the police used sham polygraphs. In 1931 Philadelphia police picked up a youth, 16-year-old Charles Donahue, as a robbery suspect. Back at the station they hooked him up to what they called a lie detector (it was just a black box with some old radio parts attached). Each time the police thought the boy's answer to a question was wrong they told him the machine indicated he had lied. Then pepper seeds were put on his tongue, causing him to complain that they burned. He was told those "pills" always "burn the tongue of a liar." Before long, Donahue broke down, implicating himself and four others in robberies during a six-month period.[2]

New York City police tried out a sham LD on two boys, aged nine and 12, in 1937 after the boys were unable to satisfactorily explain how they got a $10 bill. This LD consisted of a towel, some string and an alarm clock. With a towel wrapped around their arms and connected with string to an alarm clock the boys changed their story from one where they said they had earned the money doing errands after school and then changed it to one big bill to the "truth;" one boy found it hidden in the ice-box of his home. Initially the boys had drawn attention when they hailed a cab and told the driver to taken them to Broadway and to stop in front of a "G-man movie." Realizing the youth of his passengers, and the large bill they carried, the cabbie called a cop over to his vehicle.[3]

Gus Winkler, reportedly a lieutenant to mobster Al Capone, submitted to an LD test at Northwestern University in an effort to convince Nebraska police that he did not participate in a $2.5 million bank robbery in Lincoln. Max Towle, a county attorney in Nebraska, returned to Lincoln from Chicago and reported the tests were given under the supervision of Professor Leonarde Keeler. Towle declared the results of the tests indicated Winkler was not present in Nebraska at the time of the Lincoln bank robbery.[4]

Early in 1933 Leonarde Keeler, then 29 years old, was presented with the medal awarded annually by the Chicago Junior Association of

Commerce to the man between 21 and 35 who had made the "most outstanding civic contribution to Chicago" in the previous year. He won because of his aid in "solving" 87 criminal cases in Chicago and nearby cities. Keeler was credited with getting 54 direct confessions and eight others following trial, from 627 tested crime suspects. Like Marston, Keeler was a tireless promoter of the polygraph, although he limited that promotion to deception detection. That constant promotion went a long way in explaining why usage of the LD was highest among police agencies in Chicago, Illinois and the Midwest in general.[5]

David Roy was held for questioning in Fairchild, Maine in 1935 in connection with the murder of a 12-year-old girl. He was given an LD test by Professor Edward J. Colgan of Colby College. Those test results, declared county attorney E. Clayton Eames, "virtually cleared him of suspicion." In the same year a tavern was burglarized in Monroe, Wisconsin. Authorities gave bloodhounds the scent from a key. Quickly they led police to a suspect. Then District Attorney John D. Germann Jr. took the suspect to Chicago where he was subjected to an LD test by Keeler. Said Germann, "The lie detector said he was innocent. He was released." According to the headline of the press account, the "Lie detector test proves bloodhounds are liars."[6]

During the 1930s Keeler and his polygraph had some competition from the Reverend Walter G. Summers, head of the Department of Psychology of the Fordham University Graduate School. Summers touted his own invention, a variation of the psychogalvanometer, which measured electrical resistance of the skin only. It did not monitor blood pressure and respiration (breathing and pulse) the way Keeler's unit did. His device was used officially in New York State for the first time in 1937 when Summers personally tested a murder suspect. However, police officials and District Attorney Charles P. Sullivan all denied comment on that particular case. Nevertheless, Summers told newsmen that his LD had been used the previous year on several occasions by the Rhode Island State police "with good results." And he said the machine had been used successfully on students at Fordham. He thought it was doubtful that LD test results could ever be used in court as evidence, but added that he believed in the psychogalvanometer as a means of establishing both probability of guilt (which might lead to a confession) and certainty of innocence.[7]

At a 1937 meeting of the Eastern branch of the American Psychological Association, Summers described cases in which his device had been used. "In all instances there was complete success," he boasted. "Results were confirmed by confession, judicial procedure or subsequent investigation."[8]

One of the agencies that used the LD intensively was the Wichita, Kansas, Police Department. Early in 1933 the Wichita police purchased a Keeler Polygraph from the professor. During the year 1936, reported Thomas Jaycox, the agency's LD operator, a total of 1,262 suspected persons were sent to the "Polygraph Room" at police headquarters. Of that total, 339 were found to be lying, and of that number, 151 made full confessions of their guilt. On the other hand, 919 people were found to be telling the truth and were "immediately released" from custody. Truthseekers, thought Jaycox, devised ways of ascertaining lies. "They learned that attempted deception is usually accompanied by certain visible physiological changes such as pulsations in the throat, blinking, eye squinting, apparent dryness of the mouth and lips, and many other manifestations." The agency's polygraph room was said to operate "continuously during each working day." Suspects in all types of crimes were examined as were "vagrants who are picked up and held overnight." Over those three years, 1933–1936, the Wichita Police Department, said Police Chief O. W. Wilson, had obtained about 20 confessions per month that would not have been secured without the use of the LD. Statistics were said to show that about 60 percent of those caught lying by the instrument actually confessed their guilt. Transients, or "floaters" were examined on the polygraph to determine whether they were guilty of an offense for which they might be wanted by the police.[9]

Jaycox was back a couple years later with more statistics. The polygraph that his Wichita Police Department used recorded blood pressure and respiration simultaneously. Although Keeler had added a unit that measured electrical resistance of the skin to his polygraph before this time, it seemed to be present on some units but absent on others. Perhaps it was an optional feature at that time. By about the 1950s, though, it was a standard part of all LDs. For the years 1936, 1937 and 1938 the Wichita Police Department subjected some 4,000 people to polygraph tests, over 1,300 per year. Jaycox reported that 3,026 of that total were able to produce "clear" polygraph records—those in which no deception was displayed. Apparently many of these exams were not given in connection with a specific crime but were fishing expeditions as Jaycox reported that 1,690 examinees "were transients or vagrants picked up in the railroad yards or found loitering about the city streets." A total of 974 LD tests produced records indicating deception. From that number police were able to secure 537 full confessions to the crime under investigation. Thus there were still 437 to be disposed of. Of that number, 287 were released because complainants refused to prosecute or because sufficient evidence to prove guilt was not obtainable. Police took the remaining 150 through the courts with 112 convicted, 34 acquitted, and four cases still pending. By Jaycox's calculations, 55.1 percent of those whose LD record indicated deception confessed their crime; 74.7 percent of those whose records indicated deception, but who did not confess, were successfully prosecuted in court. In conclusion Jaycox stated that "it is safe to assume that the lie detector, in police science, will average a high score in precision and accuracy." It was an assumption that was true, he thought, only where a skilled and well-trained operator was conducting the tests. "The instrument in the hands of a novice," he warned, "would be much like calling in a truck driver to diagnose some physical ailment. The recipient of his diagnosis would suffer."[10]

Unwilling to submit to LD tests in 1938 for District Attorney Walter A. Ferris in his investigation of Port Chester, New York gambling, that village's three detectives were demoted to patrol duty by the police committee of the Village Board. Ferris wanted to give tests to check the truthfulness of the detectives' statements that they knew nothing about "notorious bookmaking" taking place in town. One of the three officers, Michael Brennan, said, "We never heard of detectives being asked before to take lie detector tests. We waived immunity and testified before the grand jury and it was an insult for Mr. Ferris to ask us to take the test." Adding to the insult was the fact that the LD machine had recently been given to Ferris by the Westchester County Police Benevolent Association, of which the three were members.[11]

Toledo, Ohio Chief of Police, R. E. Allen presented his own statistics in 1939, based on a polygraph purchased from Keeler. In 172 cases, a total of 245 subjects were given LD tests. In 55 cases, the exams were said to have aided in solution. Results from those tests indicated deception 112 times (Seven of those subjects were proved guilty even though no confessions were obtained.) and no deception 73 times (36 of those were proved innocent). Fifteen subjects confessed upon being confronted by their polygraph results; of eight who refused to take the test, seven were proved guilty. The Keeler Polygraph "is an asset equivalent to an increase in personnel and has paid for itself several times over," declared Allen. "In a great many cases, it has quickly broken down the alibis of hardened criminals."[12]

Keeler discussed the spread of the polygraph and its use by police agencies in a 1940 article he wrote. He noted that his Keeler Polygraph was made up of three separate units and that each recorded a physiological process: a) breathing, b) pulse rate and blood pressure, c) electrical changes in the apparent resistance of the skin. Emphatically he still refused to call his device a lie detector and described it as an "aid" in the operator's analysis of the subject's truthfulness. Most important part of the process, he emphasized, was the interpretation of the polygraph record. A mantra that would be used incessantly over the coming decades by the LD industry to justify itself whenever it came under attack was uttered here when Keeler said, "Its most important use both in the police and commercial field is in the elimination of innocent persons." According to Keeler, police departments in the following cities were using LDs: Berkeley, Indianapolis, Honolulu, Wichita, Buffalo, San Antonio, Kansas City and St. Louis (both in Missouri), Cincinnati, East Cleveland, and Toledo (all in Ohio), Chicago, Elgin, Evanston and Wheaton (all in Illinois). Also, the polygraph was used by the United States Department of Justice and by the state police or other state agencies in Illinois, Indiana, Michigan, North Dakota, Pennsylvania, Rhode Island and West Virginia. Keeler stressed the time saving benefits of the polygraph when a lot of potential suspects were involved. For example, if thefts had taken place at a dormitory, police could submit all residents to a polygraph. Another example he gave concerned a case in Berkeley in which an 11-year-old girl was raped. The only description the child could give of her attacker was that he wore work clothes similar to those worn by men working on a government relief project. The first 120 workers from a relief work camp near the crime scene were all given LD tests and all were cleared. However, the 121st person tested registered as being deceptive and when those polygraph records were shown to him, he confessed. Another point made by Keeler was that it was common police experience that prominent citizens were sometimes charged with crimes by "irresponsible persons or neurotic children." Frequently those crimes were said to be of a sexual nature. Again and again, he declared, the polygraph had "protected law-abiding citizens from just such situations by examining both the person charged and the one making the charge." The potential for abuse in such situations was, of course, obvious. (A criticism of LD use many decades later was that rape victims in some jurisdictions were asked to take LD tests. This was the only crime for which the request was made.) Such tests were voluntary but pressure could be applied with hints the state might not pursue the case with much vigor if the complainant refused to submit to the polygraph. Applicants for police positions in Evanston, Illinois and Wichita, Kansas, were all required to take a polygraph test; in East Cleveland, Ohio, all applicants for civil service positions were required to submit to the machine. The Chicago Park District Civil Service Commission polygraphed policemen against whom a charge was placed or on whom suspicion was cast. None of this bothered Keeler because, he said, "The honest police officer welcomes the chance to exonerate himself of charges...."[13]

One police agency that did not welcome the LD was the Federal Bureau of Investigation (FBI). In 1938, when polygraph tests administered in a murder case in Florida "proved" an innocent man was guilty and "cleared" the person who later confessed, FBI head J. Edgar Hoover told his agents to "throw that box into Biscayne Bay." Hoover completely banned the box from FBI investigations in 1964, but the Bureau brought it back and established a Polygraph Unit in 1978.[14]

When it came to being admitted as court evidence, the LD test result had little success in the 1930s. Fred Inbau was one of the device's chief proponents and practitioners. Since he felt the instrument was accurate, he asked himself why the polygraph had not been given judicial recognition. His reply was that things went in stages and he pointed to the history of fingerprint evidence, which he said took "a score of years" to be accepted by the courts. Inbau concluded that "Eventually, lie-detector testimony will probably be admitted as evidence." Besides the 1923 federal court rejection of the polygraph in the *Frye* decision, the state appellate court in Wisconsin, *State v Bohner*, had rendered a 1934 decision against the admission of LD results as evidence. The rationale of the *Frye* decision remained the guiding principle, "Just when a scientific principle or discovery crosses the line between the experimental and demonstrable stages is difficult to define. Somewhere in this twilight zone the evidential force of the principle must be recognized, and while courts will go a long way in admitting expert testimony deduced from a well-recognized principle of discovery, the thing from which the deduction is made must be sufficiently established to have gained acceptance in the particular field to which it belongs." Inbau expected polygraph results to eventually be admitted because the machine was "known to be working with a high degree of accuracy," and that it was gradually gaining acceptance. Addressing the idea that an accused person could not be forced to testify against himself, Inbau argued that compulsory submission to an LD test did not constitute "compulsory testimony" and therefore "it appears that an accused individual may even be forced to submit to the examination." It was an argument rooted in the idea that since no verbal responses were recorded by a polygraph, only physiological ones, there was no actual testimony involved.[15]

In November, 1929, Anna Gustafson was found dead in her Chicago apartment. Two policemen, William Tobin and Henry Dompke, were assigned to guard the woman's property. However, Gustafson's canary went missing soon after the woman's death and was later found dead in a pile of rubbish with its neck wrung. Both policemen were given LD tests by August Vollmer, then professor of police criminology at the University of Chicago, and Leonarde Keeler of the Chicago-based Illinois State

Department of Criminology. They reported Dompke as "clear," or non-deceptive, but that Tobin displayed "marked tension" regarding the disappearance of the bird. As a result of the polygraph tests Judge Henry Horner declared Tobin guilty of the bird's death and ordered him to pay $25 to the Public Administrator.[16]

A polygraph test was used late in 1934 in the case of a prisoner in the Michigan State penitentiary who had served 13 years of a life sentence for murder. Reportedly, the machine sustained the denials of guilt the man had long professed and, as a result, Governor Comstock gave him a pardon as a Christmas gift.[17]

Inbau was not alone in the 1930s in expressing a belief that LD test results would eventually be admitted into court as evidence. In 1935 the *Literary Digest* remarked that such material had not yet been admitted as evidence "in any court. However, it is generally considered only a matter of time until it will be."[18]

New Jersey constable Charles Fremgen was found guilty in October, 1937, of extorting $10 from a motorist when he pulled the driver over for a routine traffic stop. Seeking a new trial on that charge, Fremgen voluntarily submitted to an LD test, conducted by Summers of Fordham University and his machine. It was noted that the motorist had "ignored a challenge" to be tested at the same time. Judge J. Edward Knight said he would consider the lie detector test results, but not allow them to "preclude any other evidence." After the test Assistant Prosecutor Edward Juska of Monmouth County said he was enthusiastic about the device. "I came, I saw and I was conquered by it. I am sure it has a future." After studying the conclusions of Summers, Judge Knight commented that the report indicated Fremgen was falsifying when he testified that he did not receive $10 from the motorist. A new trial was not granted. Juska added, "I am now convinced that the detector is 98 percent correct, as claimed."[19]

When Homer Stanley staked his veracity in Chicago in 1938 against the assessment of an LD, the result cost him $93.50. Judge J. M. Braude set Stanley's fine for drunk driving at $100 and then suggested that if the polygraph at Northwestern University showed he was telling the truth when he said he had only one beer, Stanley would pay a $25 fine and Judge Braude would pay the $10 fee for the test. Otherwise Stanley would pay the $10 plus the fine of $100 and $8.50 in costs. Stanley was declared by the polygraph to be untruthful.[20]

In the spring of 1938, Raymond Kenny was on trial on hold-up charges. An earlier trial on the same charge resulted in a conviction but that verdict was set aside and a new trial was ordered, on technical grounds unrelated to deception testing. In Queens County court at that second trial, Judge Charles S. Colden admitted the results of a polygraph test (administered by Summers) and said that jurors could consider and evaluate the findings of the LD in the same manner as any other evidence. "It seems to me that this pathometer (lie detector) and the technique by which it is used indicate a new and more scientific approach to the ascertainment of truth in legal investigating," said Colden. On the stand Summers declared it was not possible for the subject to control his emotions and defeat the purpose of the exam.[21]

So unusual were the judge's actions in admitting polygraph results that the case attracted national media attention. *Newsweek* also reported that police in Michigan, Indiana, Kansas and California attributed more than 250 confessions to the Keeler instrument while Summers, using his device, had assisted in some 50 criminal investigations. Colden had admitted the test results over the strenuous objections of the prosecution and ruled Summers's testimony was as admissible as handwriting, fingerprint data, ballistics, or "other expert" testimony although he did tell the jury it was not obliged to accept the LD findings. Jurors returned a not guilty verdict. Later they told reporters they had inclined toward a guilty verdict "until they heard Father Summers."[22]

Vincent Forte was convicted of murder in March, 1937, in New York. His request to submit an LD test was denied and Forte appealed to a higher court. In November of that year, the New York Court of Appeal decided unanimously that evidence obtained by the use of a lie detector was not admissible in New York courts. Forte's murder conviction was affirmed. Judge John F. O'Brien declared "The record is devoid of evidence tending to show a general scientific recognition that the pathometer possesses efficacy." He added, "Evidence relating to handwriting, fingerprinting and ballistics is recognized by experts as possessing such value that reasonable certainty can follow from tests. Until such a fact, if it be a fact, is demonstrated by capable witnesses in respect to the 'lie-detector,' we cannot hold as a matter of law that error was committed in refusing to allow defendant to experiment with it."[23]

When the *Harvard Law Review* ran a brief review of the polygraph and the courts, it observed that any time a case involving LD results reached a state appellate court, those test results had never been found worthy of judicial recognition. Nevertheless, it was also noted that the tests were "sufficiently reliable" to the extent that a number of lower courts had admitted them as evidence pursuant to a stipulation of the parties. That is, admission was allowed if both sides agreed to the admission prior to the polygraph test being administered and without regard to the outcome of the test. To that point, it had always been the defendant who had sought to introduce LD results. This article agreed with the idea that self-incrimination was not involved in an LD test, because words were not recorded. However, it expressed a more serious objection to an eventual use of the test in a compulsory fashion, which was the "right of privacy." If polygraph results were introduced in a lower court over the objection of one party and the case went to a state appellate court, then the LD results were thrown out, or not admitted. However, if the case was not appealed then, of course, the results stood. Appellate courts in some states had allowed polygraph evidence where it had been admitted on stipulation; some states did not allow even that.[24]

During the coming years, a ghoulish use would be made of the LD in connection with death row prisoners in unsightly spectacles that were in part grandstanding and in part political. Convicted murderer Joseph Rappaport was executed in Chicago on March 2, 1937, just hours after being given an LD test in his cell on death row. Administering the test was Keeler, who concluded the condemned man lied. Just a few hours later, Rappaport was executed. Previously he had received fives stays of execution. Finally, Illinois Governor Henry Horner — said to be a "great believer" in LDs — declared he might have reconsidered his decision against a further reprieve if Rappaport had submitted to a polygraph test.[25]

International media attention was drawn to this case with mentions in *Newsweek*, *Literary Digest*, and the UK's *New Statesman and Nation*, among others. In the *Digest* it was reported that Horner would be guided in further reprieves in the case "by the machine which can't lie." After giving the test Keeler went to the warden's office, picked up the phone and told Horner "On the basis of my findings, Rappaport is guilty." In its comments the *New Statesman* wondered about the device and its accuracy and was openly skeptical that it really worked. "If the lie detector is an absolutely infallible instrument, it seems to me that criminal courts are no longer necessary," declared the publication. "If the lie-detector triumphs, the lawyer's occupation will be gone."[26]

Lie detector evidence was admitted in a worker's compensation case as early as 1935. John Nowak was a Buffalo, New York stevedore who claimed he was disabled in July, 1933, when several sacks of sugar fell on him while he was helping to unload a barge. Kenneth G. McMonigal, a federal compensation examiner suggested the test for the United States Compensation Bureau after four physicians gave conflicting testimony as to Nowak's injuries. After he agreed to take the LD test, the results reportedly showed Nowak to have been a liar. McMonigal said the decision in the case would not depend solely on the LD evidence, but that it would be used as corroborative evidence and considered.[27]

During the 1930s, usage of the lie detector moved into the private sector area for the first time. Apparently it started with banks in Chicago around 1930. Ultimately LD usage in the private sector would dwarf all other usage with the instrument being used in three different ways in the private sector: 1) to screen applicants for jobs, 2) to periodically screen existing employees, 3) to screen employees because of a specific event, such as a shortage or a disappearance of company cash. Early in March, 1931, Fred Inbau reported that within the previous couple of years, about 45 Chicago banks had started using the polygraph as an aid in detecting employee embezzlement, and also for the purpose of ascertaining whether or not a prospective employee had been guilty of any previous irregularities under former employers. In those banks, where all employees, from presidents to janitors, had been tested, Inbau declared; "the polygraph records of from ten to twenty-five percent of the personnel have indicated deception in the answers to questions pertaining to the taking of money from the institutions or from the customers. And practically all such records have been substantiated by admission of the subjects themselves."[28]

In one case, wrote Inbau, a bank desired to have LD tests made on its 56 employees to find the embezzler of $5,000. Instead of finding one liar in the group, 12 were discovered. Of those 12, nine were said to have confessed to embezzlement to that point unknown to bank officials. In another instance, six bank applicants were sent to Northwestern University's Polygraph Laboratory for tests to determine whether or not they had been guilty of converting to their own use any money or property belonging to previous employers. Only one of the six ran a clear record. Each of the other five reportedly subsequently admitted having diverted various sums of money plus other miscellaneous articles. However, not every bank employee with a guilty record was dismissed or refused employment. "The individual who admits all his irregular practices is usually retained, or employed, even in many cases where substantial sums are involved," stated Inbau. That was because such a person was considered to be a "good risk" due in part to the psychological benefit of admission and in part because he was aware he would have to take another polygraph test in six months, the outcome of which had to be favorable to him in order for him to retain his position.[29]

A year later, Fred Inbau asserted that in the previous three years, about 2,000 bank employees in 52 Chicago banks had been examined to detect embezzlers. And "Several Chicago banking institutions will not employ an applicant for a position unless he is tested on the lie-detector," added Inbau.[30]

Use of a polygraph in a public school involving a sham instrument resulted in a public outcry. Newark, New Jersey's Newton School's lie detector — merely a black box equipped with dials and electric lights—was physically destroyed in September, 1936 by the inventor of the device and principal of the school Gray Moreland. Insisting it was not an LD, Moreland called it an "experiment in psychology" that he had used only once. He had tried it on an 11-year-old boy accused of stealing a pair of gloves. Unbeknownst to the boy, Moreland pressed a button that turned on a light when the boy denied the theft. Finally the boy admitted the theft and returned the gloves. Somehow word got out and the principal found himself besieged by newsmen. After they published their accounts and it became public knowledge that an LD was in use in a school, "there was outspoken condemnation from various sources." That led school officials to launch an investigation and to order the destruction of the machine.[31]

William Marston reported in 1938 that the LD was used by "upwards of 50 banks" in testing the "honesty" of all personnel and was also used by "numerous" insurance companies, chain stores, department stores, and other commercial institutions, although he provided no specific details. It would be true over time that companies that used polygraph testing on their employees and prospective employees were as a rule reluctant to admit to using the device. Marston added that during the previous three years he had used the LD extensively in his psychological consultation work. This was on individuals who had personal problems and was not related to deception detection. He also said it was used by more than 100 police departments and by prosecuting attorneys in 10 states. Later that same year he declared, "The lie detector is here to stay. It is slowly but surely worming its way into the cancerous and parasitical habits of deception which have been gnawing insidiously at the vitals of human society for untold centuries."[32]

Will R. Shafroth, secretary of the National Conference of Bar Examiners, said in 1939 that LD tests had been used in one Midwestern state in testing candidates for admission to the bar. He thought this practice could be "extremely helpful" in cases where "reasonable doubt" about a candidate's character had arisen.[33]

Perhaps the first lengthy, substantive article in the general media about the use of the lie detector in business was the one that appeared in *Forbes* in the January 15, 1941, issue and then turned up in February in condensed form in *Reader's Digest*. It was an article somewhat in awe of, and full of praise for, the device. The article subhead proclaimed "A machine that tests employees' honesty, solves baffling thefts, protects the innocent and reforms the guilty." For 10 years, reporter J. P. McEvoy explained, many of Chicago's banks, chain stores, restaurants and department stores had

3. *A Painless Third Degree, 1930 to 1941*   33

been using the Keeler Polygraph with "astonishing results." Hundreds of inside jobs "which had baffled employers and detectives have been exposed. And, perhaps more important, thousands of suspected employees have been proved innocent." When a chain store lost $1.4 million worth of goods in a single year, Keeler was asked to test a cross section of employees. They were told results would be confidential and no one would be fired. Although six months later, they were cautioned, they would be polygraphed again and then have to live with the consequences of a bad test. Those tests were said to have shown that 76 percent of the employees tested were taking merchandise or money. Six months later, a retest declared that less than three percent were repeaters. "It proved the lie detector not only could detect, as it does consistently in police work, but could reform," enthused McEvoy. "A man caught lying by the machine has learned his lesson and is a better risk than the average employee who hasn't had the jolting experience of being found out." After testing some 25,000 people over a period of years at the Northwestern Lab, Keeler concluded that most people were honest only because they were afraid of getting caught, and therefore should be polygraphed regularly. "Sixty-five percent of those who handle money take money," asserted Keeler. "The percentage who take merchandise is even larger."[34]

Back in 1931, continued McEvoy, Henry Scarborough Jr., who represented the insurance underwriter Lloyd's of London in Chicago took the Keeler instrument to London and demonstrated it to the underwriters at Lloyd's. Since then, whenever banks used the polygraph according to the Lloyd's "formula," insurance premiums were "substantially reduced." That formula required tests for the entire staff the first year, and at least one third of the staff each succeeding year. Also, all new employees had to be tested. Thirty Chicago banks had been using the polygraph since 1931, wrote the journalist, "and defalcations have vanished."[35]

Keeler's work was said by McEvoy to be 95 percent commercial. It was reported that in one of America's largest department stores, the LD had been in constant use for six years and "has caught 90 percent of the guilty, has never convicted the innocent." One example of this store's use took place when a customer called up to say the store's delivery boy was there that morning and when he left, the customer's purse was missing. The boy was polygraphed. An official of a large detective agency said 50 percent of its commercial cases could be solved by direct investigation, "but in the other half detectives run against a stone wall. Here they have found the Polygraph 99 percent perfect." Then McEvoy asked himself if the LD was so good, why wasn't it used more often. For him the answer was to be found in "public misunderstanding." Indignant meetings by two

women's clubs protesting the tests given at a chain store and a state legis-
lator who offered a resolution condemning the lie detector as "un–American" were examples of such misunderstandings. Also, McEvoy reported
that LD tests were regularly given to collectors who gathered the coins
from telephones, jukeboxes and vending machines. Insurance companies
brought it in for tests on diamond salesmen who reported being the victims of "weird holdups," and women who had lost too many furs. Indus-
trialists checked prospective employees to see if they might be saboteurs,
"a fifth columnist need not open his mouth; his reflexes will expose him."
McEvoy concluded by saying, "The lie detector fails only on subnormal
individuals, mentally disordered persons who believe their own lies, and
some hardened criminals."[36]

Public relations, theatrical grandstanding and plain hype were also
features of the 1930s. Presumably these events did not detract from the LD
as a serious and scientific instrument while they perhaps pushed the device
more and more into the public consciousness and increased its acceptance.
A demonstration of a polygraph was given at a Rochester, New York meeting of the International Association of Identification to show what science
could do in checking stories of people who fell into the hands of police.
Northwestern University's Calvin Goddard gave the demonstration while
two Rochester men, Alphonso Camp and Tony Lalluto, arrested as suspects in the bombing of a bakery, "submitted voluntarily to the ordeal."
However, the nature of the testimony and outcome were not disclosed.
Goddard declared the LD "to be generally accurate in its findings."[37]

When Chicago residents Harriet Berger and Vaclaw Hund were married in that city in 1932 by Judge Charles B. Adams, they were strapped to
a couple of Northwestern University's polygraphs. The bridegroom's blood
pressure rapidly and steadily decreased during the ceremony; the bride's
steadily rose. According to the assessment of LD operator Charles M. Wilson "The newlyweds really love each other." Charts recorded by the instruments were given to the couple along with their marriage certificate.[38]

Bruno Richard Hauptmann was sentenced to die in 1935 for the murder of the infant of famed aviator Charles Lindbergh. This was another
case that received worldwide attention. From his cell in the death house
of the New Jersey State prison at Trenton, Hauptmann wrote a letter to
Governor Harold Hoffman in which he offered to submit to LD tests and
to "truth serum" drug tests. Not long after his conviction, the condemned
man informed his lawyers that he would be glad to submit to a polygraph
but then made no further comment about it. His letter to the Governor
was the first actual move he had made to take the test. In January, 1936,
William Marston came to Trenton with his machine and conferred with

Hoffman "who was impressed by the psychologist's claims for his mechanical contrivance to bring out the truth." Marston said his exam would cost the state or the defense $100. However, no test was ever administered to Hauptmann. Apparently Marston offered to place his expertise at the disposal of Charles Lindbergh (who did not reply) in 1932 after his baby had been kidnapped.[39]

Hollywood's "dancing sweethearts of the films," as Jackie Coogan and Betty Grable were described in a 1936 account, happened to be in Chicago when they were the victims of a jewel robber. Without a doubt, Chicago was the LD capital of the world with no other real contenders for the title. Much of that had to do with the incessant proselytizing done for the device by Keeler and his disciples at Northwestern University. Coogan and Grable submitted to LD tests to prove the $5,000 jewel robbery they reported was true and not merely a publicity stunt. Polygraph test administrator Orlando F. Scott pronounced the pair to be truthful. Digressing somewhat, Grable asked Coogan if he had loved Toby Wine (a former girlfriend) more than he then loved her. According to the LD record, Coogan truthfully said, "no."[40]

At a 1938 conference of the International Police Congress (a gathering of police chiefs), Keeler showed up to pitch his machine and to argue that deception, guilt or innocence could be diagnosed from certain symptoms — recordings on his machine — just like appendicitis. Also in attendance was Summers, who pitched his own "very accurate" lie detector.[41]

J. H. Mathews, criminologist at the University of Wisconsin, gave a 1939 demonstration of his LD in Madison, Wisconsin before 50 officials of the State District Attorneys Association. He tested one of the attending newsmen with the names of 10 girls, one of whom was the man's girlfriend. However, he picked the wrong name. Mathews explained his failure by saying "A fellow doesn't always know himself which one of his girls he feels strongest for."[42]

In the late 1930s, Marston had a column, "Problems in Living," which appeared in *The Forum and Century*. He presented a letter in one of those columns from a husband married 10 years who had "strayed" early in the marriage and been discovered by his wife. As a result, there was a lack of full confidence on her part of his fidelity ever since. Declaring he had not strayed since his early misadventure the husband wanted to know if she could be convinced of his fidelity through the polygraph. "Yes. I have tested many cases of this type with consistently satisfactory results," said the psychologist. Marston suggested the husband see himself, Larson, or go to a "first-class" university for testing. In reply to a question about the galvanometer Marston declared; "It was found unreliable for deception testing twenty years ago, during the World War, and remains equally unreliable today."[43]

In another one of those columns Marston discussed his views on lying saying that "Deception is the root of all social evil. It is the malignant psychological cancer which causes civilization continuous and exquisite pain." Destroy the power to deceive, he argued, and society could "eliminate crime; business and political crookedness; matrimonial unfaithfulness; marriage for money and other ulterior purposes; social pretense; using people whom you allure for selfish purposes; and destroying people by war (legalized murder) for self-aggrandizement in the guise of right, justice, and self-defense." Over the course of 6,000 years of known history, happiness for the human masses had only been a dream, a futile delusion, he said. "And why? Because no truly constructive reform, no matter how wise and practicable in its conception, has ever been administered by honest human beings. There aren't any. You lie. I lie. Everybody lies." Human reform, in Marston's view, could be reduced to just three words, "make lying impossible." And "a method has been found, a beginning made. A scientifically reliable lie-detector test has been discovered and established." Recalling his early years Marston declared that in 1915 he discovered "that systolic blood pressure rises uncontrollably every time a person lies." Once again he attacked the galvanometer, dismissing it as "wholly unreliable."[44]

Apparently Marston believed in the ability of the LD to bring about character reform in people. The example he used was the lying criminal who kept repeating his crimes and kept coming back as a lying criminal. But suppose that each time that criminal tried to deceive, he was caught at it and instead been made to tell the truth (through being polygraphed). "Gradually his personality changes, he stops lying." In his own psychological consulting work he reported that girls came to see him in a state of emotional conflict. They wanted to know whether they truly loved some wealthy man who had proposed to them or whether they were subconsciously seeking his money. "They want to know whether a certain man is in love with them. The lie-detector test will answer these questions," explained Marston. "Husbands and wives who doubt each other come to me — the test reveals the truth, whatever it is, and they adjust to it in nine case out of ten, avoiding separation or divorce."[45]

The December 6, 1938, issue of *Look* magazine featured the psychologist/physician/priest in a two-page article under the heading "Would you dare take these tests?" Marston appeared in the photo story attempting to resolve marital difficulties with his lie detector. Not only did the machine discover that "the neglected wife and her roving husband" still had some affection for each other, but it also disclosed that another young couple were in love, even though they were engaged to other people. Marston was a strong advocate of using the polygraph to solve "marital or other domestic problems." *Look* magazine concluded, "From the field of crime, the lie detector has entered the field of love."[46]

Moving even farther afield Marston also appeared in ads for Gillette razor blades with his device. One such ad, "Lie detector 'tells all,'" appeared in the November 21, 1938, issue of *Life* magazine. Supposedly the ad contained the actual record of one man's shave as recorded by a lie detector. Marston declared in the ad, "In conducting exhaustive shaving tests for Gillette I have discovered that the quality of a man's shave has a marked effect upon his mood and general attitude for hours to come."[47]

Deception testing in this period was not limited to the polygraph and galvanometer. A brief flurry of interest was aroused by other methods of separating the truth from lies. One of those was by the use of drugs. At least two different drugs were touted as being useful in deception detection: sodium amytal and scopolamine. The latter was an anesthetic, or sleep producer, with its use in lie detection discovered by Dr. R. E. House of Texas. He found that scopolamine had the power of submerging certain inhibitory areas of the brain. "Further investigation proved that the brain area submerged by scopolamine was the part normally used in fabricating self-protective stories— in plain language, lies," noted an account that was favorable to the drug. "And so it was established that a person under the influence of scopolamine is in full possession of all his senses, but deprived of the power of inventing falsehoods!" Until his death in 1930, House was said to have conducted several hundred tests "in many of which he procured the release of accused and convicted individuals who were subsequently proved innocent." Yet this account declared that House's own conservative estimate of success was an accuracy rate of 50 percent, which, of course, was nothing to brag about.[48]

Literary Digest reported that the theory behind scopolamine was that used in small amounts it put the subject into a drowsy state, instead of into unconsciousness. Once in that state, the subject was supposed to be too sleepy to devise any but truthful answers. However, the person who wrote this account was no fan of the "truth drugs" and declared, "The difficulty with 'truth drugs' is that the suspected persons will confess to almost anything that is suggested to them. They respond to 'leading questions' too well." With regard to the drug sodium amytal, which had a different effect causing the person to whom it was given to feel strong, confident, and friendly toward everybody, the article stated "In this condition, however, one is inclined to boast of crimes he did not commit and is hardly a reliable witness either for or against himself."[49]

At the beginning of the 1900s, scopolamine was a general birth anesthetic that, with the appropriate amount, produced a twilight sleep. To
gauge the correct amount a researcher of the time, J. Christian Gauss, after
experimentation, developed a series of so-called memory tests asking
patients questions every half an hour until the drug had deadened their
powers of recollection. Supposedly it was from that research that it was
ascertained that scopolamine could render a person unable to tell a lie.
Doctor Robert Ernest House took up the cause of the drug and, said journalist Gilbert Geis, "stands unchallenged" as the "father of truth serum."
He pushed use of the drug relentlessly in the 1920s, until his death in 1930.
Geis said, "He was exaggerative in regard to his scientific product, noto-
riously blind to its failings, grossly indulgent of its wayward behavior, and
stubbornly proud of its minor achievements." As did others in the deception detection industry, House made extreme claims for his item, such as
100 percent accuracy and that "there are no human minds capable of resist-
ing the physiological effects of scopolamine any more than they could resist
the effects of ether or nitrous acid." A legal case involving testing under
the influence of scopolamine reached the appellate court in Missouri in
1926 where Judge Robert Walker Franklin delivered a blistering attack on
the drug as "bunk," in the same category as "the magic powers of philters,
potions and cures by faith." The trail court, he held, "ruled correctly in
excluding this clap-trap from the consideration of the jury." Geis concluded the legal and scientific objections to scopolamine effectively pre-
vented its expanded usage in police work, "particularly after House, with
his crusading zeal and his ability to call public attention to his work, passed
from the scene." By the mid 1930s scopolamine had become passé as the
focus moved to other drugs such as sodium amytal and sodium pentothal.[50]

Drug usage in deception detection seemed to have been done only to
a limited degree in this period before fading into oblivion. For one thing,
drugs did not work in detecting deception. For another, the administering of these drugs was a medical procedure that had to be done in a clinic-
like setting with the appropriate medical instruments on hand. It was a
procedure that carried some risk — albeit slight — to the subject, and it
required that an anesthesiologist be present. At least that's how it should
have been done. In March, 1935, in Bellefonte, Pennsylvania, District
Attorney Philip H. Johnston disclosed that two men had been cleared as
murder suspects after they had submitted to a "truth serum"— the injec-
tion of one-fiftieth of a grain of scopolamine. Later that same year in
Arnett, Oklahoma, murder charges against two people were dropped by
county attorney Charles B. Leedy after the ex-husband of one of the

accused was given scopolamine and, under its influence, admitted he lied in giving prior details to police which put the pair under charges.[51]

Hypnotism was briefly considered as a method to detect deception. Since hypnotism was seen as a state of heightened suggestibility, it was felt that a subject under hypnosis would act according to instructions given him. It was thought possible to hypnotize a subject, instruct him to tell the truth, and then question him about the crime being investigated. Of course, it did not work with one of the problems being that very suggestibility.[52]

The psychology of color was used in the offbeat and bizarre "mirror confession chamber." In this method, the walls of the confessional were mirrors. Suspects sat in the center and were questioned through an aperture in one of the walls. As the examination proceeded, the lights inside the room were gradually changed to a greenish tinge. Being unaware of the altered illumination, the suspect saw only the "characteristic hue of guilt" upon his face. Believing his "ghastly complexion" had already betrayed him, the suspect "breaks down and tells all." This method was said to have been particularly successful with "neurotic and ignorant prisoners."[53]

During the 1930s, very little attention was devoted to the accuracy level of the LD or to its reliability and validity. This despite the fact that the developers and proponents of the device all were involved in the academic world. Articles of the era tended to focus more on the types of LDs available, the theory behind them, how they worked, and so forth. Fred Inbau outlined the early development of the instrument from the time of Lombroso onward and noted that the Keeler LD — one of several available in the mid 1930s — was the "most reliable instrument" up to that time. Keeler was then Assistant Professor of Law at the Scientific Crime Detection Laboratory of Northwestern University and was said to have conducted some 10,000 deception tests within the past 11 years. The Keeler machine consisted, in 1934 according to Inbau, of three units: one for recording respiratory changes; a second for continuously recording the pulse wave and blood pressure; and a third for recording a duplicate blood pressure curve or for recording muscular reflexes of the arms or leg. Usually only the first two units were used; the third served merely as an "accessory." Apparently the Keeler machine did not then have a galvanic skin response unit. Inbau was research assistant at the Scientific Crime Detection laboratory, sometimes just called the Polygraph Lab. Only occasionally, said Inbau, did the Chicago Police Department request the assistance of the LD, even though that Laboratory service was "formerly offered free of charge to the law." When asked why, a leading Chicago police official (with a display of his clenched fist) said "Here is the best lie-detector." Given that the Polygraph Lab was located in metro Chicago, Inbau hoped in time its presence would cause local police "to place an increasing reliance on the investigation of outside evidence of crimes instead of the extortion of confessions by brutal methods." For experimental cases run in the tight control of a lab setting the accuracy of the LD was about 85 percent, he argued. However, in criminal cases "statistical data are difficult to obtain" but he went on to declare that in numerous criminal cases confessions had been obtained in about 75 percent of those cases in which the record indicated deception. Inbau stressed that successful use of the polygraph depended on the skill of the operator and that "An instrument of this nature in the hands of an unscrupulous individual is an extremely dangerous thing." The Scientific Crime Detection Laboratory had been founded in 1930 and in 1938 it became a unit of the Chicago Police Department. Over the period between January 1, 1935 and June 1, 1938, 2,171 subjects were examined at the Northwestern Lab and of that number, said one account, only 12 mistakes in assessment of innocence or guilt "have been verified."[54]

The movement to modernize Chicago's crime detection methods started with the St. Valentine's Day massacre on February 14, 1929, when seven members of the Bugs Moran gang were lined up against the wall of a garage and machine gunned to death. Coroner Herman N. Bundesen summoned several prominent Chicago citizens to be members of his investigative jury with Burt Massee, vice president of the Colgate-Palmolive-Peet company, being named foreman. Massee was surprised to find that America's second largest city had never heard of firearms identification or ballistics. Next, Massee hired Calvin Goddard, considered an expert in the field, to study all phases of scientific crime detection in which Chicago was backward. Goddard developed plans for a modern crime detection laboratory and when Massee offered the lab to Northwestern University, it was accepted. For eight years it was a chief center for scientific experiments in crime detection in the United States. Keeler joined the lab in 1930 and later established his own private polygraph business, selling the machines, training operators, and so forth.[55]

Writing in the New York Times in 1935, reporter Waldemar Kaempffert drew a distinction between a galvanometer and the Keeler polygraph noting that Keeler believed the former was "untrustworthy" as a means of telling whether or not a man was lying. According to this account the Keeler instrument recorded blood pressure and respiration and it also included the "sensitive psycho-galvano reflex recorder."[56]

About the same time Fred Inbau returned to argue that many LDs were really only galvanometers and while changes in the galvanic skin response served as an extremely sensitive criterion for emotionality it "can not by itself" be depended upon as a means for the detection of deception. Used, however, in conjunction with the other two reactions (blood pressure and respiration) "it may be of considerable assistance." The new Keeler unit would, he said, contain a galvanic skin response unit in addition to the other two. So it appeared that it was early in 1935 that the Keeler polygraph began to record the three physiological functions which became standard for LDs. There was no love lost in the 1930s between Keeler, Inbau, other Polygraph Lab members and the galvanometer proponents and practitioners (led by Summers). The former criticized the latter as worthless in lie detection every chance they got. Yet they added such a component to their own unit.[57]

Time magazine reported in 1936 on the new gadgets, limiting mentions to Keeler's unit and to Summers instrument, then newly developed and displayed before newsmen. Summers used the card test in which a newsman picked a card from a group of five, remembered it and replaced it. Then the LD operator — Summers and his galvanometer in this case — showed the newsman each of the cards while he was hooked up to the machine. Instructed to say "no" to all five cards the operator then guessed which card the newsman had lied about from the machine's record. This, of course, was a very old carnival trick, but more about that later. With regard to the squiggly lines produced on an LD record, Summers remarked "The bigger the lie, the bigger the jiggle."[58]

When reporter Henry Pringle discussed the device in 1936, he declared the Keeler Polygraph had been in operation at Northwestern for five years with 15,000 people having been tested by it with "their experimental lies being detected with a very high degree of accuracy." Pringle observed that the polygraph had no legal standing and that a defendant could not be forced to submit and then have the evidence used against him in court as he had the constitutional privilege of refusing to testify against himself. Still, "It is difficult for an accused person to escape taking the test; to refuse is a fairly clear admission of guilt," said the reporter. "The vast majority of defendants, moreover are entirely confident that they can outwit the little black box and offer no objection." Over the following years and decades the question would often arise as to why anybody would agree to take an LD test. The reasons mentioned here by Pringle were the ones that would always surface. There was a great deal of pressure placed on a person to submit to the machine. Although the police could not use LD evidence directly in court, they could use it to produce a confession — which was admissible — or to obtain other information and go from there.[59]

Newsweek declared in a 1937 piece that the weight of evidence was on the side of the LD. When he demonstrated his machine, Keeler also used the pick-a-card routine. With a reported accuracy of 90 percent, his apparatus indicated the card that had been drawn. This article also cited the statistic that 75 percent of all suspects in criminal cases declared guilty by the instrument were later confirmed guilty by subsequent confessions. This statistic would be used repeatedly.[60]

Elevating the role of the operator of the machine was Professor Christian Ruckmick of the University of Iowa. He had concluded that the LD, in the hands of an expert, should prove valuable for crime detection. However, since it was not perfect, it became a "dangerous weapon" in the hands of any but the most competent. Mystifying the role still further, Ruckmick declared that "Only those who can see beyond the actual scores and interpret these scores in the frame of the individual mental life are competent to pass judgment."[61]

From time to time new LDs would emerge. Most quickly faded away. One of those was developed by Dr. F. K. Berrien of Colgate University whose device was based on the mechanical measure of the steadiness of a person's gaze when lying and when telling the truth. Subjects looked at a fixed white card while a beam of light was reflected from the surface of the eyeball into a recording instrument. Claiming it had an accuracy of 75 percent, Berrien said that, contrary to popular belief, "the liar is betrayed by an unwavering gaze."[62]

Sometime in the 1930s Keeler started to sell his polygraph machine. Reportedly, he sold his LDs only to police departments and to "qualified" research laboratories. Another condition of sale was that one of his operators had to go along with the machine to train the purchasing institution's operator. That training process was eight months in length. It was estimated there were only 10 to 12 Keeler Polygraphs in use in the 1930s, outside of Northwestern University. Given the conditions attached to a sale, it was easy to see why so few were in use. There were other polygraphs developed by other people, on the market. Reporter J. P. McEvoy estimated in 1941, "there are not more than 100 Polygraph experts in the United States."[63]

Most of the media accounts in the 1930s about the new scientific marvel were full of praise for the device and offered an uncritical acceptance. Undoubtedly such exposure helped establish a reputation of infallibility for the polygraph. In a 1931 account, the *Literary Digest* explained what happened to someone being polygraphed. A subject was seated in a chair, the blood-pressure cuff was adjusted above the left arm and the pneumograph placed around the chest. Pressure was pumped into the cuff with the subject cautioned not to move or speak until he was told to do so. For three minutes a 'normal' record was taken. Following that, the subject was asked three nonsignificant questions, such as "Do you live in Chicago?" Then three significant questions, such as "Did you take the cash-box?" were asked. The innocent were not especially disturbed by being questioned about the crime. However, the guilty suspect showed significant changes often both in the breathing and heart records. According to this account, some 8,000 tests had been performed on criminal suspects and of those "there have been 6 checked failures," that is, the interpretation of the test record was in error, either the subject was given a "clear" and subsequently was proven guilty or had been given a "deceptive" assessment and later was proved to be innocent. "Suffice it to say," said the account, "since it has failed in six of the 8,000 instances, it should never be considered as court evidence on an equal footing with finger-prints." Such an error rate—less than one-tenth of one percent—was, of course, a ludicrous exaggeration. John Larson had recently declined to be an LD consultant for the defense in a high profile murder case. He felt the method was not perfected and "Out of every hundred cases," he said, "perhaps as many as twenty show failures."[64]

Less than a year later, this same publication was back to declare that this new branch of knowledge was then only 10 to 12 years old "and it seems that it is developing rapidly into an exact science." A liar's blood pressure "grows jumpy" as did his pulse, his breathing changed and "even his glands secrete more or less of their products into the blood-stream and cause symptoms that can be detected. His chances of getting by are growing slimmer and slimmer."[65]

New York Times reporter George N. Coad attended a 1932 meeting of the International Association for Identification where he viewed many of the latest scientific advances in crime fighting—microscopes, ultraviolet light, blood tests, hair analysis, unusual cameras, chemicals, and other gadgets. Calvin Goddard, managing director of the Polygraph Lab at Northwestern, predicted the use of these new scientific advances and devices would be routine within a generation. He added that, with respect to court admissibility, "I venture to say that by such time even the evidence obtained with our lie-detector will be admissible." Scientific crime fighting was very much in vogue at this time, both in fiction and in real-life, and, of course, extended to the LD. It was a relatively recent development and the belief in science as a universal problem solver was strong.[66]

In his 1935 piece, journalist Henry Morton Robinson argued first that 600 years of western civilization "have not appreciably altered the use of

torture and coercion in wringing guilty knowledge from suspected criminals," and that science had recently developed a number of devices, which,
"while they are not yet in general use, they seem clearly destined to sup-
plant the barbarous torments of the third degree." Robinson thought the
most "dramatic and satisfactory" of those instruments was the Keeler
device. Asking the question why an abrupt rise in blood pressure could
indicate a person had committed a crime he wrote, "Now, when a person
is confronted by danger in the form of a question the truthful answer to
which will connect him with a crime, his reaction is naturally that of fear."
Then his whole system organized for defense, which in this case was the
"concealment of his guilty knowledge." The figure of 75 percent of suspects confessing after being confronted with their supposed deceptive LD
records was herein repeated. An even more extreme, and exaggerated, conclusion was draw when he stated, "The lie detector infallibly reveals innocence as well as guilt; in fifteen hundred cases, not a single finding has
proved erroneous." Robinson also mentioned Summer's galvanometer and
after a brief explanation of how it worked he asserted that "It is impossible to beat this machine." He also wondered why the deception tests were
not more widely used, especially if they were as good as he described them.
Robinson suggested the answer lay partly in the fact that courts were committed to a policy of caution. He worried that judges and juries not familiar with, or prejudiced against, "the solid bases on which science is
founding the new criminology gravely shake their heads and say that Constitutional rights must not be jeopardized by evidence given by blood pressure devices or by confessions made while the prisoner is under the
influence of a drug." That last was a reference to scopolamine. Robinson,
like others who wrote general media articles on the subject, had nothing
bad to say about LD tests (any of them) and described them all as accurate.[67]

Literary Digest returned with another laudatory piece in February,
1935, which rehashed the story of the LD's birth and growth. Like its previous pieces, this one was uncritical, accepting and praiseful. Also noted
was that mentions of the LD in newspapers were becoming more and more
frequent.[68]

Louther Horne wrote a long, highly positive article in the New York
Times. It was devoted exclusively to Keeler's unit and his Northwestern
Lab. Following an explanation of how the device worked Horne also used
the statistic that full confessions had resulted in about 75 percent of those
cases in which deception was detected. In dramatic fashion Horne
explained how the Keeler Polygraph was used to catch a man suspected of
murder. "Betrayed by the scientific crime revealer, [Mills] Redmond cried

out his confession and was pleading for immediate punishment almost before the inquisitors could remove the attachments through which the guilt was telegraphed into the lie detector."[69]

Proof that the lie detector had made it into America's consciousness could be found in the May, 1936 issue of *Popular Science*, which contained plans for a homemade LD. Actually, two different plans were offered, one with a blood pressure cuff only and the other being a version of the galvanometer. With regard to the homemade lie detector, reporter Kenneth Murray declared that "With uncanny accuracy it uncovers falsehoods as quickly as you can tell them. While your voice is saying 'no,' your body says 'yes' and leaves a visible record of the truth on this device." Murray advised the user of the homemade LD not to ask "serious questions" of anyone undergoing a test because "the device will always indicate when the truth is being told, sometimes with embarrassing results."[70]

While the above article may have been the first on how to make a homemade polygraph it would not be the last. *Popular Science* featured another article on the topic in its April, 1940 issue. This time the plan was for something reporter Julius Steinberg called an "electric" LD. A subject held a pair of grips in his hands, which were attached to a box. A tight grip moved a dial. A suggested test was to have someone hide an object somewhere in the house and then name the different rooms as the subject holding the grips said, "No" to all. Once the correct room had been discovered by the operator, then it was time to narrow down the location within the room, and so on. Steinberg declared that "Hundreds of tests by the writer have proved its meter to indicate correctly about eighty percent of the time...." Cost to make this device "need not exceed $2.50."[71]

Criticism of the device was not absent in the 1930s but it was not nearly as prevalent, or as lengthy, as articles that celebrated the instrument with showers of uncritical praise. The story was told in *The New Statesman and Nation* in 1931 about a professor at the University of Chicago who, after discovering a number of books missing from the library, warned the students that each of them would be subjected to a polygraph if the books were not returned within 24 hours. Reportedly, all the books were returned on the following day. "It would be the most desirable of devices if all men who lied experienced the same irregularities of pulse rate," said the article. "I wonder, however, whether it is possible to be sure that a man is lying because of a quickening of his pulse any more than one can be sure because of a change in his countenance."[72]

Edward P. Mulrooney, chairman of the New York State Division of Alcoholic Beverage Control and formerly Police Commissioner of New York City said that for a number of years in the early 1930s many LD "contrivances" had been presented to the New York Police Department. In one of the later tests a device was applied to four known criminals but, said Mulrooney, "In three of the tests the result was an absolute failure." Later, when he was Correction Commissioner in Buffalo, New York, Mulrooney declared that hardened criminals could deceive the machine, although he gave no details.[73]

At the end of the 1930s, the *Journal of the American Medical Association* briefly discussed four types of LDs. Its report was not favorable and concluded that many of those machines were being exploited by non-medical men.[74]

J. E. Winter, chairman of the psychology department at West Virginia University reported in 1936 the successful solution of a series of dormitory thefts by means of a polygraph. Of 25 females tested, the respiratory records alone showed 24 innocent and one guilty (but the wrong one), while the blood pressure records alone produced three guilty assessments (including the real guilty one who later confessed when faced with the tracings). Despite his success, Winter expressed some skepticism concerning the polygraph. Since in both cases some innocent subjects showed symptoms of guilt, Winter felt there was a "hazard in trusting too implicitly" in the polygraph.[75]

Most surprising of all the criticism was that which came from Dr. John Larson. In 1938 when he was with the Psychopathic Clinic of the Detroit Recorder's Court, he spoke before a joint meeting of the Wayne County Medical Society and the Detroit Bar Association. At that meeting he said he did not think LD tests would ever be considered as accurate as fingerprints. He objected to any court use of lie detector evidence but allowed that police officers might use the device "with some success in preference to the third degree." One account said Larson's honest scientific bent compelled him to subject his own theories to rigorous testing, and he ended up rejecting the polygraph as a "racket" and a "psychological third degree."[76]

As the 1940s began, the LD had received a growing amount of publicity and media coverage, most of it positive. Still, the machine was not widely used, being limited to a number of police agencies, some minor usage by other government agencies and to a small number of businesses in the private sector — principally banks in the Chicago area. Predominant use of the instrument was in Illinois and the Midwest in general, largely because of the influence and proselytizing work of the Keeler lab at Northwestern University. Mostly the instrument remained in the hands of academics who were the polygraph's major proponents, practitioners, trainers, and sellers of units with Keeler, Larson, Marston and Summers being the best known of that group. Criticism of the device was infrequent and weak. Rarely was the accuracy of the device challenged. For that matter, LD proponents only infrequently bothered to release numbers (self-serving) purporting to indicate the LD's reliability and validity. Concepts such as the right to privacy and the right to not self-incriminate arose only very rarely. Given that courts everywhere rejected LD results the instrument might have been expected to have perhaps fallen into the doldrums and even disappeared after the 1930s, as all the major names in the field disappeared. Marston shifted his attention to his comic book creation Wonder Woman; Summers was dead; Larson no longer believed in the LD; Keeler would die in 1949. But the world of the 1940s and 1950s was different; it was a world that favored the LD. The machine grew stronger.

4

—⌁—⌁—

The Polygraph Spreads in Cold War America, 1940s to 1950s

Leonarde Keeler's astounding invention tracks down murderers, unmasks the liars and the larcenous, and can tell just how honest you are — and intend to be.
— Alva Johnston, 1944

Chief usefulness of the gadget is as an aid to the police in scaring an ignorant and superstitious person into making a confession of crime.
— Science News Letter, 1946

I am convinced you cannot fool the lie detector.
— Senator Joseph McCarthy, 1954

[The LD] turned out to be useless when it came to detecting security risks....
— New York Times, 1953

A decision to employ an individual as a guardian of his fellow citizen and their property must be based on the best information available and nothing equals the polygraph in securing accurate information.
— John C. Lilly, Stockton, California City Manager, 1959

[The LD] is regarded by most intelligent people as a modern instrument of emotional torture that puts a man through a psychological third degree.
— New York Times, 1953

Police use of the polygraph continued in this period but it was still very much in a minority of those agencies— one reason being the continued rejection of LD records in court — and such use was not much noted in the media. Ray Holmes, chief engineer for Associated Research of

Chicago, estimated in 1948 that only 10 percent of American municipal police departments were equipped with LDs.[1]

When a Boston office of the Brink's company was robbed of $1.2 million in January, 1950, there were six employees of the firm on duty at the time. They submitted to LDs shortly after the robbery. A little over two years later, the robbery remained unsolved and those employees were asked to take a second polygraph test. At first they refused. However, a day later the employees changed their minds and agreed to take the second test "after a conference with company officials." And so they submitted "voluntarily."[2]

One of the largest LD screening operations ever undertaken in a criminal case was begun in La Crosse, Wisconsin in 1954, where 1,700 high school students and teachers were to be examined in an attempt to solve the disappearance of a 15-year-old.[3]

Charles A. McInerney was a polygraph operator at the Pittsburgh office of John E. Reid and Associates, a private LD testing company. Also, he was the polygraph examiner for the Pittsburgh and Allegheny County Crime Laboratory. McInerney argued that the LD technique for detecting deception "has a valuable application in the routine screening of individuals who, in the opinion of investigating police officers, could have been responsible for crimes in addition to those for which they were apprehended." In other words, he wanted to see the police undertake more fishing expeditions, as the Wichita Police Department had done. Although the LD "has been used extensively in the screening of employment applicants in the Chicago laboratories of John E. Reid and Associates for several years," he lamented, "it is seldom employed in the screening of criminal suspects."[4]

Philadelphia's Police Department joined the ranks of police agencies with their own polygraph when they bought their first LD, in 1955, at a cost of $1,250.[5]

Still avoiding the LD was the FBI with the Bureau only using a polygraph when a suspect who was trying to prove his innocence insisted on it. Even if a suspect requested a test, the FBI sometimes refused the request. Among the reasons cited by the agency for not using the LD was that the courts would not admit polygraph evidence and that "doctors, criminologists, and scientists do not regard the lie-detector as accurate." Also said to be behind the refusal was the following sentence from Article Five of the Bill of Rights (the first 10 amendments to the Constitution), "No person ... shall be compelled in any criminal case to be a witness against himself."[6]

A real-life crime that involved the theft of $10 from the room of one

of 81 men living in a campus dorm at Cornell University was investigated
not by the police but by two professors from the university. At a meeting,
the 81 men voted that they would all submit to an LD test, under the
penalty of social disapproval. There was a strong possibility the thief was
an outsider but the men were as much concerned with finding out if one
of their number was guilty as with finding the money. Those 81 LD records
were assessed and classified as follows: 1) insignificant response — negli-
gible reaction to all questions (31 subjects, 38.3 percent); 2) non-differential response — significant reaction to all or nearly all the queries (with
those records broken into two groups: 2S — moderate non-differential (23
men, 28.4 percent) and 2L — extensive non-differential (20 subjects, 24.7
percent); 3) differential response — more pronounced reactions to relevant
(crime related) than to irrelevant (not crime-related) questions (seven
men, 8.6 percent). The 27 subjects whose records were classed as either
2L or 3 were retested. According to the study, "After from one to five retests
all of these men showed patterns falling into categories 1 or 2S which the
writers accepted as indicative of innocence...."[7]

Polygraph evidence made no progress in being admitted in court.
Alfonse Di Lillo of Brooklyn was arrested and brought to trial in 1944 on
charges of possessing policy slips. The arresting police officer testified he
entered a building and saw Di Lillo with a slip of paper in his hand on
which were 49 sets of policy numbers. Di Lillo then threw the paper on
the floor, said the officer. Di Lillo denied all accusations. Magistrate John
Mastersen permitted the findings of a galvanometer when Dr. Joseph Kubis
of the Graduate School of Fordham University took the witness stand and
gave the history of the machine, experimental test results and the specific
results for Di Lillo. Upon completion of Kubis's testimony, Masterson dismissed the charges. Kubis had taken over the role of chief proponent of
the galvanometer after the death of his colleague Summers.[8]

That same year a criminal trial for rape in New York City attracted
nationwide attention. A man was first convicted but later was released and
exonerated on the basis of new evidence that became available after the
conviction. That new evidence was partly the result of the findings of psychologists who administered a galvanometer to the convicted man. In addition, his accuser was held on a charge of perjury. When she came to trial,
the polygraph would not be used on her by decision of the court.[9]

High courts continued to reject the machine and its findings. When
a court in Nebraska registered a conviction in a forgery case, partly on the
basis of an LD test, the case was appealed. Then in 1949 the Nebraska
Supreme Court reversed that decision and sent the case back for a retrial
after it held the polygraph had not yet gained such standing and scientific

recognition as to justify the admission of testimony deduced from tests made with it.[10]

In the mid-1950s an unusual court use of the LD was revealed. For about 16 years, a number of judges of the Chicago Municipal Court had "consistently" availed themselves of the LD to assist them in their decisions in paternity suits. Both parties had to agree to the use of the device. At that time there was no way of accurately assessing paternity. All that was available was a blood test, which could rule a man out as the father but not identify him as such. On the basis of a study of 312 disputed paternity cases, over a six-year period, it was determined that 93 percent of the tested parties lied in some respect when they testified in court.[11]

Once again the LD made an appearance in a prison death house. Theodore R. McClure was on death row in 1950 after being convicted of a robbery/slaying in Ohio. A volunteer group that investigated possible cases of miscarriages of justice intervened on McClure's behalf, after he had asked for their help claiming he was innocent. Just 50 minutes before he was slated to be executed the group won him a reprieve and arranged for him to be given a polygraph test. However, the group's spokesman Dr. Lemoyne Snyder said, of that LD exam, "after we ran the test there was not the slightest doubt of McClure's guilt." Efforts by the group to save him ended abruptly. Reportedly, McClure confessed after the test. He was later executed.[12]

A major difference in this period was that governments got involved in administering LD tests to their employees for the first time, at the federal level and then spreading to other levels of government. It started slowly and quietly. The period of the mid 1940s through the 1950s was an ideal time for the spread of the polygraph as paranoia ruled the land. It was the Cold War era, Communists lurked everywhere; it was the era of spies, of James Bond–type characters; it was a time of super patriotism, of endless accusations, of loyalty oaths; it was once again an age of gadgets and a great belief in science as the Space Race got off to a start. It was a time of distrust, of false charges; there was a need to be more American than anybody else, a need to be more truthful than anyone else. If the LD had been in any danger of slipping into irrelevancy after the 1930s, then the Cold War era breathed new life into it and gave it a robustness that it had until then lacked.

Back in 1944, at the Papago Park, Arizona prisoner of war camp, a captured German submarine crewman was found strangled to death. Investigators could not solve the crime so Keeler was called in by a Colonel Ralph W. Pierce, who had heard of his work. Keeler was able to pick out seven prisoners, all of whom were said to have then confessed to the murder and were soon executed. Impressed by the outcome, Pierce bought the first Army polygraph for the Chicago Counter-Intelligence Corps School (which he headed). This marked the first important use of the polygraph by a division of the federal government. Pierce, Keeler, and other polygraphists made the first use of the device for government security-screening purposes in August, 1945, at Fort Getty, Rhode Island where several hundred German prisoners had volunteered for police work with occupation forces in Germany. Several weeks of LD examinations screened out a third of the group as pro–Nazi or unsuitable for other reasons. The polygraph was made standard equipment in the Army's Criminal Investigation Division in the fall of 1948. Within a few years or so all branches of the armed services used the LD in their criminal work.[13]

On March 13, 1946, the Manhattan District of the Corps of Engineers (producers of the atomic bomb) admitted that the LD had been used on a "few" employees at their Oak Ridge, Tennessee weapons facility. Those employees had "volunteered" to be polygraphed. A statement released by the Manhattan District said, in part, "In the past the lie detector has been used in banks, jewelry stores and other commercial enterprises to check the honesty and loyalty of their employees…. Studies are being made to determine if the detector is a suitable instrument to assist in control of fissionable material…."[14]

A group of polygraphists, led by Keeler and including Russell Chatham (a former police officer from Indianapolis) was invited in February, 1946, by the Army Corps of Engineers (again through the auspices of Pierce) to see what they could do about clearing personnel and preventing the theft of fissionable material at the Oak Ridge facility. Those polygraphists set up an experimental program limited to the few hundred employees with access to the final-products building. Reportedly, the program was a success with the detection of some thefts of final product (the material was retrieved) and the less sinister thefts of tools, work clothing, even Kleenex (there was a paper shortage in the immediate post-war period). More ominously, the program led to the "Revelation of verbally unrevealed situations in the personal life of the personnel that could result in the disclosure of classified information under peculiar circumstances," said journalist Dwight Macdonald.[15]

On the basis of the experimental results, the authorities decided to go ahead with polygraphing and signed a contract with Russell Chatham, Inc. When the Atomic Energy Commission (AEC) took over Oak Ridge from the Army in 1947, it also took over the contract and, in 1948, extended its range to include 18,000 Oak Ridge employees. Chatham, Inc. then had six full time employees at Oak ridge asking workers there if they had been associated with subversives or talked about their work with outsiders, if they had filled out their security questionnaires truthfully, if they had any plans for sabotage, if they intended to violate the security regulations, and so on. A few employees in "sensitive" jobs had to submit to the LD every three months as a condition of employment with all the others simply invited to take annual or semiannual tests "voluntarily." Regarding the voluntary nature of the test, one of the employees in that latter group said if they refused to volunteer they were informed "that we would be regarded with suspicion, would not be allowed to handle classified work, and would be interviewed by our Security Department and reinvestigated by the FBI. I regret to say that my co-workers capitulated."[16]

Early in 1951, the AEC started a study of the Oak Ridge LD program to determine its effectiveness and perhaps also with the idea of extending it to other atomic plants if the study results were positive. When the study was completed, the AEC announced a "new and restricted" policy on April 2, 1953, with the polygraph to no longer be used in mass screening but only in specific cases of security interest. Announcement of the new policy went on to say that after studying LD use at Oak Ridge and other Federal agencies, the AEC concluded LDs offered only an "indeterminate marginal increase in security beyond that afforded by established security measures" and the cost to Oak Ridge in terms of dollars, employee morale, and labor relations, which might accrue from the use of the machine "substantially outweighed the limited advantage of polygraph use." During the seven years the program was in operation, according to Chatham, Inc., some 50,000 LD tests were made of 18,000 individuals at a cost of $361,000.[17]

When the *New York Times* reported on the AEC Oak Ridge study and its new policy there, its account was even more blunt. It declared the LD at Oak Ridge "turned out to be useless when it came to detecting security risks.... The instrument was of value only in detecting pilferers who lied."[18]

Writing in the *New York Times* at the end of 1951, reporter Anthony Leviero was perhaps the first to document the growing use of the LD in certain federal agencies and to raise alarm bells. This was a page-one story. When the AEC made its brief public mention in 1946 that it was using the polygraph, the item drew brief media coverage but was quickly forgotten. Leviero explained that the LD was being used to test the integrity of persons employed, or seeking employment, in certain federal agencies. At least four government departments were using the polygraph to supplement the existing and exacting federal loyalty investigation to test people involved in sensitive jobs related to national security. Full extent of polygraph usage by the federal government was said to be unknown as some agencies were using it secretly. Even Robert Ramspeck, chairman of the federal Civil Service Commission, was unaware that any agency was using the device until he was informed by the reporter. Agencies that used the LD, said Leviero were: the AEC at Oak Ridge; the United States State Department, which used the device only on demand of an employee suspected of wrongdoing; the Central Intelligence Agency (CIA) where it was understood the agency required every applicant to submit to the LD; the Defense Department, which did not use the LD except in dealing with people in the armed forces accused of being criminals.[19]

The Civil Service Commission was charged with the responsibility of laying down policies and regulations specifying the conditions of employment for more than two million people on the federal payroll but it had no policy or regulations regarding the use of polygraphs. In discussing the polygraph at Oak Ridge, Leviero observed that use of the device was never extended to the other atomic bomb plants. Thus, the device was not available at the Los Alamos, New Mexico facility where he thought it might have helped to trap three recently arrested spies. Since the secrets of Oak Ridge were no greater than the ones at the other atomic plants, the reporter wondered why the LD was in use at only one facility. Morse Salisbury, director of AEC information services, observed, "I think they have it there [Oak Ridge] because it keeps security uppermost in a man's mind. It is a good guard on a loose tongue. When a man knows he is going up against this machine, he thinks about it when he starts talking." When Salisbury was asked why the polygraph was not introduced into the other plants to make the practice uniform, he replied (long before the AEC efficiency study was completed), "To introduce it now in a new place might create an uproar and might break morale." The State Department said it had administered polygraphs on demand in a few instances involving security but not loyalty. People indiscreet in talk about their work or in association with disreputable persons were subject to security charges. "It was understood that the few cases referred to were persons suspected of sexual perversion," declared Leviero. He concluded, "In general the lie detector is used by the federal agencies particularly to establish whether a person has been arrested, is a sexual pervert or associates with Communists or other subversive persons."[20]

As a result of the uproar over Leviero's revelations, Senator Wayne Morse (R.–Oregon) made a speech in the U.S. Senate in which he denounced the use of the LD in testing Federal job applicants as un–American. He described the use of polygraph tests for jobs as "repugnant, foreign and outrageous." Also disclosed by Morse was that U.S. Secretary of Defense, Robert A. Lovett, had prohibited the use of the instrument in his department, after the Senator had protested. If other government departments did not cease using the machine, stated Morse, he would introduce legislation to ban the device. Senator Morse said he was informed that a private concern had been engaged to carry out the tests on defense job applicants. Lovett had told the Senate Armed Services Committee (Morse was a member) he had not known the Defense Department was using the LD on people other than those who were criminal suspects. Neither, apparently, did Leviero, in his earlier piece.[21]

Despite those assurances from Lovett, a month later it was reported that the Defense Department acknowledged that LD tests were still used on job applicants and employees in positions involving absolute security. It was said the tests were not compulsory but an applicant picked for one of those sensitive jobs sacrificed his chance unless he submitted to the machine.[22]

Dwight Macdonald reported in 1954 that, officially, the polygraph was used for general security screening in only three federal government agencies. All three were hush-hush defense agencies: the Operations Research Office (ORO), the CIA, and the National Security Agency (NSA). At ORO, all the new employees were tested and all existing workers were polygraphed twice a year. The CIA set up its own LD program in 1948 and, according to the *Army Times*; "While no worker is compelled to submit to the device's estimate of his veracity, ninety-nine percent of the agency's employees have undergone the test voluntarily...."[23]

At NSA, the polygraph program was started early in 1951 when six examiners were hired, at salaries of $6,400 a year each. NSA had some 4,000 to 8,000 employees. None of those polygraph examiners hired, it was said, had more than a six weeks' course at the Keeler polygraph school in Chicago, an institute that had fallen into disrepute after the 1949 death of its founder. At NSA, all employees and all applicants were tested. An example was given by Macdonald on how applicants were forced into taking what were always described as voluntary tests. Twenty-one successful applicants (awaiting security clearance and not yet on the payroll) were called to a meeting at which the person in charge asked them to all take the LD test to speed up those clearances. It was entirely voluntary, he explained, adding, though, that he did not know when or if those who declined to take the test would get their clearances. In a vote, the 21 unanimously agreed to take the test. Questions included, "Are you an alcoholic?" "Are you a dope addict?" "Are you a homosexual?" "Have you ever associated with Communists?" Often the questions posed were very vague, such as, "Have you ever done anything you were ashamed of?" "Are you now or have you ever been in sympathy with leftist ideas?" Examiners were said to have violated most of the rules of a good operator — be friendly, get along with people, and so on. Sometimes they browbeat the subjects, saying, for example, "Damn it, I know you're lying, the machine tells me so."[24]

Employees of NSA were not retested annually even though that was the announced policy. That was tied to a reported general feeling that if all were tested yearly it would cause a mass exodus. At some of these testing sessions, male examiners asked unmarried females questions such as, "Have you ever slept with a man?" and other specifically sexual queries. Word of that got out and three leading polygraphists— not involved in the NSA program — got together in Chicago to discuss the problem. One of them, Russell Chatham, was delegated to go to Washington to express their displeasure and concern at the manner in which the tests were being handled. "It was our information," explained Russell, "that the men conducting some of these examinations had little or no experience ... also that the polygraph tests were being used conclusively in determining whether or not an applicant would be employed." After Chatham spoke to Washington officials and left the capital, he felt the situation would be stopped or corrected. However, it was not.[25]

In the executive departments of the administration of President Dwight Eisenhower, according to White House claims, over 2,000 security risks had been found and cleaned out of government (this was a response to the paranoia and witch-hunting of the Cold War and McCarthy eras). "In the process, increasing reliance is being placed upon sex blackmail and use of the lie detector as a means of frightening employees into resigning," said Macdonald. "To increasing numbers of government workers, it [the lie detector] is known as the 'Soul-Washer.'" By the summer or fall of 1950, the State Department was using the LD in "Miscellaneous Morals" cases— most of them involved charges of homosexuality.[26]

Municipal governments were also moving into the use of polygraphs. William Carlile, director of personnel services for Stockton, California, reported that Stockton had started using the LD in its personnel selection in April, 1958. Eighteen months later, he enthusiastically said that city officials believed it to be the best method available by which to select individuals for a position of trust, whether it was the police, fire, or other departments. Since Stockton started its program, several other cities in Northern California had done the same thing and several had reportedly dispensed entirely with the traditional oral-appraisal board. "A decision to employ an individual as a guardian of his fellow citizens and their property must be based on the best information available and nothing equals the polygraph in securing accurate information," said Stockton City

Manager John C. Lilly. The polygraph test administered by Stockton lasted 90 minutes during which time the subject was asked 300 questions. It was given only after an applicant had passed all the other screening procedures such as psychological testing, physical agility exam, fingerprint check, oral interview, and medical exam. Each applicant was questioned about his previous work history, military service, physical and mental health, credit and financial stability, marital history, use of liquor and narcotics, education, and "any abnormal sexual contacts." Based on LD results only, the rejection rate was between 40 and 60 percent of the applicants. Reasons for rejection ranged from false statements to narcotic addiction, "as revealed by the polygraph."[27]

Another area of major expansion for LD usage in the 1940s and 1950s was in business, the private sector, especially from the late 1940s onward. Ray Holmes of the Chicago-based Associated Research Inc., said, in 1948, LDs were then being used at a rate 200 percent above pre-war utilization, by consulting personnel counselors who served industrial establishments. Those machines cost about $1,300 with the cost per test per employee, in evaluating honesty, averaging from $25 to $100.[28]

In an article on the subject in *Business Week* in 1951, it was reported that one of Washington, D.C.'s biggest hardware stores, Fries, Beall & Sharp, had tried to find out why its 1950 profit margin had dropped off. It decided that its workers might be stealing merchandise. To see if that assumption was true, the company hired Deception Tests Associates to subject all 122 of its employees to polygraphing. Somebody leaked the story to the papers and "This brought an immediate furor, with the store accused of everything from violation of civil rights to a deliberate attempt to break the morale of its employees." Fries president W. J. Tastet was forced into trying to justify the program and said, "We believe our employees are honest, and we're just trying to prove it." *Business Week* remarked that "Regardless of the moral issue, the fact is that the use of lie detectors in business has become pretty widespread." Alex L. Gregory, president of the International Society for the Detection of Deception (a trade lobby group) estimated there could be as many as 50 private LD practitioner firms that did polygraph work for industry and the police. That lobby group, formed in 1947 to set and maintain LD standards, and to lobby, was evidence itself of the growth of private polygraphing. Not many years earlier, there were not enough people to form such a group. Its founding motto was "Truth Through Science." By 1954, it claimed about 150 members and a new name — the Academy for Scientific Interrogation.[29]

One of those private LD firms, Associated Research Inc., claimed it had upward of 300 clients in business alone. Deception Tests Associates charged $10 per person, per test; another firm charged $15. The full extent of business usage of polygraphs was said to be unknown because everyone concerned was reluctant to talk about it. After the story broke in the papers about the Washington hardware store, another company postponed its arrangement for a similar investigation. Companies that administered such tests were also secretive and would not allow the names of their clients to be published. One exception to that rule was made by the New York LD firm, Personnel Research, Inc. It said a Chicago company that had used its services saw its annual losses drop from $1.4 million to $40,000. However, the named company denied the whole story saying it had never heard of Personnel Research; it rarely used a polygraph; and its losses were nowhere near $1.4 million. Another major firm in the private polygraph industry was John E. Reid and Associates (Chicago). Originally all its clients came through insurance companies when one of them called Reid after one of their clients claimed a loss. After that first contact, Reid generally got more business from the non–insurance concerns. The biggest users in Reid's experience were fur companies, jewelry supply houses, and banks.[30]

Reporter Marilyn French observed in *American Business*, also in 1951, that fraud cost U.S. businesses around $600 million a year. This argument would be used repeatedly in the future as a justification for instituting, or increasing, polygraph exams, although the numbers cited as fraud losses were all over the place. French cited numerous examples of miraculous work done by LDs in finding the perpetrators of fraud. "A routine lie detection test given before hiring can be handled more diplomatically than one given after a theft has occurred," said French. "Many undesirable applicants will steer clear of employment offices where they know such a test is part of the hiring procedure." When French wondered if people resented taking such tests she answered her own question by declaring, "Innocent people have nothing to fear from them. It is the person with the guilty conscience who refuses to take a test. Of course, no one can be forced to take a test against his will." As an interesting sidelight French asserted that management seldom, if ever, suspected the real culprit. She added that "Because the machine is practically foolproof, it is especially useful in certain lines, such as at insurance companies." Also, she was enamored of a new cheap unit (It quickly disappeared as it was even more worthless than the standard LD.) which cost only $200, compared to $650 to $1,300 for a regular machine. It used to take at least six months to a year to learn to operate a regular model but, "Almost anyone can learn to operate the new electronic model in 8 hours." To emphasize her conclusions, French placed them in a set-aside black bordered box in large type. "In publishing this article we do not urge companies to rush into blanket use of them without careful consideration," she added. However, when a good deal of money or merchandise would be handled by an employee, "business seems justified in taking every possible precaution to safeguard its funds and property. The person who wants a position of responsibility should be willing to undergo such a test in order to get it."[31]

Sunbeam Corporation, manufacturer of electric razors for men and women, among other items, had been plagued by thefts for three years, in the mid 1950s. To combat that problem, the company wrote rules against carrying purses or parcels into the shaver department (worst hit by pilferage), increased plant guards, and implemented other measures. But none of them made much difference. Usually parts were stolen, as opposed to complete razors, as they were smaller and easier to conceal in clothing. One theft ring broken up in 1954 (before LD use) was found to have 1,000 razors assembled from stolen parts. Sunbeam then notified shaver department employees that it was making periodic LD tests a condition of their continued employment in the department. Those who refused would not be discharged but would be shifted to other departments in which there would be little chance for pilferage. In the future, the firm added, nobody would be hired for the shaver department without first agreeing to submit to occasional polygraph tests. The International Association of Machinists, who represented the Sunbeam workers, filed objections arguing the policy violated employees' civil and personal rights.[32]

In one manufacturing firm, the company had traced some losses to an area where a number of welders worked but could not determine which specific individual was stealing. Therefore the company had deducted the amount of the latest shortage equally from each employee's paycheck. However, arbitrators agreed with the welders that those deductions were unfair. As a result, the company terminated the program but then demanded that all those workers submit to a polygraph and proposed to refund deductions to all welders who took the LD test successfully. The arbitrator concluded it would be improper to subject to polygraph test a whole group of people of whom only an unknown few are suspected. Since the company wanted a wholesale "fishing expedition" designed to pinpoint a few unknown people as guilty of a known offense, the arbitrator rejected the company's request. He ordered the company to refund to welders with no recourse to LD tests. William Lissy reported this case in the trade journal *Supervision* (aimed at factory supervisors and managers). He gave his conclusions and warnings in a black-bordered box where he declared, "Arbitrators, like jurists, are suspect of the use of lie detectors." However, he added, "Companies that have seriously threatened the use of lie detectors have discovered that pilferage, stealing and false work reports diminish rapidly."[33]

At the end of the 1950s, just one of the private polygraph firms, albeit one of the larger companies, John E. Reid and Associates reported it was administering 2,400 polygraph exams a year in the private sector; two-thirds of them were about embezzlement.[34]

As the polygraph became more widely used and discussed, the need for grandstanding with the device faded away. It was fast becoming accepted, at least in some quarters, as a serious device with a serious mandate. It also helped that one of the main grandstanders and trivializers of the machine, Marston, was otherwise occupied. However, such publicity opportunities were not entirely absent. Raymond Schindler of the Schindler detective agency arranged a demonstration in New York City in 1944 that pitted Keeler against a group of well-known citizens including M. H. Aylesworth, the former head of RKO; James A. Moffett, former vice president of Standard Oil of New Jersey; Frank Buck, celebrated wild animal trainer; and others. Using his polygraph Keeler reportedly beat them all in a series of "pick a number, any number between 1 and 20" matches. Keeler had a bit part in the 1948 film by director Henry Hathaway, *Call Northside 777* (starring James Stewart and Richard Conte). Appropriately enough, Keeler played an LD operator who gave a test to Conte's character.[35]

If grandstanding was disappearing, then it was replaced by something more fitting and in keeping with the ambience of the Cold War Era. What rose up was the demand and challenge in which an outraged well-known public figure would demand that so-and-so immediately submit himself to the device. Or, the enraged individual offered to take an LD test himself, if the person or persons accused would do likewise, all to "clear the air." Many of these challenges involved Communism in some fashion.

President Harry Truman declared in August, 1948 that the spy investigations of the House Committee on Un–American Activities were infringing on the Bill of Rights, as Alger Hiss, former State Department official accused of leadership in an alleged pre-war Communist underground, refused to take the LD test proposed by the committee. This, even though his accuser, Whittaker Chambers, consented to undergo such an exam also. Hiss notified the committee that he preferred to give the proposal further study and to seek scientific guidance. In a letter Hiss told the committee that reports he had received until then were uniformly negative as to the capability of the polygraph to conclusively separate the truth from falsehoods. Acting chairman of the House investigative group, Representative Richard Nixon (R.–California) indicated disappointment that Hiss had declined, for the present, to submit to the machine. "Mr. Hiss would be taking no greater risk than Mr. Chambers, who has consented to take the test," said Nixon. "But this test is an entirely voluntary thing. The committee, of course, cannot require it. Many persons accused take it as a means of clearing themselves. For the present we will have to drop the proposal." Hiss added, in his letter, "Both the scientific and legal experts whom I have consulted confirm the impression which I, as a practicing lawyer, had obtained some years ago that the scientific validity of mechanical tests for veracity have most definitely not been established by Dr. Keeler or anyone else."[36]

On a 1953 edition of the radio and television program "Meet the Press," Bert Andrews, head of the Washington bureau of the New York *Herald Tribune* was one of several journalists questioning James Weschler, editor of the *New York Post*. He asked Weschler whether, to disprove allegations that he was still a "Commie" at heart, he would subject himself to the instrument. That caused the author of an article in *The Reporter* to reflect on the vogue of the polygraph in fact finding and in truth checking. "Whenever anything we say is called a lie by somebody, we may be invited to take a lie-detector test," he concluded. "Our devotion to our country, to our family, or to plain decency may have to be checked by a mechanical gadget. A presumption of guilt is thus laid on the accused."[37]

When it came to issuing demands and challenges, nobody was more active than Senator Joseph McCarthy (R.–Wisconsin). It was, of course, more than a little ironic that one of America's most notorious liars should be such a singular proponent of the "truth machine." During a 1949 hearing of a Senate Armed Services subcommittee, Senator McCarthy demanded polygraph tests for a former Army officer and two aides who had been accused of brutality toward German prisoners. McCarthy said he thought the men were lying in denying the charges. However, the committee rejected McCarthy's demand. For that, and other reasons, the Senator was irate and stormed out of the investigation room.[38]

When McCarthy made his demand for an LD test at the hearing he lashed out at one witness, "I think you are lying! I do not think you can fool the lie detector. You may be able to fool us. I have been told you are very, very smart.... I am convinced you cannot fool the lie detector."[39]

Near the end of 1951, McCarthy declared that all government officials and employees in sensitive jobs should be required to submit to lie detector tests. He was described as a persistent campaigner against Communists in government positions and a long time advocate of the use of the polygraph on witnesses who gave conflicting testimony to committees of Congress. While he agreed it was unconstitutional to compel anyone to submit to such a test as that would be tantamount to requiring him to give testimony against himself, he did add that no applicant "has the right to a sensitive Government job or office unless he is willing to submit to such a test."[40]

In March, 1953, the question came up in the Senate whether Charles Bohlen, chosen by President Eisenhower to be Ambassador to the Soviet Union, should be subjected to a polygraph test. That proposal was made by McCarthy, and quickly squelched by Senator Robert Taft of Ohio. When McCarthy first proposed Bohlen submit to the machine, Taft's face became, said an account, "red in anger" and he said, "I want to know whether the Senator from Wisconsin is aware that J. Edgar Hoover is absolutely opposed to the lie detector, regards it as of no possible use whatsoever, and that he in fact is a 'leader of the opposition' to its use?" It all caused one media account to say that if McCarthy and his "acolytes" had their way, the time might come when "just as we check our weight by stepping on a scale, we may get accustomed to having our veracity tested by the lie detector."[41]

McCarthy locked horns with the U.S. Army again, in 1954. He proposed, in March of that year, that polygraph exams be given to all witnesses in the Senate investigation of his dispute with the Army. "The truth in this case is the important thing," he said. The Senate Permanent Subcommittee on Investigations was looking into an Army report that McCarthy and his chief counsel, Roy M. Cohn, made direct threats in an effort to obtain preferential treatment for Private G. David Schine. Until he was drafted, Schine was an unpaid committee consultant. McCarthy charged the Army tried to blackmail him out of investigating alleged Commies in the Army by threatening to make public the Cohn/Schine report. It came down to who was lying. When he suggested polygraph tests for all witnesses, McCarthy recalled that he used the instrument while presiding over murder trails as a circuit judge in Wisconsin and that he had complete confidence in the device. Reporters then reminded him that FBI director Hoover was "absolutely opposed" to the polygraph. However, McCarthy then denied that Hoover was opposed to such tests.[42]

As the McCarthy/Army investigation rolled along, it had reached 24 days of hearings, and counting, in June, 1954. Army counsel Joseph N. Welch voiced suspicions about the authenticity of documents on which McCarthy based his accusations against Army officials. Faced with that challenge McCarthy quickly offered to take an LD test, if all other principals in the case would and "we might be able to end this thing in twenty-four hours rather than twenty-four days." McCarthy's original request for polygraphs all around was made in March in a newspaper interview but was not pressed when the committee began its inquiry the next day. The second request was made at the inquiry. Challenges and demands made by high-profile people would remain part of the polygraph industry over the coming years, but not as pervasively as in the 1940s and 1950s. Such requests for use of the machine as made by Senator McCarthy, for example, illustrated using the LD for political reasons only, and with no regard for truth verification.[43]

Media articles with nothing but praise for the instrument continued to appear in this period, especially in the earlier years of the period. Articles which praised the device continued to appear after that time, of course, but they were more likely to include at least a little bit of caution, a negative remark or two.

The most important article to appear to that time in the general media showed up in April, 1944. It was a lengthy three-part series on successive weeks in the widely-read *Saturday Evening Post*. Its laudatory tone could be seen in the title Alva Johnston chose for her series, "The magic lie detector" and in a subhead that appeared in part one and said the series was about "How Leonarde Keeler's astounding invention tracks down murderers, unmasks the liars and the larcenous, and can tell just how honest you are — and intend to be." Enlarging the mystique, Johnston added the idea that "Getting caught on the lie detector is a sort of moral vaccination, a shot of integrity in the arm." By this time, she said, the device had been used in 60,000 cases "and its uncanny power of penetrating guilty secrets had been thoroughly established." Declaring the usage of the polygraph was expanding rapidly in the Middle West, she did acknowledge that "In some other sections of the country, the detector is still almost unknown and is classed with divining rods, rain-making machines and anti-earthquake pills." Keeler recalled that back in 1931, when he first tested job applicants for banks, he had found 62 percent of them had stolen from previous employers. Over the ensuing 13 years he had tested thousands more applicants and employees and little had changed. He said, "The average of 62 percent of dishonesty remains fairly constant for groups in a position to take small sums without great immediate danger of being caught. The percentage is higher in chain stores, where small items can be pilfered without much risk." In one case Keeler was called to a summer hotel in Northern Michigan to polygraph the workers. His machine indicated to him that 11 of 12 bartenders were guilty of irregularities. "They confessed" that they had pocketed money that should have gone into the till, short-changed customers, stolen the occasional flask, and so forth. Apparently it caused a ripple effect because, said Keeler, "The majority of the other employees confessed [before being polygraphed]." They had stolen from bedrooms, cheated guests, tapped tills and raided hotel supplies.[44]

Many specific cases in which the LD supposedly performed wonders were cited by Johnston. One involved a bank vault custodian who planned to have a duplicate key made and to steal $50,000 from a safety deposit box. Before he could carry out the plan, his bank adopted a policy of having its entire personnel regularly examined on the polygraph. When he was tested he produced a "peculiar" record. Although the LD "showed clearly" that he had never stolen anything from the bank, it did indicate "he had something exciting on his mind." On being asked more searching questions the man broke down and confessed his plan. He was fired. Over 30 banks in Chicago were then said to use periodic LD tests and that there was a 10 percent reduction in the charge for bonding employees who were regularly "run on the machine." Johnston declared that from the experience of Keeler and his Northwestern group their assessments of polygraph records were "confirmed by confessions or legal proof in 82 percent of their cases." For 17 percent of the cases the record was inconclusive, that is, the subject could not be declared truthful or deceptive. In one percent of the cases the lie detector findings were "proved wrong." However, in that one percent, "the mistake is almost invariably that of giving a guilty man the benefit of the doubt." Obviously, if there had to be an error rate, then that was the "best" kind of error to have since society accepted the concept that it was better for a guilty man to go free than it was for an innocent one to be convicted. Even more unbelievably Johnston declared that "There is said to have been only one case where the polygraph had anything to do with sending a possible innocent main to jail."[45]

A subhead for part two of Johnston's series heralded the powerful range of the device by asserting, "It airs a scandal in a sorority house, stops students from cribbing, bank presidents from tapping the till, and releases a guiltless man condemned to a lifetime in jail." Johnston argued that "The lie detector has won some spectacular victories over eyewitness testimony." Keeler was said to have tested 500 convicts at Joliet prison, many of whom claimed to be innocent. Every one of the 500 ran a guilty polygraph record. A university president gave students a test and let them mark their own papers, making it easy for them to change their answers and to cheat. Then the professor announced that evidence of cheating had come to light and the whole class would be run on the polygraph. Sixty percent of the students confessed to cheating rather than face the machine. Statements such as that helped to give the LD an image of infallibility and to mystify it, to give it powers that were almost beyond human comprehension. This was how witch doctors operated in the more "primitive" societies. It had to be that way when the item in question — the LDs or the witch doctor's concoctions — did not really work. In another Keeler case discussed by Johnston, the former was due to travel to a small town near Chicago to test a bank president because a holdup there gave indications of being an inside job. However, early in the morning of the day he was to make his journey Keeler got a call from a local judge who told him the bank president, fearing to face the LD, had killed himself.[46]

Joseph Kubis wrote an article in praise of LDs for the magazine *Electronics* in 1945, especially the galvanometer. That was not surprising since Kubis was an Associate Professor of Psychology at Fordham University and had taken over the role of chief proselytizer for the pathometer (as the machine was then called) after the death of its inventor, Summers. First Kubis explained that all lie detectors were based on the fundamental principle that the telling of a lie created a situation of conflict and attendant emotional disturbance within the individual. Though internal, that disturbance could be expressed in many ways such as blushing, paling, perspiring, shaking, fidgeting, and so forth. While the clever or habitual liar, continued Kubis, could, with a little practice, easily conceal such observable reactions, he could not control certain involuntary reactions, such as minor variations in breathing, increased reactivity of his heart and almost imperceptible changes in the electrical character of his body.[47]

Kubis briefly mentioned the Keeler polygraph, crediting it with 75 to 85 percent accuracy but stating that the interpreters of its results "require considerable skill." On the other hand, he declared the pathometer provided "easily interpreted" records and had "better than 98 percent accuracy in the diagnosis of guilt and innocence." Also stretching the bounds of credibility was the statement by Kubis that "No diagnosis of guilt or innocence made with this equipment has yet been contradicted by later evidence and already over 300 criminal situations have been diagnosed with the aid of the Pathometer." While it had been chiefly used in criminal cases, in cooperation with police authorities, Kubis noted it had been more recently used by the armed forces and also "in connection with the diagnosis of mental disorders."[48]

A dozen years later, Kubis authored another article but the galvanometer (as it was then called again) was pretty much finished. It could not compete with the standard polygraph (which, of course, had had a galvanometer component for a couple of decades) even though the galvanometer was cheaper to buy and took less time to learn how to operate. Kubis declared that "no self-respecting lie detection device advertises less than 95 percent accuracy." But that's not the same thing as achieving that figure. In dealing with the difficult issue of court rejection of LD records, Kubis was content to say, "There is no general legal recognition of lie detection procedures as valid sources of legal evidence [which was a diplomatic way of saying that every high court in American that ruled on such a case had rejected polygraph evidence]. There are, however, several instances of acceptance in lower courts." Again, there was no mention that all of those that were appealed had the LD records rejected. If some of those decisions stood, it was because they had never been appealed.[49]

Maclean's magazine (Canada's equivalent to Time or Newsweek) published a laudatory piece in 1945 that was not quite as fawning as the Saturday Evening Post effort even though the device was "almost unknown in Canada." In conclusion the piece declared the LD "has been building a very credible record since the basic methods were first used in criminal investigations as early as 1921."[50]

The New Yorker, in a 1948 article, also indirectly mentioned the mystical powers being attributed to the device. After remarking that no upper court in the nation had admitted an LD test result in evidence, but that a few lower courts had, the account declared, "It's a matter of record, in fact, that a good many criminals have been so frightened by the prospect of having to take the test that they have confessed while sitting around waiting for it to start."[51]

Articles that contained nothing but praise for the polygraph tended to become very rare after the early 1950s. Many articles full of praise for the instrument, overwhelmingly positive, still appeared, of course, but even these usually mentioned a negative point or two, at least if only in a perfunctory fashion. The days of complete uncritical acceptance were passing. An exception was a piece by William Leonard in 1959 in Science Digest. Leonard spoke to John Reid who told him that "The lie test of today is no ordeal. It never includes more than 11 questions, and none of these questions is a surprise, for our examiners show the suspect the written list of queries before the questioning begins. No test ever takes more than 3 minutes. Most of them don't last that long." When the first test was not conclusive, Leonard explained, a second test was administered, which also lasted three minutes. Sometimes there was even a third or a fourth test. Standard industry practice of the time was that all questions be given to the subject before a test was started. Supposedly this allowed for any ambiguities or problems with definitions to be straightened out beforehand. However, a three-minute test was not standard practice. Industry representatives favored 30 minutes or more, although some polygraph firms may have cut corners to increase profit margins.[52]

There was still no outside research conducted on the LD to determine its reliability and validity. When asked about accuracy in this period, the numbers usually cited were the industry-generated figures that polygraphs were accurate 95 percent of the time, inconclusive in four percent of the cases, and in error one percent of the time — with that error rate said to be much more likely to declare the guilty innocent rather than to find the innocent guilty.[53]

On the other hand, arrayed against the believers and supporters were an increasing number of skeptics and critics. *Time* magazine joined that group, in a mild way, with a 1944 article in which it remarked that courts in general considered LDs "too unreliable to admit their findings as conclusive evidence. Psychologists are equally skeptical of them." Observing that proving a polygraph's accuracy was "obviously impossible" the article asserted that "There is no way of guaranteeing that, in some cases, even the best instrument may not tell the wrong story."[54]

At a spring, 1944 meeting the American Psychiatric Association expressed its "low opinion" of the lie detector in a resolution that pointed out the machine's findings were wrong in about 30 percent of the cases and that, in any event, guilt was too complex a response to be measured by a machine such as an LD.[55]

One of the first media articles to attack the device with harsh criticism appeared in *Science News Letter* in 1946, and was written in response to the revelation that some workers at the Oak Ridge, Tennessee, weapons facility were subjected to polygraphing. The polygraph was, said the account, "an instrument of third-degree intimidation, not of scientific crime detection. Its evidence is not generally accepted in courts of law." Pointing out the LD had been in limited use for 20 years or more the article said "During that time it has not been established as generally useful. Evidence obtained by the 'lie detector' has never stood up in courts of law. In a few cases, it has been accepted by lower courts, but has not withstood appeal." In conclusion the publication declared the "Chief usefulness of the gadget is as an aid to the police in scaring an ignorant or superstitious person into making a confession of crime. An empty black box, if it looks mysterious, would serve the same purpose — and has been used for it."[56]

Reporter Anthony Leviero of the *New York Times* had broken the story in 1951 of the federal government's more-or-less secret use of the polygraph in certain agencies and was important in focusing attention on the situation, which led to an increase in criticism of the industry. Leviero returned with a 1952 attack on the LD that tried to place the machine within American society, something many of its critics attempted. "Thirty years of use have failed to accord to the lie detector a respected place in American life," he declared, but at the same time acknowledging that its use was more widespread than ever before in both government and industry. He felt two factors accounted for that anomaly, "The threat of Communist subversion," and "Expert salesmanship, which has persuaded many

private industries to apply it to employees handling money or merchandise that may be pilfered easily. Leviero declared that "Americans generally regard the use of the polygraph with repugnance except in criminal
cases, and then only as an accessory to other means of investigation."[57]

A year later, an account with no author byline in the *New York Times*
said that a lie detector did not detect lies but only recorded emotional
disturbances. Catalyst for the piece was the McCarthy proposal to
have Charles Bohlen submit to the machine. The polygraph, said the
account, "is regarded by most intelligent people as a modern instrument
of emotional torture that puts a man through a psychological third
degree."[58]

When *Scientific American* discussed the problems of the device in
1953 it titled its piece "Lie gadgets" and noted that the AEC had concluded
the instrument was not worthwhile. This piece also pointed out that two
lawyers and two psychiatrists on the faculty of Yale University had issued
a joint warning against the use of "truth serums" in criminal investigations. The use of drugs such as sodium amytal and sodium pentothal (the
successors to scopolamine) in lie detection was almost never mentioned
in this period although this account, with no specific details, claimed that
"truth drugs have been used by many police departments."[59]

One of the longest, and most critical, of the articles came from Dwight
Macdonald in a two-part series in the pages of *The Reporter* magazine in
June, 1954. Openly hostile, this series was at the opposite extreme of the
loving look at the device in the *Saturday Evening Post*'s 1944 series. In the
intervening years, there had been several critical revelations, such as that
of Leviero. Macdonald, like others, said the device did not detect lies at
all but simply recorded the physiological by-products of emotional
responses. Citing J. Edgar Hoover as the source, Macdonald wrote, "The
name is a complete misnomer. The machine used is not a lie detector....
The person who operates the machine is the lie detector by reason of his
interpretation," and "whenever the human element enters into an interpretation of anything, there is always a variance." He thought the machine
may have proved its usefulness in certain police and commercial investigations, but he was concerned with the expansion of usage in the preced-
ing five years or so to the mass screening of new employees, especially in
certain "sensitive" positions in some Federal agencies. It was an area in
which the LD results were said to be much less impressive. Questions asked
in criminal investigations, such as "Did you take the money?" were very
different, thought Macdonald, from queries in those mass screenings
such as "Is your sex life normal?" or "Have you ever had any Communist
sympathies." For Macdonald, a moral question involved was whether a

citizen accused of no crime should have to submit himself to an LD test in order to convince superiors of his honesty.[60]

When Macdonald wrote his series, the great majority of the thousand or so LDs then estimated to be in use were polygraphs. The two best-selling models were both made in Chicago and each cost around $1,300. One was Keeler's machine while the second was a close relative called the Stoelting Deceptograph; the latter had been adopted as standard equipment by the Army Signal Corps. Two other variations on the design of the best-sellers were available — the Berkeley Psychograph (it used a different system for measuring blood pressure), and the Reid Polygraph (which also recorded arm and leg movements— tensing the muscles in the limbs was one way to "beat" the device). Also available were Tremographs, Ataxia-graph, Reactograhs, Psychointegroammeters, and Behavior Research Photopolygraphs. However, only one other type of LD was widely used in practical work. That was the psychogalvanometer, which recorded only one physiological measure — the galvanic skin response. It was still sometimes called a galvanometer or pathometer.[61]

Yet another item on the market was the illegitimate child of the scientifically respectable pathometer (It was a very sensitive instrument and for that reason widely used in non-deception lab experiments.). For the previous few years, the company B & W Associates of Michigan City, Indiana, had used high-pressure to aggressively market its Electronic Psychometer, a much cheaper version of the Summers/Kubis galvanometer with the Electronic Psychometer selling for just $210. Sales brochures implied a purchaser could use the machine after eight hours or less of study and setup. It offered a guarantee that if you did not detect "lies 8 times out of 10 on future tests, you may return the machine and your money will be refunded." Macdonald reported that "Quite a few wrong-minded police departments use the B & W device." An inspector in the U.S. Post Office Department, where the machine was said to be widely used in criminal investigations, "feels that its value is about fifty percent psychological." An even simpler device was manufactured by the Merlin Electric company; it was a $24.95 LD, available in toy stores.[62]

In a poll of some 1,700 criminologists, polygraphists and psychologists conducted by the University of Tennessee, only 36 percent of the psychologists (against 75 percent of the polygraphists) agreed with this statement, reported Macdonald, "The fear of being found out and conscious efforts to deceive are the main causes of significant reactions in polygraphic tests of deception." All agreed that the operator was the key item, not the mechanical part, yet Macdonald declared, "Members of the profession itself have estimated that only ten percent of the examiners working with lie detectors today are fully qualified."[63]

After Keeler died in 1949, one of his students, Jack Harrison, bought his business and in a couple of years had turned the Keeler polygraph training school into what Macdonald called a "diploma mill." According to a Harrison associate "Jack gave 'em [diplomas] away to pay bills." Reportedly the school was operating more legitimately by 1954 and ran a series of six-week training courses with six to twelve students per course. Graduates received a letter certifying their training; they got a diploma only by producing evidence that they had conducted 150 tests in a manner satisfactory to the Keeler school. During the time this institute was a diploma mill, the Provost Marshal's office canceled its contract for the training of Army personnel and set up its own school. That school, at Camp Gordon, a Military Police installation near Augusta, Georgia, was, said Macdonald, the only other bona fide polygraph training school in the country, and almost all federal polygraph examiners were then trained there. Their regular course ran eight weeks in length.[64]

John E. Reid and Associates was one of the larger private firms involved in the industry, with headquarters in Chicago and branches in New York, San Francisco and Pittsburgh. It probably did more commercial work than any other agency and administered some 200 tests a month at an average fee of $25. Among its clients were: about 30 Chicago judges (who used the polygraph in civil suits when both parties agreed); the Chicago Police Department (It had its own machine but sometimes used Reid for consultation work.); the Office of Naval Intelligence; 15 banks; 171 lawyers; six mail-order houses, including Montgomery Ward; 19 hotels, from the swank Palmer House to the YMCA; the Chicago Racquet Club; the Armored Express Corp.; and a dozen department stores, including Marshall Field. Commenting on the geographic distribution of LD usage, Macdonald remarked that Chicago was perhaps the most "polygraph conscious city" in the United States while "New York is a barren vineyard. No big banks use the device there. Only one big store uses it, and the police use it only occasionally."[65]

Although much of the early work that led to the development of the polygraph was done abroad, noted Macdonald, "the instrument has seldom or never been used by British or Continental police — and certainly not by governments." Paul Trovillo, who also wrote on the instrument at this time agreed with that sentiment. "The instrumental detection of deception remains a typically if not exclusively American practice." Macdonald also related a bizarre proposal of a couple of years earlier for extended use of the LD, a proposal that was not implemented but which had all the earmarks of placing a blind faith in the box. Roy Post, a New York criminologist, proposed a 6th column armed with LDs to eliminate all Communist 5th columnists. Post would train 10 or 12 operators, equip them with polygraphs and send them into strategic industries that might be subject to sabotage. Once they were established, those men, said Post, could examine 2,000 people per day, about one every three minutes. Under the Post proposal, subjects would be asked only three questions, "Did you eat breakfast today?" "Do you drive a car?" and "Are you in the employ of any foreign government?"[66]

An editorial in the *New York Times* in August, 1954, said "Even the experts agree that there are only fifty or a hundred technicians out of a total of 500 or 600 who are fit to interpret the wavy lines that mean 'true' or 'false' to a technician." And because of that "it is easy to understand why polygraph evidence is not good enough for higher courts and why European police heads have no faith in it." As a last point of skepticism, the editor stated that the then late Leonarde Keeler, who was partial to using the pick-a-card gambit in his demonstrations, "had, no difficulty in fooling his own machine."[67]

Pope Pius XII said in April, 1958, that modern psychology, as a whole, was worthy of praise from a moral and religious standpoint but, he added, methods used by psychologists were not always blameless. In that connection the Pope mentioned narcoanalysis—the questioning of suspects when they were under the influence of so-called truth serum drugs. Such practices, he said, were questionable in psychotherapy and unlawful in judiciary procedures. He stated the same could be said about the lie detector. The Pope was speaking in Rome before 400 delegates from 30 countries attending the 13th congress of the International Association of Applied Psychology.[68]

Throughout this period there was a sharp increase in the use of the polygraph, especially by the federal government, fueled in part by the paranoia of the McCarthy/Cold War era. In turn that led to more media attention to the instrument and a growing number of critical articles about the machines, some of them quite harsh. Mass screenings for some government posts were especially galling to critics, although the same practice had been going on in the private sector—to a very limited extent—since the early 1930s. Some of it may have been a class bias as the government employees were mostly in high level positions, or sought them, while the small number of mass screenings in business usually applied to lower level workers. It was also an era that saw the emergence of the challenge issued to an opponent to submit to the machine. For the first time, some attention was paid to the use of the LD to intimidate and to its use for political purposes rather than any deception detection. Throughout this period as in the past, there was not a single piece of credible scientific evidence to validate either the underlying assumptions (lying leads to guilt, which leads to…, and so forth). Nor was there a single piece of evidence as to the instrument's accuracy. The few numbers that were used were all industry-generated and were too self-serving to draw any consideration.

5

-\/\--\/-

Government Use
Increases, 1960s

[The LD was used to] uncover such undesirable attributes as alcoholism, a prison record or pregnancy.
— Business Week, 1960

Is the Deputy Secretary of Defense, or the secretaries of the Navy and the Air Force, to be put in the same class with pickpockets and second-story men?
— Washington Evening Star, 1963

If we have reached the point where we have to rely upon these truth machines to tell us whether we can trust our public officials, then our nation is in sad shape.
— Saturday Evening Post, 1963

the aura of infallibility already surrounding polygraphs has led to count- less instances of coercion, intimidation, and other abuses."
— Newsweek, 1963

Throughout the 1960s the use of the polygraph continued to spread, especially in the federal government and in the private sector. Formal hearings on the subject were held by the federal legislators. Individual states began to limit the use of the instrument and to license operators of the devices. As in the past, though, courts continued to reject polygraph evidence. Colonel Maurice Levin was a member of the New York Bar and former Judge Advocate to the Surgeon General of the United States Army. He argued that the margin of error in any LD test was wide enough that the results of such tests were not generally acceptable in the scientific community. It was the rule in criminal trials in the U.S., he said, that in the absence of stipulation, LD test results were not admissible as evidence when offered to prove or disprove whether the defendant was guilty of the crime charged. And that rule had been extended so that inferential reference to the results of a polygraph exam was prohibited; a defendant could not introduce evidence of his willingness to take an LD test, and the prosecution could not show either directly or indirectly a defendant's refusal to take a polygraph exam.[1]

Levin reviewed both the 1923 Frye case and the one 10 years later by the Supreme Court of Wisconsin wherein both courts had rejected the device and its findings as not good enough. Since then a number of other courts had come to the same conclusion with a 1961 decision remarking "that there is not a single reported decision where an appellate court has permitted the introduction of the results of a polygraph or lie detector test as evidence in the absence of a sanctioning agreement or stipulation between the parties." Acknowledging the value of the LD as an investigational aid, but given the margin of error implicit in every test, Levin concluded that "the courts wisely do not admit lie detector evidence in the absence of stipulation." Without comment Levin noted the contradiction involved in admitting polygraph evidence pursuant to stipulation compared to the rule that did not admit results in the absence of stipulation. That is, if LD results were not good enough to be admitted with no stipulation how did admission under stipulation change that?[2]

As 1969 drew to a close, the New York State Court of Appeals reaffirmed that the results of an LD test could not be admitted as evidence in criminal cases because they were not reliable enough "to warrant judicial acceptance." It was a unanimous decision by the seven justices of the state's highest court. Associate Justice Matthew Jasen said, in his written opinion, that the data did "not adequately establish the reliability of the test to be admissible in evidence." He added that "We are all aware of the tremendous weight which such tests would necessarily have in the minds of a jury. Thus, we should be most careful in admitting into evidence the results of such tests unless their reasonable accuracy and general scientific acceptance are clearly recognized." This was the second time this high court had rejected the polygraph.[3]

In cases before government boards and labor arbitrators, generally, the instrument did not fare any better. Livingston and Sons was a retail store suffering losses that finally insisted all its employees submit to the machine. Forty-four workers refused and, as a result, either quit or were fired. On the employees' application for unemployment benefits the Unemployment Compensation Board of Review decided there was no just cause for firing an employee whose only misbehavior was his refusal to submit to an LD test.[4]

William Lissy reviewed the arbitration situation in a 1965 article in a trade publication aimed at foremen and supervisors. Arbitrators, he said, usually frowned upon the use of the device in industry. A few felt its use might be proper if an employee voluntarily agreed to take it, but more disagreed with that position. They felt an employee could be disciplined or discharged on competent evidence but not incompetent evidence. Polygraph results, being "incompetent evidence according to most courts," he declared, "cannot be made competent ... by an employee's voluntary submission to it." Since the use of LDs in pre-employment tests did not come within the scope of union contracts, it meant that management was free to use them in that situation. However, in an effort to stop their use in that area, unions had reportedly been successful in getting some states to pass laws restricting their use. A law in Massachusetts (one of five states which then had such a law) stated that "no employer shall require or subject any employee to any lie test as a condition of employment or continued employment." Writing in The *Arbitration Journal*, Lee Burkey remarked on the controversial nature of the instrument and concluded by saying, "It seems proper to conclude that an employer can no longer soundly contend that as a management prerogative he is entitled to subject any or all of his employees to polygraphic tests. To do so is to violate the employee's right to privacy and his right against self-incrimination. The emphasis will probably shift from science to civil rights in future cases." Lissy concluded his article with advice to supervisors contained within a black bordered box and set in a larger typeface. The three points were: 1) LDs were not free from error; 2) "Arbitrators usually will not uphold their use by management"; 3) union members were being urged by union officials to refuse to submit to the machine.[5]

Within the area of government use, most of the media interest focused on polygraph usage at the federal level. Occasionally, though, there was a report from another level of government. George Washnis was an administrative assistant to the city manager in Evanston, Illinois. Polygraph tests were used by that city as an aid in the final screening for new policemen and firemen, starting early in 1961. Those tests cost Evanston $15 to $20 per applicant and were administered by a private firm based in Chicago. An LD test was given after the civil service eligible list had been posted but before any applicants were appointed. Purpose of the test was to scrutinize the background of job applicants with respect to theft, "homosexualists," narcotics use, and "other detrimental characteristics." When the first 1961 list of eligible applicants was posted it contained eighteen names; five waived appointment for refusing to take a polygraph or for other reasons; six of the remaining thirteen were not hired as a result of the LD

tests. When the second eligible list of 1961 was posted, the first nine people on the list were asked to submit to the machine. Two passed, four
failed, two refused and waived appointment and one was asked to take
a second exam. "The tests have shown persons with long histories of
theft, serious undetected crimes, homosexuality, serious debt problems,
communist sympathies, use of narcotics and other undesirable traits,"
explained Washnis. "Most of the crimes were undetected. The persons
tested readily admitted these traits to professional interrogators." Washnis enthusiastically concluded by declaring "The polygraph program has
been highly successful in eliminating undesirable persons who otherwise
might have been appointed to the police and fire departments."[6]

Senator John J. Williams (R.–Delaware) complained in 1960 that the
Internal Revenue Service (IRS) had subjected some of its employees to LD
tests in an effort to find out how the Senator had uncovered scandals in
the service. He charged that one of the tax agency's officials was dismissed
after refusing to submit to the box because he felt it was an insulting
request. Williams declared that individual had given him no information.[7]

A Federal Aviation Agency (FAA) clerk was discharged in 1960 when
he admitted, while being polygraphed, to participating in four homosexual acts in his youth. That admission came during an LD test that was part
of the procedure for a change in jobs, to the Central Intelligence Agency.
Not only did he not get the CIA position but he was fired by the FAA. Four
years later, in 1964, he won reinstatement with back pay.[8]

Enough complaints about the use of polygraphs in the federal government had surfaced that in June, 1963, Representative Cornelius Gallagher (D.–New Jersey) announced a congressional subcommittee would
investigate the use of LDs by federal agencies. He said a House Government Operations subcommittee had drafted a questionnaire to measure
the extent, manner, and cost of government polygraph usage and the rights
of individuals subjected to the machines. All this came on the heels of a
report that the U.S. Defense Department alone owned 440 LDs and
employed 560 "polygraph experts."[9]

Early in 1964, Gallagher released preliminary figures from his still not
completed investigation, in response to numerous requests on its progress.
During the fiscal year ending June 30, 1963, reported Gallagher, the federal government carried out 23,122 LD tests and the government owned
525 machines for which it had paid $444,000. Leading the way in owner-
ship was the Army (261 machines), the Navy (86), the Air Force (72) and
the FBI (48). There were 656 authorized polygraph operators in the employ
of the government. Of the 24 agencies that permitted the use of LDs, only
seven of them had formal regulations regarding their use. Five agencies

that used the devices did not make the test results available to the employees who were tested. The figures, said Gallagher, did not include the use and ownership of the instruments by the CIA (who declined to reveal the numbers), which may have been the most prolific user. Of the total tests administered in fiscal 1963, the Army gave 12,494 with 3,494 of them administered to Cuban refugees seeking to enlist in the U.S. Army. Some 8,084 of the Army exams were described as being for security reasons. Reportedly the FBI did not use the polygraph for personnel screening. That agency was acknowledged to have the most skilled operators. Gallagher, who first took an interest in the topic after a complaint from a constituent, said he was deeply disturbed by the lack of ground rules for the protection of individuals being tested. Also revealed was that some of the military men who were also LD operators had only five days training and were required to have only a high school diploma. Further, the House Committee on Government Operations reported the polygraph had been found to be only 72 percent accurate in judging falsehoods, a far cry from the 95 to 98 percent accuracy figures so regularly cited by the industry.[10]

A *New York Times* editorial on the Gallagher report noted that operators of the devices were "often high-school trainees without the ability to form pertinent questions and weigh responses; these are matters which cannot be left to machines." Nor was the editor happy that the study disclosed questions had been asked of examinees about political affiliation, union and organizational memberships and even social friendship. "Many Americans feel that there is something repugnant about underhand detection or even open detection tests as a condition of employment," said the editor.[11]

On April 7, 1964, public hearings on LDs were held by the House Committee on Government Operations, chaired by John E. Moss (D.-California). Cornelius Gallagher (not a member of the committee) was denied permission to question the appearing witnesses and stormed out of the hearing room yelling, "whitewash." He said, "If I am not going to be able to ask questions I feel the hearing has taken on the nature of a whitewash of the polygraph industry. I am appalled." Slightly different figures disclosed that 19 federal agencies affirmed ownership of 512 LDs costing a total of $425,000. With 638 polygraph examiners employed to conduct the tests, the annual operating costs neared $4.5 million. Generally, the hearing was held to determine if the government should use polygraphs and, if so, to what extent, and so on. Professor Fred Inbau of Northwestern University (a well-known, long-time proponent) suggested in his testimony that untrained operators were responsible for a lot of the errors and about 80 percent of existing operators "are not measuring up to the standards we feel are required." George Lindberg, of John E. Reid and Associates, quoted the old, oft-used error rate of "as low as 1 percent." Challenging that figure was committee member Henry Reuss who said, "As of now, I think the lie detector is largely bunk." Inbau stated that LD tests were "not susceptible to actual statistical analysis."[12]

A couple of days later at the hearings, the Army, Navy, and Air Force all admitted they used hidden microphones and two-way mirrors when conducting LD tests and people subjected to those exams were informed of those things "only if they asked about them." Major General Ralph J. Butchers, provost marshal general of the Army, explained it was "absolutely essential" to monitor tests of women. He did not say why that was the case, but other witnesses said it was to guard against false accusations against polygraph operators. Rear Admiral Rufus Taylor, director of Naval Intelligence, tried to explain that the Navy used such methods "mainly to protect the person taking the test"—to ensure the operator was following proper procedures. All witnesses claimed polygraphs were used only in criminal and intelligence investigations by the armed services and not to screen job applicants.[13]

At the end of April, 1964, the U.S. Defense Department ordered a "sharp curtailment" in the use of polygraphs and that anyone asked to submit to one had to be told he could refuse, and that he was to be informed if the session was monitored, and so on. Apparently that resulted from the investigation by the Moss committee. Hearings resumed with testimony from Dr. Joseph Kubis, psychology professor at Fordham University, who described the polygraph as an "instrument of distrust." He criticized its use in such "trivial situations" as attempting to determine whether someone would steal in the future or make a good employee.[14]

Reporter Elinor Langer observed, in discussing the hearings, on the large number of government tests done but said, "Even the figures do not reflect the true veneration in which the lie detector or polygraph is held." It was announced in February, 1963, she explained, that the Pentagon had taken to using portable lie detectors in Vietnam, to flush out Viet Cong agents infiltrating the government forces. The polygraph model in question, about the size of an electric razor, was regarded "even by real proponents of lie detection, as better suited to parlor games than to criminal interrogation." In the first couple of weeks of hearings, she noted, witnesses representing both the lie detector industry and the Pentagon — the heaviest known government user of LDs—"could come up with no statistics, studies, or figures to indicate why they believed the instrument was so satisfactory." During fiscal 1963, the AEC (Atomic Energy Commission) conducted just one polygraph test while the space agency, NASA, had only conducted two LD tests in its history. The FBI administered 2,314 exams in that year. A Navy witness at the hearing stated the instrument was 70 percent accurate while Henry Reuss (D.–Wisconsin) did his own calculations and came to the conclusion the device had an accuracy rate of only 18.9 percent. But, said Langer, "Since no evidence was brought forth to support any of these claims, they had more the appearance of mystical revelation than of reliable fact."[15]

Later in 1964, Moss said the pattern of LD use at the time was one of rapid growth and expansion of the use of "these imperfect machines in the hands of inadequately-trained, imperfect individuals." Moss declared it amounted to a major invasion of the privacy of individuals not even suspected of a crime "where the price they must pay for seeking employment is probing on a broad basis in their subconscious mind ... dossiers are built up and transferred from one employer to another and permanent prejudice can be created."[16]

The strangest revelation that resulted from the investigation came in June, 1964, when the Moss subcommittee unearthed a two-year-old secret Pentagon report that "belittled" the reliability of polygraph tests. Yet the Pentagon did not curtail the use of such tests at the time despite that report for which it paid about $50,000. Prepared for the Department of Defense by the Institute for Defense Analysis, the report was submitted on July 31, 1962, and was immediately classified. It was not declassified for almost two years and even then only at the insistence of Moss's committee. According to the secret report, there was no scientific evidence to show that LD tests were worthwhile. Dr. Jesse Orlansky (the report's author from the institute), also said there was evidence that people could be trained to fool the devices. An example of the faith in such devices, wrote reporter Jack Raymond, was to be found in the proposal, cited by an unnamed government official, that in any disarmament treaty between America and the Soviet Union, a provision would call for regular lie detector tests of heads of states as an assurance that the treaty was not being breached.[17]

When the House Government Operations subcommittee delivered its report in March, 1965, it declared "There is no lie detector, neither machine nor human." Although the government had spent millions of dollars on polygraph machines and although investigators had given thousands of tests, research, continued the Moss report, "has failed to prove that polygraph interrogation actually detects lies or determines guilt or innocence." People, it concluded, had been deceived by a myth that a metal box in the hands of an investigator could detect truth or falsehood.[18]

Dr. Stefan Possony of Stanford University's Hoover Institution on

War, Revolution and Peace (He had served a total of 18 years in U.S. intelligence agencies.) prepared a study on polygraph use in the CIA, at the
request of Gallagher for the Moss committee. Possony said the LD, used
routinely in pre-employment screening by the CIA and in other government agencies, was "ineffective" because it tended to weed out "the active,
all–American, conscientious and virile types most urgently needed as
spies." Conversely, he said, the polygraph helped open the way to employment of "homosexuals, laggards and trained Communist agents." With
regard to the questions posed in exams by the CIA, "One point of emphasis is usually sex." Most virile young men were brought up in a tradition
that sex was a private matter, Possony felt, and responded uneasily to
bureaucratic questioning about their sex experience. That caused the polygraph to register doubt and, in security cases, "doubts tend to be resolved
against the applicants." By contrast, he continued, homosexuals lacked
any guilt feelings about their sex lives and "probably will pass the lie detector with flying colors." The Russians, he presumed, had trained all their
agents to pass LD exams.[19]

The Defense Department issued a directive in July, 1965, which further curtailed the use of LDs and the scope of questioning in cases where
such devices were still authorized. Moss hailed the directive signed by
Deputy Secretary of Defense Cyrus Vance as "the first step taken by
any Government agency to curtail the widespread use of so-called 'lie
detectors.'" Under the directive, polygraph usage was limited to the criminal investigations of a crime punishable by death or a year or more
confinement. Although he applauded the general direction of the Defense
announcement, Moss questioned why each armed service branch was still
to be permitted to determine the training programs for polygraph operators. "Presumably this would allow the Navy Department to continue its
five-day training course," Moss worried, "and the Army to continue its
seven-week training course — both totally inadequate."[20]

Moss announced in December, 1965, that President Lyndon Johnson
would establish a government-wide committee to take up the problem of
LDs and to recommend guidelines for using the machines. The Moss subcommittee made a recommendation the previous March for such a committee. However, it did not happen.[21]

Business use of the polygraph continued to expand in the 1960s. *Business Week* estimated in 1960 that about 80 percent of all LD tests administered by private firms were given to the employees of industrial and
commercial companies. Firms wanted to know if their employees were,
ever had been, or might become dishonest. "More and more companies
are making use of the lie detector on a more or less regular basis," declared

the business publication. Long established firms like Chicago's Keeler Polygraph Institute and John E. Reid and Associates (also Chicago-based) said their volume of business was eight to ten times what it was a decade earlier. They each administered over 3,000 tests a year. The New York office of the William J. Burns International Detective Agency, which offered LD exams as one of its industrial security services, reported that phase of its activity had more than doubled in the last year. More than 400 other firms then offered polygraph services to management and to the police and, said the account, "new organizations are springing up all the time."[22]

The reason for the increased LD usage, thought *Business Week,* was a growing worry over employee dishonesty, "although no one knows if it is increasing in business." Roy Taylor, a business control analyst, told an American Management Association conference that a million or more people stole from their firms every year. Consultant Norman Jaspan put business's daily loss of cash and property at $4 million, but no specific details on how those figures were derived was given. The controversial nature of the polygraph was mentioned along with the fact that it was not being accepted by the courts, and the possibly that it was in violation of employee rights, and so on. A Massachusetts law prohibited employers from requiring employees or job applicants to take LD tests. For accuracy numbers, this account cited Associated Research Corp. (a polygraph manufacturer) as stating that in lab experiments the device was accuracy 95 percent of the time. According to Associated Research, the polygraph's finding of deception had been followed by verified confessions in about 80 percent of personnel cases and in about 60 percent of criminal cases. Purchasers of machines from Associated were virtually all police departments, research laboratories, and independent LD examiners. It was estimated that no more than 2,000 LD units had been made in total and the annual sales, including replacements and conversions "probably do not exceed 200."[23]

Most business use of the instrument, said the *Business Week* account, involved trying to track down missing cash and property in specific cases of loss. Another common use was said to be in periodic personnel checks. Questions asked of subjects in those periodic tests tended to be more vague than those used in investigations of specific instances. One Midwestern bank reportedly got 80 percent of its employees to admit to thefts averaging $2 a week or more. A supermarket operator discovered 90 percent of his employees were taking home one or two dollars a week or more in cash or merchandise — for a total of $1.5 million plus per year. Yet a re-examination of those same employees six months later turned up only three percent as repeaters. Often employees were not fired for these small thefts. Instead, many employers claimed, a major advantage of periodic LD checks was that they served as a psychological deterrent to dishonesty. Leo Bramson, president of the Chicago department store, Bramson's said, "The best workers are those who have been caught once. They have too much on the line to risk the embarrassment of being caught again." Supermarkets reported that, generally, only about 10 percent of employees flunked a second test.[24]

Pre-employment LD testing, said *Business Week*, "though still small, is probably the fastest-growing polygraph application." In those cases, noted the account, the instrument was used to verify statements on the employment application and to "uncover such undesirable attributes as alcoholism, a prison record, or pregnancy." A St. Louis drug distributor used the device to identify and screen out narcotics users applying for positions. Companies that used a lot of temporary help were said to find the LD faster to use than reference checking in the peak season. Bramson claimed he cut his firm's losses in half the first year after introducing periodic personnel checks. After three years of polygraph screening, First Distributors, a Chicago mail order house that handled a lot of jewelry, concluded its losses had been cut by $6,000 to $10,000 a year and insurance premiums had been reduced 20 percent per year. Chicago's Lake Shore Bank screened all job applicants and re-examined workers after five years. One out of every three applicants who otherwise seemed acceptable failed the LD test, reported the bank, "and a significant percentage never turns up for the test at all." An average pre-employment screening test took about 30 minutes and cost a firm about $20 per hour. A number of firms that used polygraph exams in hiring seasonal help asked the potential employee to put up the test fee. If he passed, the company refunded his money; if he failed he forfeited it.[25]

When it came to validity, *Business Week* admitted "The courts' attitude has done lie detector testing a lot of harm." Even more disturbing, said the publication, were the disagreements within the industry. The Keeler and Reid organizations were said to be at odds on points of technique such as the types of questions to ask subjects and both were highly critical of all other training and equipment. "They accuse most other polygraphers of charlatanism and even corruption, asserting that they would not trust themselves to be examined by more than a few dozen of their competitors." Admittedly, said the account, there was some basis for those charges. One self-trained Midwest examiner who advertised "confidential lie detection tests and honesty screening" went on to declare, "I have lie detectors to back me up, but usually I can look applicants straight in the eye and tell whether they are lying or not." In this publication's view, a big problem was the lack of regulation in the industry. Not a single state had set minimum standards for licensing polygraph examiners.[26]

An October, 1961 account in the *Wall Street Journal* had a similar tone to the earlier *Business Week* piece. Reporter William Carley said the use of LDs to uncover employee wrongdoing was growing and that the fastest growing area of polygraph use was in pre-employment screening. It was still hard to know which specific companies were using the machines because most were reluctant to talk about the subject. But on the roster of known polygraph users were major companies in steel production, copper refining, auto manufacturing, meat packing, food processing, oil, electronics, and mail order retailing. As well, dozens of smaller concerns such as liquor stores and vending machine operators were regular users. Lee R. Keener, president of Truth Verification Inc., with offices in Dallas, Fort Worth, and Houston, said the number of LD tests his firm administered for business rose from 4,985 in 1959 to 6,896 in 1960. John E. Reid and Associates (Chicago and San Francisco) gave 3,400 commercial tests in 1960, up 28 percent from the previous year. The cost of the machines then ranged from $675 to $1,800, depending largely on the number of physiological responses to be measured. Charges for commercial polygraph tests usually ranged from $25 to $50 per employee for pre-employment and periodic tests up to $35 to $150 for testing on specific instances of loss. "In a few cases which have never been appealed, trial courts have accepted lie detector findings," concluded Carley. "But every appellate court that has ruled on the issue has denied admissibility when the evidence was offered over the objection of opposing counsel."[27]

The trade journal *Restaurant Management* declared in 1962 that restaurants were thinking more seriously about using LDs due to the increasing problem of pilferage and losses. One outspoken proponent of polygraph testing was William McClure, owner and manager of McClure's Charcoal Steak Restaurant, in a Greensboro, North Carolina shopping center. Upset by escalating pilferage at his restaurant, he decided to try and control his problem with the use of an LD. From this emerged a firm called Truth Incorporated, a company "dedicated to the proposition that honesty can be enforced." Assumed by the company was that an employee would not pilfer "if he knows he may be questioned about it in such a manner he can't fib his way out." McClure got into the truth business when he brought an LD into his restaurant, after learning that the county coroner had such a device. When he first got his machine McClure gathered his workers, told them of the pilferage problem, and said his only solution appeared to be to put everyone on the polygraph and got their agreement to submit, if requested, to a lie test in the future. Employees signed a one-line agreement "I agree to take the lie detector test if requested to do so." McClure asserted, "Our profits have been better ever since."[28]

Other restaurant people watched this reportedly successful move by McClure and deluged him with queries and with pleas for him to do the same for them. He then formed Truth Inc. After two years Truth Inc. had grown to such an extent that McClure stepped down as president to devote himself to his restaurant. By then the firm had about 100 restaurant clients as well as some in other business areas. According to statistics, supposedly from bonding companies, 25 percent of people were honest; 25 percent were dishonest; 50 percent were just as honest as the system under which they worked. Ed Pontifex, new president of Truth Inc., said, "To date we have had less than one tenth of one percent [of employees] refuse to sign this agreement [to submit to the machine]." Pontifex claimed a restaurant could effect a savings of at least two percent in food cost through using LD tests. A Truth Inc., technician made regularly scheduled visits to restaurant clients but "Only a handful of employees are actually checked." The tests themselves were administered by a "licensed technician" (but there was no such thing). In the experience of Truth Inc., to that point, it was said a "small percentage" of employees would leave a company within a week or 10 days after the polygraph system was introduced, but before any tests were administered. Truth Inc., was also said to have an effect on employees similar to that which the sign "You are being watched by radar" had on drivers. "By and large the drivers slow down."[29]

Writing in the *Saturday Evening Post* in November, 1962, Alex Gregory, self-described as a private investigator of personnel problems and user of polygraphs for 25 years, devoted much of his article to brief descriptions of miracles he had performed in the field in various business cases. He did estimate that employees rob American businesses of $1 billion a year in cash and merchandise. Of that amount, one hundred million dollars was from supermarkets alone. Two hundred million was from department stores. Gregory screened job applicants for some firms in Detroit where he lived but most of his polygraph work involved specific losses or other personnel problems. "Perhaps the greatest achievement of the polygraph," he declared, "is in helping prove people innocent, lifting the cloud of suspicion from honorable employees." For many business firms, he argued, LDs had become the most efficient aid to security. He also estimated that 30,000 to 40,000 firms were then using polygraph examiners, either on a consulting basis or as permanent employees on their security staffs. One large drug company reportedly employed three full-time examiners. Gregory, and most experienced operators, were said to charge from $150 to $200 per day for work with groups, and a minimum of $25 per person for testing job applicants.[30]

One of the first articles to deal solely with business use of the instrument, but to do so in a harshly critical manner was authored by Richard Sternbach, Lawrence Gustafson and Ronald Colier and appeared in the November, 1962 issue of the *Harvard Business Review*. They estimated that employee theft cost American business $4,000,000 a day in 1961 ($1.2 billion for 300 days). If traditional screening procedures were not effective enough to detect dishonesty or disloyalty-prone employees, what then was the answer? One response they identified was "a great increase in the number of polygraph operators in business." From a handful who specialized in lie detection before World War II, there were then "over 500 companies in major cities throughout the nation." Authors of this article argued that 1) polygraphic measurements were not valid; 2) those results were not reliable; and 3) moral questions surrounded "trial by polygraph." In 1962, the devices marketed by Associated Research and the C. H. Stoelting Company, the two largest manufacturers of polygraphs for lie detection "offer only slight modifications from the models used more than 25 years ago," stated the authors.[31]

The National Board of Polygraph Examiners, a short-lived organization of polygraphists that disbanded not long after its formation, approved certain instruments as being adequate and set forth the minimum standards for LDs but, observed Sternbach et. al., "These standards were so simple that virtually any instrument that recorded breathing and a crude index of blood pressure could qualify." They regarded the relatively primitive devices used by commercial LD operators, compared to those in use in laboratory non-deception applications, as only part of the instrument's limitations. "It is no exaggeration to say that commercial operators are using the equivalent of biplanes in a rocket age."[32]

Sternbach et. al., reported the often cited statistics that some commercial operators claimed an accuracy rate of 95 percent, an inconclusive rate of four percent, and an error rate of less than one percent. Similar claims had been made in a book coauthored by John Reid and Fred Inbau. However, in the *Harvard Business Review*, the authors analyzed the data and determined that only 18.9 percent of the 4,280 cases mentioned in the book were actually verified by some other criterion as correct. The remaining high degree of accuracy came solely from the LD operator's assessment. It was all a far cry from the claim of 95 percent accuracy. Other claims of accuracy figures offered no documentation at all. "There are no publications in respectable journals, no facts, no figures, tables, or graphs," concluded Sternbach. "In short, there is nothing to document the claims to accuracy or effectiveness except bald assertions." Only a few useful studies of accuracy had been done and those had been performed by academic researchers, mostly physiological psychologists. Results from them indicated an accuracy rate of about 70 percent. Those controlled labora-tory studies had been vehemently criticized by the commercial operators as being contrived and artificial, not real life situations.[33]

Using the accepted scientific standards of validity and reliability, Sternbach concluded the LD process was defective. "These defects are inherent and render the polygraph virtually useless." Until acceptable lev-els of accuracy were properly produced and documented, "businessmen should not endorse the use of polygraphic lie detection in industry." They regarded the use of LD procedures to avoid hiring certain persons as con-stituting a subversion of judicial process to "trial by polygraph." An indi-vidual was "persuaded" by social pressures to testify against himself through "a distorted, error-ridden medium." As a result, he could be denied the right to work without ever knowing why and he had no defense against the LD report since it was not known to him and he had no rights with respect to how it was used. The polygraphic method, said the authors, "will be effective only as long as people believe it is a real 'lie detector,' and confess their guilt when confronted with funny-looking squiggles on chart paper."[34]

Much more sympathetic to the machine's use in business was reporter Philip Shabecoff in the *New York Times* in June, 1963, when he estimated that employee theft, on the "rapid rise," cost U.S. business $2 billion a year in losses of money and merchandise. He also came up with a new figure, one that would also be often invoked in the future. Shabecoff estimated that three to seven percent of all business failures were attributable to employee theft. Until that point nothing had stemmed the rising tide of thievery but there was a growing belief, he said, in the efficacy of the lie detector. Dale Systems, a business investigating service, chairman Leonard Lowell called LDs "probably the most effective weapon for combating employee stealing." Of the three uses businesses made of the polygraph (specific cases of loss, periodic checking of existing employees, and pre-employment testing), Leonard believed the most effective use of the instru-ment was in pre-employment screening. He liked the periodic screening of employees because a firm could keep an employee found to be stealing (from an LD assessment) if it wanted to do so, "knowing we can keep him from stealing by periodic polygraphs," but he did not advocate the peri-odic mass testing of employees. He did, though, proselytize for the wide use of the instrument in pre-employment screening. When administer-ing pre-employment tests, Dale asked the same questions as on the appli-cation form and also obtained information "on the applicant's drinking and gambling habits, his morals and his intentions on job permanency." Polygraph tests, stated Lowell, were "at least 95 percent accurate." (This, of course, was the old standard figure). At a large drug store the LD testing of all employees was said to reveal that "100 percent of the employees were stealing merchandise and two of them were stealing cash." Shabecoff's article contained nothing critical except a brief mention of the limited court use of the device. Most of the article was devoted to Dale and its opinions, which were uncritically accepted.[35]

H. B. Dearman and B. M. Smith were, respectively, a psychiatrist and psychologist at the University of Virginia School of Medicine who warned in 1963 against the increasing and largely unrestricted use of LDs in business and industry. They argued that an examiner usually sought to impress the subjects with the idea that the machine could not be beat, and so to encourage confessions he "uses deception in his effort to detect deception." Dearman and Smith concluded that polygraph tests should not be conducted by private companies and that the use of such tests by public agencies "should be carefully and continually scrutinized, lest we find George Orwell's *1984* is upon us."[36]

The trade publication *The Office* presented an account of LD use by businesses in a 1964 piece presented as a series of questions and answers with *The Office* interviewing Lincoln Zonn, described as "a world renowned expert on the use of the polygraph," (although his name had not appeared before in the literature on the subject). Zonn declared the polygraph to be 98 percent accurate. When he was asked if it was true that test results could not be used as evidence in court Zonn declared, "This is not true," pointing out that some states admitted the use of the lie detector and its results into evidence by stipulation. However, in 28 states the courts would not admit the results even with stipulation. When Zonn was asked about employee refusal to take a test, he replied that "very often a refusal to take a test pinpointed the person or persons involved." With regard to the issue of invasion of privacy, Zonn believed that in pre-hiring, there should be no such objection "because we are merely asking a person to verify and validate the information given on his application." If a person objected to a test at that point, his advice was to think carefully before hiring that person because "Our experience has been that the individual who states that he resents this type of thing normally has something to hide."[37]

George Linder, associate director of John E. Reid and Associates, said his company ran nearly 5,200 LD tests in 1964, and nearly all of them were for private companies. This number was up from about 4,400 in both 1963 and 1962. "Almost every big company uses lie detectors at least occasionally," Linder added. Andrew Smith, chairman of Truth Verification in Dallas, said his company conducted 42,000 tests in 1964, against 26,000 in 1963.[38]

Bruce Gunn authored a long piece in *Business Topics* in the fall of 1966 that bent over backward to put LD usage in business in the best possible light. He remarked that "One day the public hears that the technique is a panacea and the next that it is a hoax." Gunn declared that pilferage amounted to over $2 billion annually with employees outstealing professional thieves by a five to one ratio and shoplifters by a 15 to one ratio. He used the estimate that three to seven percent of all business failures were caused by those shortages. Consultant Norman Jaspan said that if all commercial dishonesty could be eliminated, prices could be reduced by 15 percent. When such figures were cited, often exaggerated and invariably without detail or explanation, they were used as a justification for taking drastic measures to stem the supposedly astronomically high losses. It was expected that such figures might mute criticism. That is, if the polygraph had negative points to it, if it violated privacy, it all paled beside the greater problem of business losses. In that sense, such numbers needed no explanation or sourcing because their accuracy was never the point. Business losses, or shrinkage, as the concept was called in the trade, was due to three factors: employee theft, shoplifting, and all other. In the latter category were a large number of items ranging from wholesalers accidentally or deliberately short-shipping (99 items in a box marked 100 and where the receiving firm counted the number of boxes times 100 rather than counting within each box) to owners stealing from their own firms to people making honest mistakes at the cash desk, and so on. No one knew how much each item contributed to the losses. However, if the media did an article on shoplifting, virtually all of the shortage amount was attributed to shoplifters; if it did an article on employee theft, virtually all of the shortage amount was attributed to employees pilfering. The amount of shortage should have been fairly easy to calculate—closing inventory minus opening inventory plus all purchases in over the year minus all purchases out. Yet the number was all over the map, apparently adjusted to suit the dramatic needs of the article.[39]

Gunn remarked that the Illinois Retail Merchants Association reported that employers who checked their job applicants thoroughly (in the usual fashion without any LD tests) found that about two percent of them were rejected because of information obtained from prior employers and references. Overall, he said, "about 21 percent of applicants are rejected as a result of pre-employment investigation, but 40 percent are rejected after a polygraph examination." Using another mantra depended upon by people who favored the device but were worried by criticism he added, "Quite possible the greatest value of the polygraph is to exonerate the innocent from suspicion and prosecution. Examiners across the country report that the most satisfying factor in the work is that more innocent people have been cleared by the polygraph's use than the guilty discovered."[40]

With regard to the polygraph's accuracy, Gunn claimed that "no objective information has been developed to conclusively measure the aggregate effectiveness of the polygraph technique," which, of course, was not true. Yet Gunn then went on to cite Richard Arther, a nationally known polygraph expert and his five-year study of thousands of cases with a purported accuracy of 96 percent, three percent inconclusive and an "actual known error during that period to be less than one twentieth of 1 percent." Gunn then did admit those figures were challenged by studies conducted by academics, who indicated an accuracy closer to 70 percent and that the lab people claimed the practitioners' figures were "highly optimistic and so the controversy rages on." If a controversy raged, it was only because the media insisted on reporting numbers indicating high accuracy, which were put out by those with a vested interest in the industry, and giving them an uncritical publicity. Gunn failed to mention that Arther had reported on his own cases and also failed to mention that Arther ran a training school for polygraph operators.[41]

Founded by Arther and Cleve Backster, the National Training Center of Lie Detection opened in New York City in April, 1960. It offered a six-week course in LD operation. That first class contained six police officers, who had been sent by their police departments for training as polygraph examiners, and one private security person, Donald Mauro of the security department with the City Stores Mercantile Company of New York. Arther opened that initial six-week course by telling the students, "When you're a polygraph examiner, people think you're infallible. Of course you're not. But actually in a way you're playing God. You've got a lot of responsibility because you're judge, prosecutor, jury and law enforcement agency all at once."[42]

Dealing with the issue of operator incompetence and training schedules, Gunn argued, "Ironically, many police and governmental agencies have added to the problem by pressuring polygraph schools to provide six-week courses so the agencies will not lose the services of their employees for more than a short period." However, he presented no evidence to support that claim, not even anecdotal. He did have praise for an Illinois law that licensed polygraph operators. Under that proposal, a candidate for a license had to have a four-year bachelors degree, complete at least a six-month internship under the supervision of a licensed polygraph examiner, and then pass a test of competence prepared and administered by the Board of Polygraph Examiners. In his conclusion Gunn declared that

"Quite possibly the primary step in objectively ascertaining the merit of polygraph technology may well be to uniformly regulate through statutory means the qualifications and competence to be required of applicants seeking admittance to this vocation." He added that "At such a time as the polygraph gains further legal status and public acceptance, the courts would be free to reinterpret its role in criminal investigations." Although Gunn's article title indicated a question of whether the polygraph was a "hoax or a panacea," he devoted almost no space to presenting evidence or dealing with the idea that it might be a hoax.[43]

When C. Glenn Walters and Bruce Gunn assessed the use of LDs by retailers, they estimated the losses from employee theft at $3 billion annually; they also used the three to seven percent bankruptcy figure. The authors' purpose, they said, was to analyze the possible consequences to the employer who used the polygraph as a management tool and not to pass judgment on whether or not it should be used in business. "Since large number of retailers have already decided to use this investigative aid," they reported, "the question of whether the polygraph is a valid management tool appears rhetorical." The National Polygraph Association estimated that over 400,000 people were given polygraph exams in the U.S. in 1967. The accuracy of that number is not known, but it seemed to have been the first estimate. Walters and Gunn argued it was understandable why so many retailers were turning to the use of an LD since it gave them "in one instrument, the potential means to obtain trusted employees, to keep these employees honest, and to reduce to a minimum the cost of stock control and shrinkage."[44]

For use in pre-employment screening, the authors cited the Council of Polygraph Examiners as indicating that 30 percent of all applicants were rejected by LD tests and "Out of this 30 percent, 90 percent are rejected on their own admission of serious criminal behavior." Retailers who used the polygraph to conduct periodic exams of employees preferred to use periodic random testing since testing all employees periodically was regarded as too costly and time consuming. Walters and Gunn did point out that opinions on accuracy differed, that employees objected to the LD as an infringement on the right to privacy in violation of the Fourth Amendment and that such tests constituted self-incrimination in violation of the Fifth Amendment to the Constitution. Also noted was that unions such as the Retail Clerks International Association and the International Brotherhood of Teamsters had been fighting the use of polygraphs for years.[45]

Because the LD was used most effectively when all employees agreed to its use, Walters and Gunn declared, "either direct or subtle pressures are most likely to be applied by management to assure that everyone complies." Examples of "moral suasion" could include the loss of opportunities for promotion, smaller pay raises, transfers to undesirable departments, and so on. Before outlining their guidelines for using the polygraph in retail management they first stated, "The evidence indicates that the polygraph can be an important retail management tool for screening employees and the control of dishonesty." One of the points in their guidelines declared, "Management should begin a public relations program to indoctrinate employees on the instrument before its use."[46]

During the 1960s, a number of states passed laws that restricted the use of polygraphs while a number of states also passed laws that licensed polygraph operators. The labor federation AFL-CIO was instrumental in getting restrictive laws passed. Groups that favored laws restricting the use of LDs usually were opposed to laws that licensed operators since they felt that helped to legitimize the LD and to lead to an increase in polygraph usage. By 1963 Kentucky and New Mexico had licensing laws with one then awaiting Governor Nelson Rockefeller's signature in New York (it would be vetoed) while four other states had licensing laws under consideration. A glaring weakness in those, enacted or under consideration, was the "grandfather clause" that allowed those previously active to continue in the business, no matter how far short they fell of the bill's requirements.[47]

By around the same time reporter Elinor Langer noted that the AFL-CIO had been influential in getting laws passed in Massachusetts, California, Oregon and Alaska forbidding the use of the LD in personnel screening.[48]

Early in 1965, the Executive Council of the AFL-CIO began a drive against the use of LDs by public and private employers. "We object to the use of these devices not only because their claims to validity are dubious but because they infringe on the fundamental rights of American citizens to personal privacy," said a statement from the federation. "Neither the Government nor private employers should be permitted to engage in this sort of police-state surveillance of the lives of individual citizens." George Meany, AFL-CIO president, said he was "appalled" by the widespread use of polygraphs and that the Executive Council had instructed him to appoint a committee to start a campaign of education, legislation and other appropriate action to discourage the use of lie detectors.[49]

When *Wall Street Journal* reporter John Grimes reported on this labor offensive against the LD, he conceded organized labor was winning some restrictions on the instrument, noting the AFL-CIO was fighting at the bargaining table and in state legislatures as was the largest union in the land, the Teamsters, who were independent and not affiliated with the federation. Unions objected to the device on many grounds: LDs were not reliable; many employers fired workers for refusing to submit to the machine; some firms demanded their workers sign pledges giving management the right to test them, and that violated Constitutional rights. In March, 1965, the Washington state legislature — with strong labor backing — easily passed a measure ruling out an employer's use of the polygraph in questioning current or prospective workers. Washington was the sixth state to enact such a law; half a dozen other states had bills in various stages of consideration. Also, state labor federations in a number of other states had been lobbying their legislatures to take similar measures.[50]

Around that time, at the urging of the United Rubber Workers, said Grimes, the Akron, Ohio city council adopted a city ordinance outlawing the use of LDs as a condition of getting or keeping either a public or a private job. Many unions were writing prohibitions into their contracts with employers. Meanwhile, the Chicago-based Council of Polygraph Examiners warned the "passage of anti-polygraph laws in more states will be disastrous for both employers and employees." J. Kirk Barefoot, security director for the large pharmaceutical manufacturer and wholesaler McKesson and Robbins, Inc., told an Ohio State Senate committee that passage of an under-consideration anti-polygraph bill "would virtually open our doors to all those persons who would desire employment for the purpose of gaining access to these drugs."[51]

If the passage of laws restricting LD usage went fairly quickly in some jurisdictions, the process appeared unending in others. New York's State Senate unanimously approved a bill in March, 1961 outlawing the use of LDs in the screening of job applicants as a condition of employment. Many lawmakers were said to have expressed surprise at the widespread use of the device with chain stores and banks among concerns using the instrument and with at least half a dozen private firms in the metro New York area that administered such tests. Senator Thomas Laverne (R.–Rochester, and sponsor of the bill) denounced LD usage as "offensive and degrading to the dignity of labor." Senator Daniel G. Albert (R.–Nassau) declared that requiring a job applicant to take a polygraph exam "was a Gestapo thing." That legislation was filed as a result of a labor dispute in Rochester in which an employee was dismissed when a polygraph indicated he had been stealing. When the worker demanded a second test, the results of it were assessed as inconclusive and he was reinstated. Laverne said, "Real liars have been known to pass the test and sensitive people to have flunked it." He added, "If an employer may use the lie detector test cannot it be said that he can also use psychoanalysis, hypnosis or truth serum to learn the inner working of his employee's mind?"[52]

One of five Rochester firms using polygraphs was drug maker McKesson and Robbins, who urged in a telegram that the bill be defeated. McKesson claimed the LD had been invaluable in the prevention of theft by aiding in "the selection of trustworthy types of employees." That was important, said the firm, where narcotics were available. Usage of polygraphs was also defended by Cleve Backster, president of Backster Associates of New York, which specialized in the pre-employment examination of bus drivers. In a letter to the Senate, he said polygraph tests were useful in detecting "potential child molesters, on-the-job drinkers, narcotics users and accident-prone persons."[53]

Just a few days later, in the wake of that proposed New York State law John Theobald, Superintendent of Schools in New York, announced that the fingerprinting of all applicants for school-bus driver positions would soon be required by the Board of Education. He declared the LD tests were the "only recourse at present for the protection of children against the possibility of molesters or sex deviates." Fingerprinting was then used in the screening of all new teacher applicants. Theobald did not set a date for the implementation of the new system but indicated he would wait until after the Legislature had acted on the lie detector bill. That bill later died.[54]

New York State Governor Nelson Rockefeller vetoed a bill in May, 1965 that would have made it a misdemeanor for an employer to require a job applicant to take an LD test. Rockefeller described the bill as unnecessarily vague and difficult to enforce. A year later the New York Senate unanimously passed a bill prohibiting LD tests as a condition of employment for anyone but law enforcement officers and employees in the wholesale drug industry. The Assembly had already passed a very similar bill. However, as the *New York Times* reported, Governor Rockefeller "has vetoed laws prohibiting lie detector tests for the last four years." Change that to five. Once again, in 1967, Rockefeller vetoed a bill that would have made it a misdemeanor for an employer to require any person to take an LD test as a condition of employment.[55]

Challenges and macho posturing by the well-known were not absent in the 1960s. At the end of the 1950s, a major electrical equipment price fixing scandal hit the U.S. Later, 29 electrical manufacturers and 44 of their officials were adjudged guilty with seven of those executives serving 30-day jail terms. Fines totaling nearly $2 million were imposed on the firms and the officials. In a 1961 appearance before the U.S. Senate Antitrust and Monopoly Committee, the executive vice president of General Electric, Arthur F. Vinson, denied under oath that he had known about or had directed meetings between subordinate officials and competitors to fix prices. (The indictment against Vinson had been dropped by the government prosecutor.) Four general managers of the company, all dismissed for their part in the price fixing conspiracy, testified under oath that Vinson had personally ordered and approved their activities. Subcommittee chairman Senator Estes Kefauver (D.–Tennessee) expressed surprise that someone in Vinson's position would have no knowledge and reminded Vinson that his four accusers had submitted voluntarily to a polygraph test given by the FBI in which it had been assessed that they were "not falsifying." Kefauver wanted to know why Vinson had refused to submit to such a test and invited him to do so then. Vinson explained he considered doing so earlier but thought better of the idea "when strongly advised against it" by his attorneys. He added that he was then "overwhelmingly grateful" for that advice "because if they could pass this test on something I knew didn't happen I'd be very reluctant to take one."[56]

Wallace Butts took a polygraph test in March, 1963 concerning his alleged participation in the fixing of a football game. His attorney announced the former University of Georgia football coach and athletic director "passed with flying colors." A media story alleged Butts had given Georgia football secrets to coach Paul (Bear) Bryant of Alabama prior to a 1962 game between the teams. Favored by 17 points, Alabama went on to win by a score of 35 to 0. Bryant and Butts both denied the allegations. Bryant also took a polygraph with University of Alabama officials declaring he had passed. A third party in the case, George Burnett, also underwent an LD test after he went before the Georgia Athletic Board with his complaint. In the media story Burnett said he accidentally overheard a telephone conversation between the two coaches in which Butts gave the information to Bryant. According to the Georgia Athletic Board, Burnett passed his LD test, that is, he was not falsifying his allegations.[57]

In the spring of 1963, the U.S. Air Force was conducting an investigation into a news leak in the TFX airplane controversy. A total of 120 Pentagon employees (apparently all possible suspects) were each asked to sign a paper agreeing to take LD tests. All employees, except four, did in fact sign the paper, including three high-profile people, Secretary of the Air Force Eugene Zuckert, Secretary of the Navy Fred Korth, and Deputy Secretary of Defense Roswell Gilpatric. Those three positions were at a high enough level to be presidential appointees. When word of the proposed tests leaked, the whole thing was canceled and no polygraph exams were given. President John F. Kennedy told a news conference the idea of giving LD tests had been a mistake. On the following day the *Washington Evening Star* (to whom the initial leak about the airplane was given) editorialized, "Let's stop and think for a moment about what kind of madness this really is. Is the Deputy Secretary of Defense, or the Secretaries of the Navy and the Air Force, to be put in the same class with pickpockets and second-story men?"[58]

Even the *Saturday Evening Post* felt compelled to editorialize about the "polygraph-happy Pentagon" because of this situation. Arguing he had no quarrel with the polygraph per se and that it had proved itself to be a useful investigative tool under some conditions, the editor added, "But there is a time and place for everything, and we submit that polygraph tests for high government officials have no place in our democratic society." The *Post* editor added, "That this odious episode could have occurred in our Government is appalling.... That incident is an insult to the Government of the United States. If we have reached the point where we have to rely upon these truth machines to tell us whether we can trust our public officials, then our nation is in sad shape." Also, this incident pointed at a distinct class bias in criticism leveled against the proposed tests. Apparently what offended critics was not just that Pentagon employees were asked to submit to the machine but that high ranking officials were asked to be polygraphed.[59]

Television viewers across America got to see a live murder when they watched Jack Ruby shoot and kill Lee H. Oswald, the alleged assassin of President John F. Kennedy, in the basement of the Dallas, Texas city hall on November 24, 1963, two days after Oswald's arrest on charges of murder. On December 1, agents of the FBI questioned Ruby in the presence of his lawyer Melvin M. Belli. Under Belli's instructions, Ruby volunteered to submit to a lie detector or truth serum test for the FBI. Sometime later, at the Warren Commission investigation of the Kennedy murder, FBI head J. Edgar Hoover, still opposed to the machine, told the Commission that "the lie detector is not in fact such a device."[60]

One of the more notorious killings in America took place in December, 1969, when the police broke into a Black Panther apartment in Chicago with Panther members Fred Hampton and Mark Clark being killed in the ensuing gunplay. On December 11, State Attorney Edward Hanrahan held a press conference to present evidence that the Panthers had opened fire first. The Black Panthers contended that the police came in shooting and that Hampton and Clark were shot dead in their beds. Another reason Hanrahan called the news conference was to publicly "challenge the seven surviving Panthers in the apartment to take a lie detector test, saying that his policemen would do the same." No LD tests were given but, of course, in time the Black Panther version of events was found to be accurate.[61]

In other areas Richard Arther, director of the New York–based Scientific Lie Detection, added to the mystification of the profession by arguing that all the physiological changes tracked by an LD could only be interpreted "by an expert." He also believed, "The entire testing procedure has a decided psychological effect in inducing offenders to confess their crimes." Contrary to what one might guess, he said, the average employee "looks forward" to routine periodic polygraph exams. That was because they had taken to stealing from their employer because they saw others steal and get away with it and so they joined in, but they were not content with their actions. "So, when a logical reason for their stopping — periodic polygraph tests — appears, almost everyone immediately becomes a disciple of the goddess of honesty." And the innocent were "more than glad" to submit to the machine so they could prove their innocence while the guilty almost always take the tests too, since they feel they "must" take it if their declarations of innocence were to be believed. Arther cited the usual figures on accuracy — 95 percent correct, four percent inconclusive, less than one percent error. He claimed he had done a study of 7,400 actual cases done by his firm over a seven-year period and the "actual known error for the past 7 years is less than .0003." That meant Arther suggested his assessments were wrong in just two cases of the 7,400; both were said to have involved reporting a guilty person to be innocent.[62]

If expert operators were as important as Arther and others suggested, then James Bennett, director of the Federal Bureau of Prisons agreed. From various people in the field, he elicited an opinion of the number of qualified examiners there were in the U.S.. Most of those whose opinions were elicited "estimated about a half dozen. One charitable correspondent thought there might be as many as two dozen. But that was the highest estimate I received." Bennett then went on to note there were some 2,000 polygraph examiners then practicing in America, "most of whom have received no more than 6 weeks' training in the use of this device."[63]

Critics of the polygraph industry continued to attack it in the 1960s, especially in the wake of high-profile events such as the Moss report and the Air Force proposal to polygraph Pentagon employees. *Newsweek* presented an overwhelmingly negative article in 1963 citing, among other things, the Pentagon Three and the *Harvard Business Review* piece, after noting the LD had "recently undergone an amazing upsurge in popularity." The article added that "the aura of infallibility already surrounding polygraphs has led to countless instances of coercion, intimidation, and other abuses." Chicago lawyer John Coghlan complained "The theory of the polygraph is so tainted with fraud and deceit as to violate the most elementary principles of law."[64]

Elinor Langer remarked that most private polygraph concerns claimed the results of an LD test were considered as only one part of a total investigation and that decisions affecting a person's welfare would never be made on the basis of an LD test alone. But Langer argued that while favorable polygraph results could no doubt be outweighed by other evidence, "it is far harder to overcome the suspicions arising from a polygraph finding of deception." Although most practitioners would deny it, she said "there is no doubt that at least one use of the lie detector borders on intimidation, on the hope that fear of the machine will induce confessions." What amazed Langer was that the rapidly increasing use of the instrument had developed on little more than the claims of the polygraph promoters themselves that the tests were extremely accurate. Reporter Bruce Frisch observed that the polygraph was easy for people to use and rely on but "By using it they tend to persuade themselves it isn't necessary to search for real evidence."[65]

Critics of the machine were often well-known personalities. One such person was Stewart Alsop, who wrote an outraged editorial-style piece against the device in a June, 1964 issue of the *Saturday Evening Post*. He told of a Russian agent in the employ of the Defense Department (discovered by means other than the LD) who had been given polygraphs by the Pentagon's best operators, but who was assessed as truthful, that is, not a spy. He had been through a course in the KGB espionage school that trained Russian spies how to beat the machine. "The process is so successful that the KGB very rarely uses the polygraph in counterespionage work, on the assumption that no trained agent can be caught by it." Alsop was especially upset that the use of the LD had spread from the CIA throughout the government and then into large sectors of the private economy "like some horrid fungus." And what surprised Alsop was that so many ordinary American citizens "tolerate without protest the most shameless invasion of their privacy.... The invasion of privacy will only be halted when a lot of people get angry about it."[66]

Writing in *The Nation* in 1964, Stanley Meisler summarized some of the criticism against the machine. Dr. John Lacey, a psycho-physiologist at Antioch College told a government hearing that "the field of lie detection has ... developed outside of the confines of any of the recognized scientific disciplines." Dr. Kubis said, with regard to LD use in personnel work, "The growing use of lie detectors in many vital aspects of our life is unwarranted, dangerous and degrading." When used by the inexperienced or unscrupulous operator in checking employees and prospective employees, Kubis said the LD became a "blindly probing instrument that can severely damage the inner life and reputation of the person tested." Meisler declared the device "is certainly unjust, imperfect and dangerous" and that as a personnel screening device, "it can produce nothing but harm (and profits for polygraphists)...." He wanted to see Congress demand the end of its use within federal government personnel offices and to use its influence to persuade private companies to discontinue it. If necessary, he added, Congress should pass legislation against the machine. "The polygraph is a pernicious instrument that has been seized upon by a society obsessed with gadgetry," concluded Meisler. "It should be relegated to a Smithsonian Institution exhibit case as a monument to an American craze."[67]

At the beginning of 1965, reporter Walter Goodman estimated there were between 2,000 and 3,000 polygraphists in America with three states— New Mexico, Kentucky, and Illinois— licensing the occupation. About six polygraph training schools were then said to be in operation in the U.S. with a typical course running six to seven weeks. A Pasadena, California firm, which had been patronized by the United States Post Office Department, charged $575 for its four-week course. Five states— Alaska, California, Massachusetts, Oregon, and Rhode Island — then restricted the use of LDs in job screening while "some police chiefs still cherish the instrument for its ability to cow suspects into a confession without leaving marks," said Goodman. Although the New York Police Department did not then own a polygraph, and publicly was cool to its use, at least three of its officers had recently taken Cleve Backster's six-week $525 course at his New York City school. Deputy Police Commissioner Walter Arm insisted the officers did it on their own time and at their own expense.[68]

Time magazine related an unusual case in November, 1966. In Fort Worth, Texas a prosecutor gave a polygraph test to Donald Carter, who had spent three months in jail awaiting trial for a burglary he insisted he did not commit. Carter passed the test so the police rechecked his story and discovered he was telling the truth. Carter was in state prison on another charge at the time of the burglary. Of course, that brought up the obvious question as to why the police had not checked the story in the first place. According to *Time*'s estimate, some 3,000 polygraph operators gave 200,000 to 300,000 LD tests a year. Senator Sam Ervin Jr. of North Carolina compared the widespread use of polygraph tests to probe federal job applicants to witchcraft. "Does the flesh of the applicant burn when a hot iron is applied to it? Heaven help us if we are reduced to alchemy as a technique of screening applicants for highly sensitive positions in the federal bureaucracy."[69]

Reporting in *Scientific American* in 1967, Burke Smith observed that one industry practice, "which is certainly not rare, is simply to show the subject some oscillations on the tape, accuse him of a lie and thereby elicit a confession."[70]

Chicago lawyer Lee Burkey authored a long article in 1967, which discussed the general place of the instrument while at the same time being harshly critical of the device. Polygraph testing was most commonly used, he said, in those businesses engaged in the sale and distribution of drugs and in those concerns engaged in the manufacture of small parts, but it was also widely used in banking, insurance, steel production, copper refining, automobile manufacturing, meat packing, food processing, automatic food vending, oil, mail order, and other retail operations. A decade earlier, when the device first began to move into the world of business, it was mainly limited to determining the honesty of employees on the payroll. However, the opposition of organized labor delivered some setbacks to the LD industry, notably that failure to pass a lie test was not "just cause" for dismissal under labor agreements. Thus, polygraph usage spread more rapidly to those with little or no protection from its abuses— the job applicants. The classified telephone directory in Chicago listed some 33 private polygraph firms while the one for New York listed over 50.[71]

Burkey remarked there was no impartial evidence to back up the claims of 95 percent accuracy, but "Nevertheless, the commercial polygraph interests, in selling their services to the business community, have carefully fostered the myth of infallibility ... a flagrant disregard of the truth.... A careful consideration of the theory of polygraphic investigation and a look at the actual results of its use, will cast grave doubts on its value." At a more basic level prominent critic Jerome H. Skolnick had said, "There seems to be little evidence that upholds the claim to a regular relationship between lying and emotion; there is even less to support the conclusion that precise inferences can be drawn between emotional change and physiological response." Because of those basic theoretical limitations Skolnick saw little reason to believe that a lie test with a high level of accuracy would ever be developed.[72]

Following the Frye court decision back in 1923, wrote Burkey, 12 state high courts had upheld the exclusion of LD evidence in court proceedings: Wisconsin, New York, Michigan, Kansas, Nebraska, Missouri, Maine, New Mexico, Pennsylvania, Minnesota, Hawaii, and Illinois. Although some magistrates in Cook County, Illinois had resorted to the use of LD tests in paternity cases and domestic relations cases, that trend was checked in Illinois in 1966 when that state's appellate court reversed a paternity suit decision that had been based in part on polygraph evidence. California, Iowa, and Arizona had recently approved the admission of polygraph results if all the parties stipulated in advance to their use in the proceedings. "Of course, it is difficult to understand how the polygraph method is improved merely because the parties stipulate to be bound by it," said Burkey. Other critics had pointed out the same contradiction. The Arizona trial judge was also left with the discretion to deny admission of the stipulation if he was convinced the polygraph examiner was not qualified. Concluding his legal survey Burkey reported that labor arbitrators and administrative agencies, including the National Labor Relations Board and Unemployment Compensation Boards of Review, had followed the majority view of the courts and "flatly excluded" polygraph evidence in their proceedings. In several recent decisions, the courts had ruled that Civil Service bodies did not have just cause for the dismissal of an employee if he refused to take a lie test, or even if he took one and failed it.[73]

Burkey also reported that 10 states—Massachusetts, Oregon, California, Rhode Island, Alaska, Washington, Hawaii, Maryland, Delaware, and New Jersey—barred employers from imposing LD tests on employees as a condition of employment. Some civil suits had already gone against the polygraph. A jury awarded $36,000 in 1961 to an employee of a meat packing firm after his polygraph test was assessed to indicate he was a thief. An employer, an LD testing firm, and a polygraph operator paid an engineer $24,500 in a 1965 out-of-court settlement when he charged he had been unlawfully deprived of his job as a result of a polygraph test. "Probably the polygraph will continue to be regarded as a valuable investigative aid, particularly when it evokes confessions from those who believe in its infallibility," concluded Burkey, "but its use by employers, both public and private, to the exclusion of a thorough investigation of extrinsic facts, can no longer be justified and can no longer be indulged with impunity."[74]

During the 1960s, the federal government's use of the polygraph increased to such an extent that Congress became involved by holding hearings, issuing reports and making recommendations. Business use of the instrument also increased dramatically, especially in the pre-employment testing of job applicants. That group had no union protection and was particularly vulnerable. For the first time, states enacted legislation that restricted the use of LDs, usually banning their use in the mass screening of job applicants and existing employees. Often it was organized labor unions who were instrumental in bringing about the passage of such laws. As usage of the machine increased, so did the media attention devoted to it. A greater proportion of that attention was critical, increasingly harshly critical as opponents pointed out the glaring faults and deficiencies of the instrument. The day of the full-of-praise, uncritically accepting article was long over. Many articles in the 1960s were definitely in favor of the machine, but even those writers felt compelled to mention at least some of the faults and criticisms, if only briefly and perfunctorily.

6

$-\sqrt{}-\sqrt{}-$

The PSE: A New
Truth Machine, 1970s

[The PSE] could change forever the relationships between husbands and wives, witnesses and juries, political leaders and voters, businessmen and customers.
— Time, 1972

The sale of PSEs constitutes the biggest fraud being perpetrated on America today.
— Howard Rothman, 1979

Perhaps the strangest development in the lie detection industry took place in the 1970s with the emergence of a new lie detection machine. A rival to the polygraph, it was, of course, new and improved. A number of media articles appeared that were full of praise for the new device and full of uncritical acceptance. It was a pattern remarkably similar to that displayed by initial articles back in the 1930s about the polygraph. This device, though, was utterly worthless in its stated objective of separating truth from lies and was well on the road to oblivion within a dozen or so years of its first media notice. But, for a time it was heralded as a miracle arrived.

The voice analyzer developed out of research by the Army during the Vietnam War when Army intelligence officers were looking for a simpler, preferably covert, alternative to the polygraph for interrogating prisoners. With all seriousness they focused for a time on body odor, which seemed promising; supposedly everyone gave off a distinct odor when under stress. However, body odors turned out to be too numerous and too easily adulterated or dispelled to be measured accurately. A career intelligence officer with a background in electronics, Lieutenant Colonel

101

Allan Bell, then claimed he had learned that certain vibrations or "microtremors" in the voice changed when a speaker was under stress. He and Lieutenant Colonel Charles McQuiston, an army polygraph "expert," set out to create a device to chart the inaudible fluctuations of those vibrations. But the Army's decided lack of enthusiasm for their idea discouraged the men, and in 1970 both retired from the Army and set up a business on their own. It was there they devised their voice stress analyzer or Psychological Stress Evaluator (PSE) as they called it. The company they founded, Dektor Counterintelligence and Security, started to produce and market PSEs. Another inventor with Army funding, Fred Fuller, designed a similar gadget that, in the late 1970s, was called the Mark II voice analyzer. "We did the original work back in 1963," he recalled. "It could have been built back then, but it would have been 10 feet long. We had to wait for the state of the art in electronics to catch up with us before we could design this thing as it is now."[1]

One of the first general media accounts of the new truth machine came from Fred Graham in June, 1972, in the *New York Times*. He reported the device could detect psychological stress by analyzing a person's voice. While it had not yet been used to test the truth of politicians and other public figures at news conferences or on television, such a use of the device to test the veracity of televised remarks was implicit in Dektor's promotional brochure. A claim therein said the device was tested by monitoring 25 segments of the television program "To Tell the Truth" in which three contestants appeared before a panel with each claiming to be John Doe. Through questioning, the panel had to guess who was the real John Doe. The device picked the person telling the truth 94.7 percent of the time, said the brochure. Behind the device the theory was, reported Graham, that the human voice normally operated in both audible and inaudible frequencies. The exception was said to be when a person was under stress. Then, according to Dektor, the inaudible FM vibration disappeared from the voice. To the human ear there was no difference, but the machine traced the fluctuations on a chart. Graham reported that intelligence agencies within the government had purchased three or four of the machines. However, an intelligence source told Graham the devices were not yet being used because "definitive testing is not complete." Graham also declared that it was not in dispute that those voice fluctuations occurred and that the device charted them. The only negative comment came, not surprisingly, from a member of the polygraph fraternity. J. Kirk Barefoot, New York security official and former president of the American Polygraph Association, said he had doubts about the reliability of the PSE and "even if it could be done, it would be an improper invasion of privacy."[2]

During that same month, both *Time* and *Newsweek* magazines heralded the arrival of the new device. Both discussed supposed recent successes when the PSE had, by agreement of prosecution and defense, been used in four court cases in Maryland and was spectacularly correct in all four instances. Phone conversations could not be recorded without the consent of both parties, but that did not effect the PSE, since the device worked on live conversations coming over the phone, or television, or radio. For that matter, it was equally accurate if the voice was recorded and the analysis done later. Both *Time* and *Newsweek* predicted a host of futuristic uses for the device. "It could change forever the relationships between husband and wives, witnesses and juries, political leaders and voters, businessmen and customers," enthused *Time*. "It could sharply reduce the output of talk all over by making everyone think twice before speaking."[3]

As might have been expected, people with PSEs were monitoring the Watergate hearings in 1973 to try and determine who was lying in the huge amount of conflicting testimony. At least three independent operators, monitoring the hearings on separate PSE devices, said an account in *Newsweek*, had reached similar conclusions about the testimony. Yet the only conclusion reported was their unanimous one in which John Dean "gets the machine's highest credibility rating."[4]

Later in 1973, Dektor president, Allan Bell, said they had tested the PSE with the Howard County (Maryland) Police Department where they polygraphed suspects and then ran tapes of the polygraph sessions through the PSE. "The P.S.E. was right 100 percent of the time on all observable details out of 40-odd cases," boasted Bell. When someone bought a PSE they also received a three-day training course. John Reid of the major polygraph firm John E. Reid and Associates complained that three-day course given PSE buyers was inadequate. "We spend six months teaching the polygraph and then the person must work some time with an expert," explained Reid. "They run a three-day thing and you're an expert. This kind of stuff is bunk." Still, Dektor was reported to be selling some 350 PSEs annually (at $3,200 each), compared to sales of around 400 polygraphs a year ($1,600).[5]

A lengthy summer 1975 account in the *Saturday Evening Post* started out with a number of anecdotal accounts of miracles performed by the new truth machine. This article presented the PSE inventors as having searched for a better LD, a way of avoiding the confrontation inherent in polygraphs. "It could well be that these few thoughtful men have indeed found that elusive method — the one which treats innocent and guilty alike with electronic dispassion and operates in an area beyond the control of the will of the one being examined," elaborated the account. Those machines were then sold for $4,000 to people "who have some qualifications to comprehend the intelligence technique involved." A training course was part of the purchase, but it was not mentioned that the training was only for three days. According to this account, the PSE was tested on 100 "To Tell the Truth" programs and was accurate 97 percent of the time and "The errors are said to have been due to noise factors in the studio or other distractions, since the test was not in the studio, but straight from the loudspeaker of an ordinary household TV unit." This eight-page article was completely and uncritically in praise of PSEs; it did not contain a single criticism or doubt. At the end of the article was the following editor's note, "The author of this article was tested by the PSE concerning the authenticity of his statements and opinions. A reading of the graph indicates that he has not knowingly told a lie at any point in these pages." Yet the author of the article was never identified, which was unusual for such a long article, and unusual in general in 1975.[6]

Allan Bell also claimed his PSE was "the first lie detector that can be used on a dead man," because it could function simply with a tape recording of a voice. Writing in *Science* magazine toward the end of 1975 Constance Holden noted the amount of publicity received by the new device with articles on the PSE having appeared in *Playboy* and *Penthouse* as well as publications directed to security personnel and law enforcement people. An advantage of the PSE was that it was more versatile than the polygraph because the subject was not required to be hooked up immobile to a machine. In fact, the subject did not even need to be present. Dektor reportedly had sold more than 700 machines ($4,200 each) to this point — mostly to retail and industrial firms. Sales continued going up, said Holden, whose account was one of the first with a mostly negative tone, despite cold water being thrown on the PSE by a report produced by the Army in 1973. The Department of Defense bought five PSE machines and turned three over to the Army whose Land Warfare Laboratory paid Joseph Kubis, a psychologist and polygraph researcher at Fordham University, $27,500 to conduct a comparative study of the worth of the polygraph and the PSE. Kubis, using laboratory subjects, gave the polygraph a 76 percent accuracy rating and the PSE a rating of 33 percent accuracy (that was the same as the chance level). While declining to officially endorse the Kubis report, the Army still acted on its findings. It assigned one of the units for use in research not related to lie detection and "destroyed" the other two, said a spokesman for the Army, who was "emphatic about disassociating the military from the PSE."[7]

Holden raised another obvious concern about the machine; it could be used without the subject's knowledge, and this raised ethical objections to its use. Bell emphasized that anyone who bought a PSE had to take the three-day training course in its use, "and if the customer flunks there is no sale, or he can pay for more training until he passes." Chief critic of the PSE was the 1,200-member American Polygraph Association (APA) that passed a resolution in 1973 saying none of its members would be allowed to operate a PSE unless it was used in conjunction with a polygraph. In the view of the APA, any LD device worthy of the name had to measure at least two physiological responses. The PSE did only one. Also, the APA wanted to see longer training for the PSE. Bell shot back that the APA was hostile because his device posed a threat to their existence. A fledgling organization had recently been set up — the International Society of Stress Analysts with some 200 PSE, polygraph and voice analyzer users as members.[8]

Berkeley Rice authored a long piece on the new machines in the June, 1978 issue of *Psychology Today*. This article was highly critical and must have gone a long way toward completely destroying the credibility of the PSE. At this time Fuller's Mark II was sold by Law Enforcement Associates (LEA), a police and industrial security supply concern in Belleville, New Jersey. Both the Mark II and the PSE sold for about $4,000 — roughly twice the price of a standard polygraph. Dektor claimed to have sold 1,300 units to that time; LEA declared 300. Each attacked the other. Dektor marketing vice president Edward Kupec said, "They try to make the Mark II sound like it does the same thing as ours, but I'd say it's only about 70 percent as accurate." Fred Fuller remarked, "I have nothing against the PSE, but basically it's a dinosaur compared to ours in a sense of technological growth."[9]

Rice mentioned the "highly flattering" account in the *Saturday Evening Post*. That article had also invited anyone who believed they had been falsely accused of a crime to contact the magazine with the *Post* promising to arrange a PSE test via telephone for people who wanted to prove their innocence. When Rice phoned the magazine to see what happened, a *Post* spokesman said they had been forced to drop the project. "We thought it was a good idea, but it kind of got out of hand. The mail just came in truckloads," explained the spokesman. "We got so many letters we had to quit, because we couldn't go through them all and still put out the magazine. Part of the problem was weeding out the nuts." A Dektor handout listed such satisfied PSE users as Cumberland Farms Dairy Stores in Massachusetts, Li'l General Stores in Florida, Jim Dandy Fast Foods in Texas, and Shopwell Supermarkets in New York. Some employers ran periodic checks on all employees— all "generally means lower level, not executives," added Rice.[10]

Reportedly, several hundred police and fire departments and county sheriffs then used the PSE in criminal investigations. "Like the polygraph, the voice analyzer is also quite effective in eliciting confessions," remarked Rice. "When confronted by a skillful examiner with the machine's seemingly conclusive 'evidence' of guilt, many subjects break down and admit to the voice-analyzer test as a 'painless third degree.' Critics call it a 'psychological rubber hose.'" Yet, neither the military nor other government agencies were buying voice analyzers. Dektor claimed it had not been pushing such sales, yet, when Rice checked around, he got a different story. "Those customers simply don't believe the new machines work." While various military and other intelligence agencies did buy and test a few voice analyzers when they first came out in the very early 1970s, "most of those machines have since been discarded, dismantled, or destroyed." The Pentagon's National Security Agency tested PSEs and found them insufficiently reliable while the Air Force's Office of Special Investigations conducted 60 PSE tests and found the device to be "not useful." After examining the evidence of various federal agencies, including the CIA and the FBI, the House Subcommittee on Government Information and Individual Rights concluded in 1976 that "The nature of research undertaken … and the results therefrom have done little to persuade the committee that polygraphs, psychological stress evaluators, or voice stress analyzers have demonstrated either their validity or reliability in differentiating between truth and deception, other than possibly in a laboratory situation."[11]

Both the PSE and the Mark II, reported Rice, made frequent claims of 95 to 99 percent accuracy and pointed out carefully, at least to journalists, that the devices were not lie detectors but stress detectors, with the rest of the situation being left to the skill of the operators. Nevertheless, in their ads, Dektor offered "To Catch the Truth" describing the PSE as "proven by over 2,000 examiners in thousands of field tests." LEA's ads for Mark II called its device "The Truth Machine" and declared it produced "an accurate measure of truth or lies." Frank Hovath, a lie detection researcher at Michigan State University's School of Criminal Justice said of the PSE, "It doesn't do what they say it does." David Lykken, professor of psychology and psychiatry at the University of Minnesota's Medical School and a major figure in lie detection research said, "I review most of the articles on the voice analyzer for the professional journals, and I haven't seen the slightest bit of credible evidence to support its validity." When Rice asked for proof of the Mark II's validity, LEA sent him a file of 10 studies that purported to show the instrument as being accurate. Yet all the studies were unpublished and only two listed the name of the researcher — an apparently independent testing firm called Technical Development Inc. (TDI). When he checked TDI out, Rice discovered its president was none other than Fred Fuller, inventor and owner of the Mark II. Rice asked him who had authored the other eight studies sent by LEA, to which Fuller replied, "I did. I did them all." When Dektor was pressed for evidence to support its claims of accuracy, that company also produced studies, with many of them also being unpublished, although they claimed an accuracy rate of 95 percent or more for the PSE. Dektor relied heavily on two unpublished studies. One was by Michael Kradz of the Howard County (Maryland) Police Department. Not long after completing that study, Kradz joined Dektor as its chief instructor. The second study was by a private researcher, John Heisse, who soon joined Dektor as a consultant to it in developing new PSE equipment. In discussing the people in the voice analyzer industry, David Lykken said that about 99 percent of them were non-scientists and non-psychologists. "They're mostly ex-policemen and entrepreneurs who've gotten into it because of the money. They're generally people with limited education." As for the length of their training, Lykken added that "a weekend or a week or even six weeks is really just superficial. It would be just a bad joke if it weren't for all the victims who get screwed out of their jobs."[12]

Rice dropped in on the Dektor PSE training school in Springfield, Virginia, where four students had completed their five days of training and were taking their final exam. That exam consisted of trying to discover which of the three Dektor secretaries had the instructor's car keys. All three denied possession. Of the four students only two picked the right one; nevertheless, they all received their diplomas. Already the voice analyzer came in a home or office model called the Hagoth, the creation of promoter Rick Bennett. Much smaller and simpler to operate than the PSE or the Mark II, it cost only $1,500 (compared to $4,000 for a standard PSE). Bennett declared he had sold thousands, mostly to executives who, he said, used them when engaged in million-dollar deals on the phone. Roughly the size of a flattened cigarette carton, the Hagoth weighed just two pounds. Because it was much simpler to operate than its bigger rivals, Bennett said "any fool can use one" after a weekend of practice. When skeptics asked for studies proving the accuracy of his device Bennett said, "I give them my banker's phone number. That's my study."[13]

Journalist Malcolm Browne reported at the end of 1979 that academic experts in criminology in recent interviews had said that in the past few years some 300,000 voice stress analyzers costing up to $6,000 each had been sold to police departments, businesses and private citizens in the U.S. (surely an extremely exaggerated figure). Reduction in the cost of components had produced a new generation of the device costing less than $200. More bizarrely, a $30 "acoustic lie detector" designed to look like a wrist watch was promised to be on the market for Christmas. It was not. Howard B. Rothman, of the University of Florida's Department of Speech and Criminal Justice, felt the sale of such devices "constitutes the biggest fraud being perpetrated in America today." Apparently for the first time, physiologists from Rothman's department, pointed out that no evidence existed that there was such a thing as a "microtremor" in the vocal cords. More and more those units, said Browne, were used by business for pre-employment screening either with the subject's consent or covertly. Although the administration of an LD test (including voice) was illegal in such situations in many states Browne noted, "the practice has become widespread, experts said." Rothman related that "I know of five of these things being used by businesses just in the small community of Gainesville, Fla., and in the Tampa area many businesses with voice stress analyzers interview their employees each quarter. Business does use these gadgets, and executives make decisions that are grossly unfair and unjust to employees." Some consultants in this industry offered a telephone service. An employer played a tape-recorded interview with a job applicant over the phone with the consultant then providing a quick voice stress analysis.[14]

Lawsuits involving the voice devices, said Browne, had become common with some of the suits charging misleading advertising while some alleged invasion of privacy. No existing form of voice analysis, including the voiceprint method of identifying speakers was "either accurate or reliable." Bell Laboratories had developed the voiceprint technology, but a spokesman for Bell said the company dropped research in the field a decade earlier. Dr. Aaron Rosenberg of Bell Laboratories said, "The parallels sometimes drawn between fingerprints and voiceprints just don't hold up." Telestar Inc., of Wormleysburg, Pennsylvania, claimed to have sold 12,000 of its $150 voice analyzer "Truth Machine" in 1979, and further claimed its machines were "92.7 percent accurate" and "entirely acceptable for police departments and private investigators." Fostering the myth of the machine's infallibility, and the use of showmanship were recognized, remarked Browne, as important elements of "operator expertise." Telestar's manual said, in part, "The very presence of your Microtronics Voice Stress Analyzer, Series IV, is likely to influence or persuade the individual with whom you are speaking to utter only accuracies." Summing up the various scientific studies that had disproved voice stress machine claims of high rates of accuracy, Browne observed "but scientific criticism appears to have little impact on sales."[15]

Writing in the trade publication *Security Management* in 1980, Robert

Peters, criminal analyst at the Wisconsin Crime Laboratory Bureau and a polygraph examiner for eight years, looked at the voice devices and declared that five scientifically acceptable studies of independent researchers had investigated voice stress analysis as a lie detection method. All reached the same conclusion that voice analysis was "not an accurate means of lie detection and to use those devices in the light of that research would be "not only an ethically questionable act, but of little actual usefulness in determining an individual's truthfulness."[16]

One of the claims Telestar Inc., made for its $150 device was "The Truth Machine — simply turn it on and if anyone ever tells you less than the truth, you'll know." It was a claim that was not only too good to be true but also fraudulent, as alleged in a 1981 criminal fraud complaint against the principals of the then dormant company, Larry Leeds and Donald Dowell. They knew the claim was false or should have known it, alleged the complaint. A ban was placed on the delivery of postal money orders to the company in May, 1980. Then a continuing investigation led the U.S. District Attorney's office in Harrisburg to conclude the two men knew their advertising claims were false, which led to their indictment on fraud charges. Telestar and Hagoth (the Issaquah, Washington producer of the low-cost device) were both sued in 1979 by the California State Attorney General's office for their advertising claims. Both companies soon ceased operations. Dektor's Allan Bell did not regard those events as indictments of the entire voice analyzer industry because he dismissed the cheaper devices as merely "toys."[17]

Howard Timm, assistant professor at the Center for the Study of Crime, Delinquency and Corrections at Southern Illinois University, Carbondale, Illinois, also noted, of the studies done on the PSE accuracy by researchers with no vested interest in the outcome of that research, that "without exception, those studies ... have indicated the instrument simply does not detect deception effectively." Despite the negative findings from those studies, the manufacturer, added Timm, continued to sell the device "and has developed a strong and vocal group of loyal PSE users." He thought one of the reasons for that may have been due to the information the maker handed out concerning the machine's accuracy — studies done, for the most part, by its own employees. An obvious paradox existed in that situation. Timm believed it was difficult for people to try and change a strong conviction, especially if the convinced person had some investment in his belief such as time, money, effort, and so on. Of those PSE users, Timm speculated that "Undoubtedly their roles as PSE experts or analysts have also become internalized as part of their identity and served as a source of prestige and recognition for them." Therefore, given the choice between admitting to a wrong decision and facing the possible internal and external consequences of that admission, "it is not surprising that most of these individuals continue to be ardent supporters of the instrument."[18]

Another factor, Timm believed that accounted for some of the PSE's continued support came from the psychological power of the instrument as an interrogation tool, apart from its accuracy. "Undoubtedly, numerous suspects have confessed to crimes merely because they were confronted by the machine, the questioning process, or simply by the suggestion to take a PSE examination." Also, PSE supporters engaged in vigorous lobbying efforts anytime a threat arose. When federal legislation against LD devices was considered in 1978, Dektor contacted PSE examiners, said Timm, "urging that they express dissatisfaction with the antidetection of deception bill that was being considered." Also, Dektor had advertised a good deal in a campaign directed at law enforcement and security personnel in trade magazines aimed at those groups.[19]

Voice stress analyzers then rapidly disappeared from view. Media accounts quickly became overwhelmingly negative, often harshly so, and swamped any remaining PSE supporters. The polygraph was rooted in good science; the voice machines were not. That is, the non-deception polygraph had a long, honorable, and accurate reputation within the scientific community while the voice devices were based on something (microtremors in the voice) which was not acceptable as valid within that community. The question was not why the voice instruments disappeared but, rather, why they got any kind of a foothold to begin with.

7

‒‧‒‖‒‖‒

Business Embraces the Truth Machine, 1970s

We use the LD to identify agitators, job hoppers and professional or amateur thieves, as well as to determine permanency intentions.
— Ray Chambers, Li'l General Stores, 1977

How often do you change your underwear? Have you ever done anything with your wife that could be considered immoral?
— Questions from a Coors
brewery test, 1977

Decline [an LD test] and as it now stands in all but 16 states, you could get fired from a job or turned down as an applicant.
—*Business Week*, 1978

I have great confidence in the polygraph. If this machine says a man lies, he lied.
— Philadelphia Mayor Frank Rizzo, 1973

I don't know anything about polygraphs and I don't know how accurate they are, but I know they'll scare the hell out of people.
— President Richard Nixon, 1970s

During the 1970s media accounts concentrated predominantly on the ever-growing business and commercial use of the LD. Little attention was paid to government use of the device, compared to the 1960s. One more do-it-yourself article appeared on building your own lie detector in the magazine *Popular Science*, which had last featured such an article over three decades earlier. The one featured in 1973 was a galvanometer that the magazine claimed could be put together by the home handyman "in just a couple of short building hours."[1]

One area of government usage mentioned was at the local level when, in 1973, LD critics began to receive strong support from numerous police officers around the country. Police officers were objecting more and more to polygraph tests being used to screen applicants for jobs as police officers and they were even more strongly opposed to mass LD screening when charges of corruption were leveled at a force or a specific part of it. In cities such as Dallas, New Orleans and Miami, for example, it was reported the polygraph was used to test police candidates for "criminal records, unsavory associations, drug use and homosexuality" and an average of one in every three applicants was rejected for a position as a result of those LD tests. Many big city forces, including New York and Chicago, had continued to resist the use of the machine to screen job applicants. Illustrating the type of conflict that sometimes arose was the situation in Seattle where Police Chief George Tielsch thought the polygraph was necessary to "maintain the integrity" of his department and that "It's a very useful tool." On the other hand, Seattle King County Councilman Edward Heavey observed the polygraph was not applied uniformly to all people in a position of public trust. "Why should it be just cops? You can't use it on judges, attorneys, building inspectors and city councilmen," he explained. "The police feel that everybody's picking on them. You know what kind of a state of mind that encourages."[2]

During a moment of acute concern over leaks of government secrets, President Richard Nixon summoned two of his aides and suggested they come up with a classification so secret that only numbered copies of the documents would be put into circulation, to people whose names were recorded. Then if a leak occurred, all the people who had access to the document in question would be given an LD test. This plan was never implemented.[3]

High praise for the business use of the LD came from a 1970 issue of the trade periodical *The Office*, which stressed that the capability of declaring those under suspicion as innocent was "the primary purpose of the lie detector or polygraph." Said Gene Sandacz, of the Scientific Lie Detection firm, "So the instrument is more of a truth verifier … than it is an actual lie detector." More and more, declared the piece, business was turning to the use of polygraphs. That was said to be due to an increase in employee crime, although the account did not cite any detail or numbers. Sandacz's firm took up to two hours to do a pre-employment LD test while if it performed one of the other two business functions, periodic re-exam of existing workers, or testing in a specific loss investigation, the time taken was up to 1.5 hours for each one. According to the account "The polygraph firm has found very little opposition to the pre-employment test on the part of job applicants." Sandacz explained that most of those candidates were "eager" for the LD test because it was a quicker method than the ordinary background investigation. Also, this publication declared "the instrument has proved remarkably accurate." In addition it cited Sandacz who mentioned the usual numbers; 97 percent accurate, three percent inconclusive, and a maximum error of one percent. Any error, he claimed, would more likely "label a lying person truthful rather than call a truthful person a liar."[4]

New York's famed jeweler, Tiffany and Company, announced in 1970 that from then on, everyone who was hired would be asked to immediately submit to the machine. "It's not really a lie detector," explained Walter Hoving, chairman of the board. "It simply registers the truth and for many years all our employees have had it on their personnel card that they would be willing to take such a test." Finally, the company was implementing that policy with new hires. A good many of the questions asked at the Tiffany polygraph exam had to do with the taking of narcotics. "People who have a dope habit have to steal to support it and we'd rather they'd steal from someone else," declared Hoving. Results of the LD tests given already under the new policy proved to Hoving how badly Tiffany needed the test because "about 40 percent of the people aren't making the grade; that includes those who decide not to show up for the test."[5]

Another famed New York retailer, Bonwit Teller, the Fifth Avenue specialty store, announced in 1971 that it had administered LD tests to about 30 employees as an "experimental step" in the fight against pilferage by store personnel. Those who took the exams were described by the company as management-level "volunteers." But a majority of Bonwit Teller sales people and stock clerks who commented on the tests to the media — despite objections from their supervisors — were outraged and indignant. Several personnel executives of other New York department stores said it was the first case in the city of polygraph tests being administered in department stores. Macy's personnel executive Joseph Douglas described LD tests as "kind of an extreme measure" and a "probably unwarranted" practice. With all the criticism raised against it Bonwit said the store was chiefly interested in "testing the test, not the employees."[6]

Just a week after its announcement that tests had been given, Bonwit president William Fine stated the store would discontinue its "experiment" with LD tests, or "polygraph interviews." Fine said, "Our testing of the test proved it was ineffectual for our purposes." Also, he said he was disturbed by the reaction of many employees who thought its use might become general but the main reason for abandoning the experiment was "the kind of thing we wanted doesn't show up — how much of our stock loss is from internal theft or external theft or simply disappears on paper."[7]

Reporter Ben Franklin produced a lengthy page-one account of the subject in the *New York Times* in November, 1971, in which he put corporate losses from pilfering, embezzlement and outright theft at $3 billion a year while noting LD tests were "quietly coming into far wider use" in business. He cited an estimate that 200,000 people in private employment — excluding employees and applicants at all government levels — would be subjected to the machine that year. Tests given by Federal agencies were said to number about one-tenth of those conducted for business by private practitioners. LD firms charged around $50 an hour and Franklin estimated there were 4,000 to 5,000 polygraph operators in America. In the face of numerous studies that showed the LD technique to be flawed, Franklin reported that its critics traced the machine's continued acceptance to a self-perpetuating circle: belief in the machine's accuracy produced confessions; a high number of confessions produced a belief in the machine's accuracy. Success of the polygraph industry in obtaining employee confessions, thought Franklin, was the device's "chief selling point." John Reid boasted, "We get better results than a priest does."[8]

While a number of polygraph examiners insisted in interviews with Franklin that no one taking a routine polygraph as part of a job application should be asked questions about his sex life, "nearly all of them acknowledged that such questions are asked fairly widely." Chicago labor lawyer Lee Burkey, who had successfully reversed a dozen or so dismissals based on LD results at arbitration hearings, said that at its most basic element, the polygraph was "a deeply ideological thing used by people who desperately long for law and order." He saw employer after employer depending on the lie detector and only perpetuating the lack of order in America "by going through this magic ritual, with all its terrible injustices." Burkey felt the "truly amoral people" breezed through the test while the introspective, nervous, sensitive person "who probably is guilty of some wrongdoing, but perhaps not the theft under investigation, shows all the 'wrong' tracings, believes the machine knows all, and makes damaging confessions." John Reid argued that industry critics should help the field get better licensing laws as a way of eliminating the corrupt and the incompetent. "We have the best investigative thing in the world going and they want to put us out of business," Reid complained. One of the standard text books on the LD (*Truth and Deception* by Fred E. Inbau of Northwestern University and John Reid) suggested the recorded observations of a secretary or receptionist as to the subject's general conduct and behavior while in the waiting room "will be very helpful to the examiner in assessing guilt or innocence." Reid dismissed criticism of the LD on the grounds that it was an invasion of privacy by arguing all tests were voluntary. Also, he brushed aside arguments against the device because it involved self-incrimination by stating that during a test, no trial was taking place. Over the course of his long article, Franklin had nothing good to say about the instrument.[9]

One year later, Stanley Klein produced an account which stated that LDs were used more and more by business. Harry Winston, Inc., (Fifth Avenue jewelers) then subjected all job applicants to polygraph exams as a condition of employment. At the Flying Tiger Corporation, job seekers looking for work in the company's air cargo facilities were given LD tests to detect, among other things, those candidates who neglected to report any past claims for workmen's compensation. Of special interest to Flying Tiger were claims for back and neck injuries. Discount department store, Twin Fair, with outlets in Ohio and upstate New York, administered LD tests periodically and randomly to a sample of employees, in addition to exams given to all new hires. Twin Fair employed a full-time polygraph specialist on its security staff.[10]

A study prepared by the American Civil Liberties Union (ACLU) on the use of the instrument by private industry, wrote Klein, explained the reasons for its rapid growth in business by asserting "One of the quickest and cheapest ways to verify a large amount of information coming from a large number of applicants is to use a lie detector instead of a background check." An average LD test costs $25, compared to more than $100 for a background check, according to Saul Astor, president of Management Safeguards, a consulting firm that specialized in loss prevention. "As a result," he said, "polygraph examinations have become a routine part of doing business for many corporations of all types and sizes across the country." One woman tested at Harry Winston said they asked her, "Did you ever cheat?" "Were you ever treated for mental illness?" and "Did you get along with your family?" Another woman was asked, by the CIA in response to her job application, "Have you ever done anything that you were ashamed of?" That ACLU study recommended the outright banning of the LD as a personnel tool adding that the process was "degrading to human dignity"; that it went against the notion a person was innocent until proven guilty and that it "forces one into a position of self-incrimination." Twelve states then had laws restricting the use of the polygraph in personnel work. "But the majority of these laws are laden with exemptions, semantic loopholes and weak enforcement provisions," according to the ACLU. However the ACLU believed even weak legislation against the machine served as a deterrent to its use by business. Ten states then had laws licensing LD operators.[11]

Business Week profiled the industry at the beginning of 1973. It opened by stating that $3 billion a year was stolen from business by employees and that five years earlier, "the top estimate was half the present figure." Added to that were the supposedly growing industry fears of alcoholism, drug use, and so on, and the result was a growing demand for polygraphs to screen prospective employees. Walter Van de Werken of the Stoelting company, a major polygraph maker said his business had doubled or tripled in the past few years. U.S. Senator Sam Ervin Jr. (D.–North Carolina) had then proposed a bill to ban LD tests as a condition of employment or prospective employment at the national level. Clearly worried about such a possibility happening, two security concerns which administered a lot of polygraph exams, Lincoln M. Zonn, Inc., of New York and Foresight Security, of Minneapolis, had formed a joint venture, Fact, Inc., which was preparing a different way to screen job applicants. Fact planned to use computer analysis of a paper and pencil questionnaire to spot potentially untrustworthy employees. That questionnaire was to be based on the standard psychological questionnaire, the Minnesota Multiphasic Personality Inventory (MMPI), which was normally used to evaluate a person's mental health.[12]

Corporate use of LDs had grown "phenomenally" over the previous few years, declared *Business Week*. J. Kirk Barefoot, past president of the American Polygraph Association (APA), estimated one-fourth of all major corporations used the instrument, a figure that other experts regarded as high "but not completely out of the ballpark." A typical LD exam was said to cost from $25 to $50. Companies that used the device to screen job applicants included numerous banks, Hertz, Avis, McDonald's, Tiffany, Remington Rand, Foremost-McKeeson, Braniff International, King Kwik, Pinkerton's, Southland Corp., Centennial Liquor Stores, Marshall Field, Levitz Furniture, National Tea, and Goldman, Sachs and Cluett, Peabody. Most companies on that list were identified by the APA or the polygraphists who administered the tests for them. Companies that used the instrument to screen employees tended still to be reticent about acknowledging it. Zale Corporation was a Dallas-based retail jewelry chain that had tested over 40,000 job applicants and believed it had saved substantially on pilferage as a result. Between 10 and 15 percent of all applicants failed the Zale LD test, according to the company. Most concerns using the device in pre-employment screening claimed to only be checking basic honesty and to verify the information on the application firms. Yet one applicant for a superintendent position with a national business machine company was asked, "Do you and your wife engage in any unusual sexual practices?" "Are you dissatisfied with the political process in this country?"

Challenged regarding those questions, the examiner explained "An unstable person could damage the company's equipment or programs."[13]

That above mentioned test was in a state with no licensing requirement for polygraph operators; sixteen states had licensing laws, while the number of states that restricted LD usage was still twelve. Twenty-two states lacked both licensing laws and bars against commercial use. Even in states that banned polygraph tests as a condition of employment, the polygraphist might still prosper, reported *Business Week,* since "the law usually permits voluntary testing." Given the choice between starting work the next day if he passed an LD test or waiting a week or more for a background check, "an applicant often chooses the test — especially if he senses that his potential employer prefers it." According to Richard Arther, president of the New York–based polygraph firm Scientific Lie Detection, there was then more pre-employment LD screening in California than there was nine years earlier, before California passed its polygraph-restricting law. To the ACLU, using polygraphs for pre-employment screening was "an inexcusable invasion of privacy" while Ervin's proposed bill (which went nowhere) would have banned such usage all together. Other strange devices were on the market to detect lies then, besides the PSE. One was the Movement Recording Chair with receptors in the seat and backrest to record muscle movement; the Voice-Instituted Pickup used an air tube wrapped around the neck under the lower jaw to register involuntary throat movements. Then there was the Plethysmograph that used reflected light to record the amount of carbon monoxide and dioxide in a person's bloodstream plus the volume of blood moving through the subject's veins — all said to be "measures of his anxiety." All of these oddities apparently disappeared almost as quickly as they surfaced.[14]

When *Time* did a 1973 piece, it explained that more and more companies were using LDs on their workers as an "easy way" to cut down on employee stealing, estimated here at $3 billion a year. Both Burger King and McDonald's had reportedly used the polygraph on some of their workers, but McDonald's had just ended the practice at its California outlets under pressure from the state labor commissioner. *Time* used the figure that one-fourth of all major U.S. firms used the LD to some extent, attributed here to "polygraphers" instead of just the actual person who had made the estimate. According to this account, the number of professional polygraphers in America had increased 50 percent in the previous five years to 1,200, which was a much lower figure than most other estimates. Also estimated was that as many as 400,000 tests were administered in the previous year by commercial LD firms, which was a much higher figure than most other estimates.[15]

Later that same year, B. Dunham, vice president in charge of personnel and administrative services at G. H. Walker Laird investment bankers, estimated about 40 percent of brokerage firms used polygraphs and said, "Personally, I don't like it. I think it's a great invasion of privacy, but on a dollars-and-cents basis I recommend it to my company." From his experience, five percent of people did not show up for the test and 25 percent of those who did take the test failed, "but 90 percent of the time it isn't on the polygraph readings; it's on an admission the person made — use of hard drugs or something." Rudolph Caputo, director of investigations for Smith & Wesson, a security firm that grew out of the small-arms company, opposed the periodic testing of employees because "It's demeaning and it degrades the polygraph." Reporter James Collier then remarked that "acceptance" of the polygraph throughout society in general was spreading (actually, usage was spreading but not necessarily acceptance).[16]

West Virginia pharmacists and graduating pharmacy students were urged in 1974 by their state association not to take jobs with companies that required them to submit to LD tests as a condition of employment. It was a move said to be aimed at the Rite-Aid drug store chain and its West Virginia subsidiaries, Cohen and Fountain. The West Virginia Pharmaceutical Association adopted a resolution on the issue after students at West Virginia University pharmacy school complained about being subjected to polygraph exams at pre-employment interviews. Rite-Aid president, Louis Lehrman, said the chain used polygraph tests routinely in screening employees in order to weed out drug users and that they also used it for specific investigations. That adopted resolution said, in part, "the administration of polygraph tests to pharmacists is unprofessional, demeaning, and unnecessary in view of the rigorous educational and licensing standards" of the state pharmacy board. According to the first "security survey" conducted by the National Association of Chain Drug Stores (NACDS), 68 percent of drug chain companies used polygraphs at some time; 25 percent used them routinely in pre-employment screening; 32 percent used them on employees suspected of theft or other crime; 46 percent used them "whenever warranted." NACDS concluded in its report on that survey that in states where LD exams were legal and not restricted at all, they were used "extensively" by drug store chains.[17]

7-Eleven, a national chain of some 4,000 convenience stores (as of 1974) had then been using polygraphs on its workers for 12 years. Clayton Day, of the Charlotte-based Carolina Polygraph Consultants said, "I don't know of a single national company that doesn't use the polygraph in one way or another." Actually, the percentage of major companies using the machine was always way below 50 percent. Writing in *The Progressive*, Frye

Gaillard estimated there were about 4,000 polygraph firms in America and that "There was surprisingly little controversy during the 1950s and 1960s, as the private use of lie detectors increased by 1,000 percent." Of course, this was not correct. There was a great deal of controversy and criticism of the device in both of those decades.[18]

The business magazine *Nation's Business* had a "Sound off to the editor" feature in its pages in 1975. One of the questions posed to the readers was; whether or not LD screening by private enterprise should be outlawed. By a margin of four to one, the readers said no. William K. Smith, vice president of Manufacturers National Bank in Detroit added a comment to his vote that "One by one, the tools for finding honest, conscientious employees are being chipped away." Edward F. White, president of United Piping Company of Greensboro, North Carolina, said, "Only those with something undesirable to hide need be concerned" by polygraph screening. Those who wished to outlaw LDs argued that there were other ways of checking on employees. The Reverend Howard W. Marsh of Harlandale United Methodist Church in San Antonio, Texas, observed, "Personnel managers have many tools in their arsenal to weed out undesirables; the interview, the FBI computer bank, former employers, persons used as references, academic records, and school counselors— to name a few."[19]

U.S. News & World Report did an article about the growing use of LDs in business and the growing concern over it, but not until early in 1976. Saul Astor of Management Safeguards said, "In the minds of businessmen, the polygraph is now an accepted form of screening people. They have almost no alternative." Critic David Lykken observed the irony wherein the U.S. Constitution protected a criminal suspect from going to prison for failing a lie detector test, but nothing protected a man from losing gainful employment for the same reason. New York City polygraphist Rudolph Caputo remarked, "For $1,750, anyone can go out and buy a polygraph and set himself up as an expert. There are many, many abuses in the field of lie detection." Heavy polygraph users, government bodies such as the CIA, the Justice Department and the Law Enforcement Assistance Administration, reported the article, "all say their reliability remains unknown in real-life use against suspected criminals." Astor estimated that in New York City thousands of companies then tested their employees with polygraphs. The attraction of the polygraph for business was said to be its relatively low cost —$25 to $75 per test — and its speed, in comparison with traditional investigations of job applicants. Firms that shunned pre-employment screening often resorted to polygraph usage in cases of suspected employee theft. Retailers such as Marshall Field in Chicago, Montgomery Ward, and Sears, Roebuck fell into that category.

By this time 11 states licensed polygraph operators while 13 States barred employers from requiring LD tests of workers or prospective employees. However, only four of those states— New Jersey, Alaska, Connecticut, and Delaware —"prohibit business from even requesting such tests." That is, in the states with laws restricting the use of LDs, an employer could not demand that a prospective employee submit to the machine, but in a majority of those states, the employer could "request" the employee take the LD test, all, of course, strictly "voluntarily."[20]

The following account probably outlined better than most the kind of management attitude that roused so much criticism and anger over use of the polygraph. Ray Chambers, vice president of loss prevention at Li'l General Stores (a chain of convenience stores) wrote the article for a 1977 issue of the trade publication *Security Management*. He estimated retail losses at in excess of $7 billion annually with 70 percent of that (nearly $5 billion) due to employee theft. Chambers went on to describe his firm's workers by saying, "The majority of the employees in the retail industry, (to include convenience stores) are drawn from the lower end of the wage scale. Most of the individuals functioning at this economic level do not possess the education, skill or motivation to enter other fields." Then he argued that from the standpoint of protection of citizens, constitutional rights and prevention of invasion of privacy, "the use of the polygraph ... is similar in application to conducting airport searches of passengers." For him, a polygraph test was no more a violation of Constitutional rights or privacy than was that airport search. Also, it was cheaper and faster to use an LD, he said, than to conduct the traditional pre-employment checks.[21]

Li'l General had four polygraph operators on its staff who each used a Psychological Stress Evaluator (PSE) and who were called Personnel Suitability Analysts. One of those analysts conducted a polygraph exam of each new employee that lasted two hours on average. Its purpose, said Chambers, was to verify the employee's education, employment history, medical history, physical limitations, chronic alcoholism, drug addiction, accident history, workmen's compensation claims, "and to identify agitators, job-hoppers and professional or amateur thieves, as well as to determine permanency intentions." Prior to employment, each employee was required to complete a statement that he had been advised that the PSE exam was "a condition of employment." A couple of paragraphs later, Chambers confused the situation by stating that each employee candidate "is advised that the PSE examination is voluntary." That is, he signed a card to the effect that it was voluntary. Still later in the article, Chambers said, "Although submission to the PSE examination is voluntary, it is specified as a condition of employment, and all employees are required to submit to the procedure. In the event of refusal to submit to the test, the employee will either not be hired or will, if already hired, be terminated."[22]

Among the questions asked at the Li'l General LD exam were, "Have you ever stolen money from an employer?" "Do you have any serious health problems that you haven't told us about?" "Have you ever been injured on the job?" "Have you ever drawn workman's compensation?" "Do you use any drugs illegally?" "Do you use alcohol to excess?" and "Do you currently smoke marijuana?" Chambers concluded that "Legislation which would deny the use of this technology would result in a chaotic situation, which would prevent the retail sector from protecting itself against disastrous depredations from dishonest employees." Denial of LD systems to the retail sector by legislation, he warned, "would be a wanton and irresponsible act which can only result in detriment to the economy, the people, the government and national prestige."[23]

Journalist Anna Quindlen wrote about LD tests being used with increasing frequency in pre-employment screening and cited a 1977 estimate by the ACLU that 300,000 polygraph tests were given yearly in America. Allen Coppage, director of Industrial Security Analysts, said his New York security firm gave polygraphs to 35 to 40 job applicants daily, for some 200 client companies. One of those client firms was Tiffany, which started LD screening six years earlier. Industrial Security served about 100 other jewelry companies, besides Tiffany. ACLU director Trudy Hayden said her group would oppose LD tests even if they were 100 percent accurate because "There are points beyond which an employer should not go." A spokesman for Tiffany said she could not remember the last time anyone was hired after refusing to take the test. Coppage remarked that the percentage of applicants deemed unacceptable (and not hired) after a polygraph at his office "is about 40 percent, usually because of gambling or drinking habits, or a history of theft." Tiffany added that part of the reason it used LD tests was because those tests were more economical, $25 to $40, compared to a traditional security check costing $50 or more.[24]

Workers at the Adolph Coors brewery in Colorado began a lengthy strike in April, 1977, when the company sought to diminish the power of the union. Coors was a well-known backer of right-wing causes and groups such as the John Birch Society. Another point the union was upset over was the firm's use of LD tests. In a series of affidavits collected by the union, striking employees charged that polygraph tests used by the company to screen job applicants required them to answer such questions as "What are your sex preferences?" "How often do you change your underwear?" "Have you every done anything with your wife that could be considered immoral?" "Are you a homosexual?" and "Are you a Communist?"

Union business manager David Sickler commented, "When you get through being grilled on that lie detector you feel dirty." Coors's executives said they did not know that such questions were on the tests since an outside firm administered them, and that now there were no more questions about sex. The union wanted the tests stopped completely maintaining they were invasions of privacy. Company chairman William Coors argued the tests helped reveal "whether the applicant may be hiding some health problem" and ensured "the applicant does not want the job for some subversive reason such as sabotaging our operation."[25]

At the beginning of 1978, *Business Week* did another lengthy piece on the growing use of LD tests in the private sector. It was estimated here that one-third of 1,500 U.S. companies that went bankrupt each year did so "because of dishonest workers"— a much higher estimate than in the past. Another estimate was that two percent of America's largest firms then used LDs to some extent. Back in 1958 only seven firms offered LD testing by listing themselves in the Manhattan Yellow Pages. By 1968 it was 17; in 1978 it was 31. The Jack Eckerd Corporation of Clearwater, Florida, expected to spend $500,000 that year to polygraph employees in its 16-state 800-outlet chain of Eckerd Drugs. A Maryland manufacturer reportedly offered employees a profit-sharing plan in return for their submission to PSE tests. They accepted. Kemper Corporation was using PSEs in Massachusetts to test tape recordings it routinely made of auto insurance claims. In about 20 percent of the tests, which were conducted on "suspicious" claims and "usually without the claimants' knowledge," it was said, the PSEs had detected "stress" that led to further investigation.[26]

The majority of business users of the LD devices were said by *Business Week* to be "satisfied customers" with a significant number of them contending that workers were actually pleased by the prospect of submitting to the machine, to show they were honest. Stressed here, as in other accounts, was that lie detector exams were quicker and cheaper to administer than were background checks or full investigations. Cited here was an estimate from the National Retail Merchants Association that "employees of member companies steal as much as $40 billion in goods from their employers each year"— an estimate some 10 times higher than earlier figures, including some from this publication. According to Lincoln Zonn, president of a national polygraph service, half of all internal theft was due to laxity on the part of management. "They just aren't controlling things properly by systems and procedures." Companies were also reported to be increasingly using LD tests to screen out applicants with health problems without resorting to more expensive physical exams. Bill R. Cannon, owner of a Dallas-based security firm, revealed that his customers wanted polygraphs to disclose if a job seeker had a history of filing "too many" workman's compensation claims. Some employers wanted to spot applicants who would not stay on a job long, to avoid putting them in expensive training programs. Others wanted to know if an applicant held "extreme political opinions."[27]

Many polygraph operators contended, continued the *Business Week* account, that their clients shopped price before accuracy which was "an attitude that opens the door to abuse." Polygraphers said a proper exam should last an hour or more, costing around $50. Nevertheless, some firms paid as little as $15 for a quickie exam. That attitude was also obvious in the number of firms that used the cheaper PSE device even though nothing objective indicated it operated at better than the chance level. William Krupa, director of security for the Pontiac, Michigan–based Perry Drug Stores, said every one of his company's 1,000 employees took a 10- or 15-minute polygraph test each year. He believed they were an excellent deterrent to theft. Los Angeles polygraph operator Jerry Wohl declared that of the estimated 3,000 examiners in the U.S., "no more than 50 are truly competent." One security officer for an oil company said, "I've come to the conclusion that polygraphs and similar equipment are only investigative crutches." A security officer for a large Chicago bank that regularly used polygraphs said, "I've seen operators that I wouldn't have enough faith in to ask if it's raining outside." Of the 19 states that then required LD operators be licensed, just three — Arizona, New Mexico, and Michigan — also restricted the types of questions that could be asked. Sixteen states prohibited the pre-employment use of LDs "but some fail to enforce the statue with much vigor, and others have worded the law so vaguely that it is essentially toothless."[28]

John Belt and Peter Holden, both with the College of Business Administration, Wichita State University, Wichita, Kansas, conducted a survey of business usage of LDs in 1978. As a background, they mentioned there was a consensus that the number of tests given and the number of firms giving them were rapidly increasing and that anywhere from 200,000 to 500,000 LD tests were given yearly in the U.S.. Among the 15 states restricting LD use, those laws came in one or two basic formats: those that forbade employers from requiring that employees undergo such tests and those that prohibited employers from even requesting such a test; ten states fell under the former condition and five came under the latter.[29]

Belt and Holden mailed a questionnaire to 400 major U.S. companies nationwide to assess polygraph usage; usable responses were received from 143 companies (35.7 percent). Asked if they were currently using polygraphs, 29 companies (20.3 percent) said yes and 114 (79.7 percent) replied no. Thirteen companies (48.1 percent) had used polygraph tests for five to ten years; seven (25.9 percent) for 10 to 15 years; four (14.8 percent) for over 15 years, three (11.1 percent) for less than five years. Of the companies that did not then use the device, 90 (93.8 percent) indicated they had never used the polygraph while six (6.2 percent) said they had discontinued usage. From the data it appeared that most companies who used the instrument had done so for a long time, with only a few turning to it recently and fewer still discontinuing its use. "These data, at least, belie the notion that polygraph usage is increasing rapidly, at least among the major firms," said Belt and Holden. Polygraph usage among major U.S. corporations, by industry category was: transportation, 25 percent; retailers, 50 percent; diversified-financial, 0 percent; commercial banks, 50 percent; life insurance, four percent; industrials, 12 percent; all firms, 20.2 percent. Of the firms using the instrument 10 (34.5 percent) used it for employment applications verification, but only three of the firms gave the test to all applicants. The same number of companies, ten and three respectively, used the polygraph to periodically test existing employees; 26 firms (89.6 percent) used the machine to investigate specific instances of theft or other irregularities.[30]

Belt and Holden found a tendency for employers in states which had licensing requirements established by law for operators to require the tests more and request them less than employers located in states that had no such legislation. In the former case, 38.5 percent of companies required their employees to submit to polygraph exams and 23.1 percent requested submission. Within states devoid of licensing laws, 25 percent of the firms required tests to be taken, 37.5 percent requested them. An analysis of the three industrial sectors that used the polygraph most frequently (retailing, commercial banking, and transportation) revealed "that a significantly greater proportion of firms located in states which have licensing statutes use the polygraph than do firms which are located in states without such controls." In conclusion the researchers declared, "it would appear that state licensing legislation has had the effect of generating a greater confidence in polygraph examiners and establishing a higher degree of credibility for the profession as a whole."[31]

Business Week published a guide on what to do if one was asked to submit to the machine. It was concluded that a person had "little to gain" by taking a polygraph test. "Agree to it, and the consequences range from loss of privacy to loss of a job. Decline, and as it now stands in all but 16 states, you could get fired from a job or turned down as an applicant." Advice on the best course of action was that "firm resistance to the polygraph — up to reasonable limits — may do you the least overall harm."

Other advice offered including checking on whether you could be denied state unemployment benefits if you got fired for refusing to submit, and to check to see if your state allowed your employer to tell other prospective bosses about your refusal to submit. By this time, it was said, 23 states licensed polygraph operators, "but requirements are often lax." Professor Edgar A. Jones Jr., an expert on labor law at UCLA said, "Lie detector tests are like Russian roulette, innocent employees are found to be deceptive; guilty employees come up innocent — there is simply no reliable correlation." As a last piece of advice, *Business Week* suggested if you failed a test to get a second opinion and to keep copies of both tests, "You may have the makings of a malpractice suit."[32]

The trade publication *Drug Topics* explored what drug stores were doing, in 1979, to stop shrinkage, and financial losses — estimated here to run from 1.6 percent to 3.2 percent of gross sales, with as much as 75 to 80 percent of that loss ascribed to employee theft. One new procedure discovered was the "Behavioral Analysis Interview" developed about a year earlier by John E. Reid and Associates. Designed for situations where a store, warehouse or other facility had detected theft, "the test is administered by an interviewer who asks employees to reply orally to a series of questions. The interviewer notes the answer while watching the employee's facial expressions and physical movements." That rather bizarre procedure could perhaps best be described as the polygraph test without the polygraph. It was claimed to be highly effective. Many drug stores still used the LD, but a worrisome increase in state laws restricting use of the machine and a threat of a federal law imposing restrictions had apparently bothered the Reid firm to the extent that it had tried to come up with an alternative if the worst case situation came to pass — a full ban on the instrument. Coming into wider use in pre-employment screening at one drug store chain were paper and pencil psychological tests with one prominent one, the Reid Report, said to come within three percent of agreement with the polygraph. However, that statistic was provided by the Reid Report creator, John E. Reid and Associates. Another one of these well-known paper and pencil tests was London House's PSI-5, "which gives a psychological profile in the areas of honesty, drug abuse, and violence."[33]

Researchers Philip Benson and Paul Krois declared that "it appears that the polygraph may function to detect deception at levels that exceed chance, but not without some chance of error. On the other hand, research on the PSE indicates a strong possibility that the instrument is not a lie detector." Despite that obvious belief to some extent in the polygraph, they argued that restrictions on the use of the lie detector were needed. "The use of such techniques in periodically assessing employee loyalty amounts to little more than a witch hunt." They also wanted to see the device banned in applicant screening, with the possible exception of continuing to use it to screen law enforcement personnel. Benson and Krois also argued to have limits imposed in the use of polygraphs to investigate specific incidents such as thefts as well as a limit on the types of questions that could be asked — nothing on sexual attitudes, religious beliefs, and so forth. Using an assumption that LDs were 90 percent accurate and five percent of the population were liars, the researchers observed that to weed out a high proportion of liars, 68 percent of those who failed the test would be telling the truth. Because of a perceived growing popular support for restrictions on the devices, Benson and Krois stated that "it seems highly likely that some sort of legislation will be passed at the federal level to control the use of polygraphs." In their view, many issues remained to be resolved including what constituted a qualified examiner and what research was needed to prove polygraphs were highly accurate and "unless such issues can be resolved, an outright ban on use of lie detectors in business is preferable to the current state of affairs ... it seems that no use of the lie detectors is better than unrestricted use."[34]

Lincoln Zonn, head of the Zonn security firm, told retail grocers at a loss prevention seminar toward the end of 1979 that when a loss prevention program based on polygraph testing was put into effect a promise of amnesty for past transgressions might be the best way to avoid employee resentment — and mass firings. Zonn marketing vice president Ronald Vickers remarked that since the average company had 70 percent of its workers steal from it, getting rid of all the thieves might not leave enough workers to open up the outlet. An approach taken by Zonn was to designate the day the LD program was introduced as "day one." Employees were told at an orientation meeting that they would never be asked about their activities before that day, but they would be held responsible from that day onward. Polygraph tests were given monthly to a random selection of a store's employees, with each worker asked to take the test twice a year. From month to month, Vickers explained, there was a 20 percent overlap of people called in for a test, which meant that no employee could be sure he would not be asked to retake the test during a given month. Compliance with the program was voluntary, said Vickers, but the participation rate among employees was said to be 96 percent. What about any dishonest people hiding in the four percent? Vickers explained the chances were good they would be caught by one of the questions given the 96 percent, "Since day one do you know of anyone stealing from your store?"[35]

Legal activity continued through the 1970s as more states took action and the federal government threatened, but failed, to enact any legislation. In a related area, Martin Markson looked at the fate of LD usage in labor arbitration cases. His report in 1971 found that in the previous two decades in 16 reported labor arbitration cases, the results of lie detector tests or refusals to submit to such tests had been barred from evidence by the arbitrators. But, in a minority of 11 other cases, arbitrators admitted such evidence even while holding that it had "slight" value. Looking more closely at the 11 cases Markson found that 10 of them had a tie-in with other evidence or various special circumstances. He concluded, "Thus, it is in but one case, out of 27 adjudicated, that evidence of the result of a lie detector test or of a refusal to submit to such test was held sufficient by itself to justify a discharge." And even in that one case, the evidence of refusal to submit to the exam was admitted to sustain a charge of no cooperation, not of an underlying crime. Markson, though, argued the right of privacy was the "vital" and the "controlling" consideration and that "Industrial security does not, we submit, require the balance to be tipped the other way, in favor of permitting the gross administration of lie detector tests." To protect workers not covered by arbitration clauses in collective agreements he wanted to see LDs banned from use as a condition of employment or continued employment.[36]

Writing in the trade journal *The Office* in the summer of 1974, John Janssen declared he was happy because in the previous seven years no prohibiting state or federal legislation against the polygraph had been enacted. Rather, in the same period, no less than 13 states had enacted legislation to "permit and regulate polygraph examination." Janssen argued that this "acceptance" by state and federal legislators had lessened the "dramatics" of the LD and increased its acceptance by both management and employees. Also, Janssen, an obvious believer in the instrument, threw in the old cliché that more often than not the LD tests were used to "clear innocent parties who willingly seek confirmation that they are telling the truth."[37]

After many, many years of attempts, New York State finally passed a law, in 1978, prohibiting employers from "requiring, requesting, suggesting, or knowingly permitting" employees or applicants to take or be subjected to truth machines, but only PSEs and other voice analyzers.[38]

At the federal level Senator Sam Ervin introduced a bill in the Senate to ban the use of LDs by companies whose activities involved interstate commerce. His bill sparked a massive lobbying and letter-writing campaign by members of the American Polygraph Association and many of their clients. Probably at least partly because of that campaign, no action was taken on the measure during the 92nd Congress. Ervin reintroduced the bill in 1974, but again nothing happened. The Senator conceded that

John Reid might have been right in that a lot of people, when strapped to an LD would confess to all manner of things. But Ervin contended such confessions flowed from the "myth of infallibility" that surrounded the polygraph. It was a myth, said Ervin, that was "self-fulfilling and self-perpetuating."[39]

The U.S. Senate Judiciary Committee in 1974 proposed legislation to prohibit both private industry and Federal agencies from "requiring, requesting or persuading any employee or applicant for employment to take any polygraph test." Then, in February, 1976, the House Committee on Government Operations recommended that "the use of polygraphs and similar devices be discontinued by all government agencies for all purposes."[40]

In 1978, U.S. Senator Birch Bayh (D.–Indiana) had a bill in the Senate that would ban LD tests in pre-employment screening of job applicants or periodically on existing employees in the private sector and in all government agencies except two, the CIA and the National Security Agency. He favored prohibition because he felt polygraph use in those circumstances was contrary to America's basic idea of freedom and individual rights. "It's a kind of police-state treatment contrary to a free society," explained the Senator.

Cited was Richard Nixon who said, on one of his Watergate tapes, "I don't know anything about polygraphs and I don't know how accurate they are, but I know they'll scare the hell out of people." Bayh was asked how the LD test was different from forced airline searches and blood alcohol tests administered to drivers. The biggest difference, he replied, was accuracy; the other two tests could be proved right. Noting that 20 percent of employers used LDs, Bayh wondered why the other 80 percent didn't do the same and why did giant retailers like J. C. Penny or Sears not use them if they were such a panacea. "The lie detector is just a lazy person's way of trying to keep a 'bad apple' from getting in his shop," said the Senator. Bayh was opposed to any type of federal licensing of operators because he was afraid it would lead to greater use "because people would feel that licensing meant the tests are credible."[41]

Saints Roller Skating Centers of St. Paul, Minnesota asked all of its employees to be tested before being hired and thereafter at regular intervals. When a 30-year-old Winnipeg woman applied for a caretaking job at the Saints Center in Manitoba, she was asked to submit to the machine. Saints claimed the test was not mandatory and was used to detect honesty as most employees handled cash. But the Winnipeg woman was asked questions about drug addiction, alcoholism and whether she was hiding any medial ailments. She filed a complaint with the Manitoba Human

Rights Commission. Support for her came from the provincial Federation of Labor and the Chamber of Commerce (groups not usually on the same side of an issue). The Chamber of Commerce objected that such testing was "American," therefore un–Canadian and "damaging to the business image." Then Manitoba announced it would ban the use of polygraphs and voice analyzers by private parties on applicants for jobs, credit, insurance, or rental apartments.[42]

In the case of celebrity testing, National Football League Commissioner, Pete Rozelle, acknowledged in 1972 on the CBS television program "Face the Nation" that he had given LD tests to football team owners in regard to gambling on professional football games. They all passed. Additionally, he had given polygraphs to players and fined or suspended some of them for gambling.[43]

The U.S. State Department admitted in 1973 that three of its officers were given LD tests by CIA personnel in 1971 at the request of the White House as part of an administration attempt to stop news leaks. Those polygraph exams were given at the request of Egil Krogh Jr., formerly a White House adviser on criminal practice matters to John Ehrlichman, President Richard Nixon's recently resigned chief domestic affairs adviser. Krogh, in 1971, headed the so-called plumbers group, charged with investigating the sources of news leaks. Secretary of State William P. Rogers, in a September, 1971 news conference, acknowledged an investigation had taken place but declined to go into detail about investigative procedures. Those three unnamed men all passed the LD test and were still working for the State Department. When it admitted in 1973 that LD tests had been used, State Department spokesman, John King, explained that as part of the investigation in late July, 1971, the White House asked three State's employees and one from the Defense Department to submit to the machine and that the CIA would do the testing. King said the CIA did the testing because FBI director J. Edgar Hoover "did not permit his agency to give lie detector tests to employees of other Government agencies."[44]

Early in the Senate Watergate hearings, Jeb Stuart Magruder testified that former Attorney General John Mitchell had authorized the break-in and other misdeeds. Mitchell denied all allegations. Subsequently it was revealed that Magruder had submitted to the machine, and passed. As the government debated the bringing of charges against Vice President Spiro Agnew, Assistant Attorney General Henry E. Petersen had the main witnesses against Agnew undergo polygraph tests. Petersen reported the results gave him "confidence that there were no deliberate misstatements," and on that basis the move was made that led to Agnew's fall from power.[45]

One man who did beat the machines in a very public way was author

Clifford Irving, famous for his Howard Hughes biography hoax. At a time when Hughes's lawyer was saying that the meetings between Hughes and Irving (which the author claimed had taken place so he could write a biography of the reclusive billionaire) had never taken place, Irving declared that if the lawyer would take a polygraph, so would he. Results of Irving's test were assessed as being inconclusive.[46]

Peter Camiel, chairman of the Democratic party in Philadelphia, charged in 1973 that Philadelphia Mayor Frank Rizzo, offered to let him name architects and engineers for city jobs if Rizzo was permitted to name the Democratic candidate for an upcoming district attorney's race. Rizzo denied the allegations and both men agreed to take an LD test, as did Rizzo's deputy Phillip Carroll. As he was being prepared for his polygraph Rizzo stated, "I have great confidence in the polygraph. If this machine says a man lies, he lied." According to the polygraph examiner's assessment of the test results, Camiel told the truth while Carroll and Rizzo both lied. On learning he had failed Rizzo exclaimed he was "baffled" by the result.[47]

Conservative political pundit William F. Buckley Jr. received a letter in the summer of 1974 from Dr. William Shockley about a debate the two were shortly to have on Buckley's television program. Shockley suggested he be wired to a polygraph and that the graph of its tracings be visible on the television screen to home viewers, but not to Shockley. Buckley declined the offer.[48]

Polygraph operator, Rudolph Caputo, discussed the questioning format that had become standard in the industry from the 1950s onward. Three types of questions were asked: 1) relevant questions such as "Did you steal the money from the foreman's desk?" 2) irrelevant questions such as "Is your name James?" 3) control questions such as "Have you ever stolen?" that were expected to be lied about. If properly posed, the control and irrelevant queries established norms on the machine for both lying and truth telling. "If you can't establish your control questions, you can't get results. You've got to find something that the suspect will lie about," explained Caputo. In the past, he continued, a lot of polygraphists asked questions about sex, such as "Have you ever masturbated since you were married?" to which the average person was expected to lie. "Today, I like to stay away from questions like that, especially with women. It makes them hostile to you.... Furthermore, the woman many suspect your intent, or simply react strongly to sexual matters. When you have emotion, you will get a reading on it, and it may be misleading." If Caputo was investigating a case of theft he might use a control question like "Did you ever between the ages of 18 and 25 steal a significant amount of money?"[49]

Although articles of uncritical praise for the instrument had significantly fallen off, they were not entirely absent. Writing in the *Journal of Police Science and Administration* in 1977, researchers Stephen C. Carlson, Michael S. Pasano and Jeffrey A. Jannuzzo came to several decidedly minority conclusions, including, "Several studies have shown that the modern polygraph technique has a very high degree of both accuracy and reliability." Other conclusions drawn included "It is becoming increasingly difficult to rationally argue that lie detectors are any less accurate and reliable than other types of evidence the courts freely admit," and "Lie detectors are accurate and reliable enough to be used extensively in business, government, and police investigation." However, given the publication's title, its intended audience, and the fact it was published at Northwestern University, perhaps the conclusions were not so unusual.[50]

Critics of the machine were much easier to find. Organized labor continued to fight against the device. At the start of the 1970s, a group of 41 unions affiliated with the AFL-CIO called for federal legislation to outlaw the use of polygraph machines, even in national security cases. That call for a total ban was contained in a 174-page report on polygraph usage in industry, prepared by the Maritime Trades Department of the AFL-CIO, which called the polygraph "clearly an unreliable device for the measuring of truth or deception." While waiting for passage of federal legislation, the report called for state laws to ban use of the instrument and for the inclusion in all collective bargaining agreements of a clause prohibiting management from using LDs on their employees, or prospective employees.[51]

Writing in *Harper's Bazaar* in 1972, journalist Patricia Beard used an accuracy figure of 75 percent for the polygraph and put that number in perspective by asking her readers to imagine depending on a contraceptive that "only" failed 25 women in 100. She believed that most people faced with a polygraph test "feel that simply refusing to answer the questions probably would jeopardize a job just as much as actually giving incriminating answers." When she added the faults of the PSE to those of the polygraph, Beard declared that "might convince Congress to impose strict controls on lie detection devices—for all our protection."[52]

One of the major critics of the instrument in the 1970s, and beyond, was university psychologist, David Lykken. He drew three main conclusions about the LD: 1) accuracy estimates given by polygraphers on the basis of their own experience were "essentially worthless," 2) laboratory studies could not provide adequate validity estimates; and 3) adequate criteria against which to measure LD test validity was next to impossible to obtain in the field. He gave an example in which 1,000 people were tested (assume the polygraph was 90 percent accurate, assume five percent were liars). In that case 45 of the 50 liars would be identified, but at the same time, 95 of the innocent truth tellers would also be expected to fail the test (false positives). Thus, of the 140 people who failed the test 68 percent (95) would actually be innocent. Lykken concluded that "The general use of the lie detector in employee screening cannot be justified, however, and psychologists have a professional responsibility to oppose this growing practice."[53]

Because of recommendations by polygraph operators, one of every four potential employees was barred from a job, according to the New York Civil Liberties Union. Group director Barbara Shack said rejection of job applicants jumped from two percent after traditional background screening and reference checks, to as high as 40 percent after the use of polygraphs. The ACLU sent a questionnaire to 750 people chosen at random — one-third were returned. Fifty-seven percent of the respondents would prohibit the use of polygraph tests as part of the hiring procedure.[54]

Journalist Jonathan Kwitny did a piece in the *Wall Street Journal* in 1977 in which he was relatively critical of the device. Some eight months later, he did an expanded article on the subject for *Esquire* magazine — a piece that was much more harshly critical. Kwitny, at the suggestion of *Esquire*, arranged to take an LD test himself even though he viewed it as something of a gimmick. He called Richard Arther, widely known in polygraph circles, who told Kwitny to come to his office. When he arrived, Arther bawled him out for his previous *Wall Street Journal* piece and said neither he nor any other established polygraphist in New York would give him a test because he would use it as a "gimmick" and they did not like what the journalist had written. "You have to have something at stake for the polygraph to work," exclaimed Arther. Then Kwitny, using many examples, launched into a scathing attack on the polygraph, letting his readers in on the LD's "dirty little secret," which was that "Lie detectors lie." People in the business had told him "that if the average citizen stops believing that lie detectors are infallible, lie detectors will become even less reliable than they are. Blind faith from all concerned is crucial." If people did not fear the machine, Kwitny explained, they would be less likely to confess and the LD industry would lose a lot of clout "because the extraction of confessions is a primary object of lie detection in law enforcement." Polygraph operator Jerry Baker acknowledged that "a lot of times" mistakes were made. Finally, he conceded to Kwitny, about LD results; "You can't rely on them too much." Secrecy about actual test results was common and was one reason that polygraph results were not challenged more often than they were. That is, people subjected to tests and their lawyers never saw the results.[55]

Researchers at Lackland Air force base in Texas reported in 1978 that training subjects in biofeedback and autohypnosis could help people beat the polygraph. Thirty volunteers first took LD tests in which they tried to deceive the polygraph operator about their selection from a set of cards. The examiner got 53 right (88 percent) and seven wrong. Subjects were then divided into three groups. One received a month of biofeedback training in which they learned to monitor and control the galvanic skin response. The second group was taught to use autohypnotic suggestion to relax and control their level of physiological arousal. The third group, controls, received no training. At the end of the month all subjects went through the same polygraph tests again. This time the examiner got 10 hits and 31 misses for the first two groups (24 percent — less than chance). There was no change in the examiner's results for the third group.[56]

Law professor Richard Underwood remarked in 1978 that "It is common to confront the suspect with a recording and then accuse him of lying without going into the interpretation process at all. Apparently, this is a fairly successful method of eliciting confessions."[57]

Interest in the LD in the 1970s focused mainly on an increasing business use of the device. In the wake of a sometimes acknowledged fact that many of the state laws restricting the instrument were less efficient than they appeared, more attempts were made at the federal level to enact some type of national restrictive legislation. However, nothing came of those efforts. At the same time criticism continued, often coming from business-friendly publications that might have been expected to emphasize the instrument's supposed good points to a greater extent. The addition of such bizarre items as the PSE to the field of LDs helped to further weaken whatever little credibility the polygraph industry may have had, and increased the pressure for more sweeping and national legislation.

The Government
Blocks the Box, 1980s

The lie detector has no more place in the courts or in business than a psychic or tarot cards.
— David Lykken, 1981

the lie detector does work as long as the subject believes it works. A good examiner scares the crap out of you. It's theater.
— Leonard Saxe, 1986

a coin toss would be more accurate.
— U.S. Representative Jack Brooks, 1985

lie detector tests are not worth a damn.
— Roy M. Cohn, 1985

An LD is an insidious Orwellian instrument of torture.
— Douglas Williams, 1986

As the 1980s began, reporter Nancy Faller complained about victims of sexual assault being given polygraph tests by police departments. She remarked that women who had been raped made up the only class of crime victims whose honesty was routinely tested. Supposedly those tests were only given voluntarily, but Faller argued that pressure was applied. "Whether or not the rapist is prosecuted may depend on whether or not she satisfies the doubts of a dubious device," she wrote. When the Detroit police department finally yielded to public pressures and stopped running polygraph tests on rape victims, Chief William L. Hart stated the possibility of "deterring even one woman" from reporting a rape made him change his mind.[1]

In the area of court use of polygraph results, the device actually made some minor gains in the 1980s, despite the fact that criticism against the instrument had been increasing dramatically. By 1985, it was reported that the polygraph was widely used by prosecutors in deciding whom to prosecute or in plea bargaining. David Lykken stated that nearly half of the states admitted polygraph evidence in court provided both sides had so stipulated in advance. Appellate or supreme courts of the following states had ruled LD evidence inadmissible under any circumstances: Alaska, Colorado, Hawaii, Illinois, Kentucky, Maine, Maryland, Michigan, Mississippi, Missouri, Montana, Nebraska, New Hampshire, North Carolina, Oklahoma, South Dakota, Texas, Virginia, West Virginia, and Wisconsin. High courts of the following 14 states had ruled that LD evidence could be admitted under prior stipulation of the parties: Arizona, California, Delaware, Georgia, Indiana, Iowa, Kansas, Massachusetts, Nevada, North Dakota, Ohio, Oregon, Washington, and Wyoming. Admissibility in other jurisdictions was determined by local tradition — case law — and varied from never, as in Minnesota, to regularly, as in Florida. Lykken reported that in a number of jurisdictions, rape charges would not even be investigated until the alleged victim had passed a polygraph exam. He said he knew of specific instances in Florida, Maryland, Michigan, Texas, Washington, and Wyoming.[2]

Arguing against any reassessment of the LD's role in the criminal justice process if it meant increased usage were psychologists Victor S. Alpher and Richard L. Blanton. They argued the use of fallible LD results (from devices having a substantial error rate) "would place upon judges, juries, and attorneys the task of determining the validity of a body of data which cannot be reliably interpreted, but which nonetheless possesses an aura of scientific truth." Alpher and Blanton also declared the methods utilized by polygraph operators were "unreliable and invalid" and that the admission of "such weak, debatable evidence under the guise of science would perpetuate costly errors and social injustice."[3]

Also arguing against any court room expansion was a 1988 article in the *Harvard Law Review*. It reported that several state courts had recognized wrongful discharge claims brought by at-will employees who were fired for failing an LD exam, or for refusal to submit to one, holding that type of employer conduct constituted a violation of public policy. This account argued that courts in all states should permit employees who were fired for failing or refusing an LD exam to bring a civil cause of action for wrongful discharge based on a public policy exception to the employment-at-will doctrine. And that judicial support should be extended to job applicants.[4]

Federal government usage of the instrument increased dramatically in the 1980s and it drew a great deal of media coverage, much of it highly critical. The U.S. Justice Department was wiring some of its own employees to LDs in the summer of 1980 as it investigated the unauthorized disclosure of details from an investigation — the Abscam inquiry. Peter F. Vaira, the U.S. Attorney in Philadelphia and Thomas P. Puccio, chief of the Federal Organized Crime Strike Force in Brooklyn, testified in Federal court that they had taken polygraph tests in the department's internal investigating. In another case, the Justice Department recommended the previous December that President Jimmy Carter dismiss Herman Silas Jr., the U.S. Attorney in Sacramento, after he reportedly failed two polygraph tests in which he was asked about allegations that he had taken a $7,500 bribe. Silas denied all the charges. Attorney General Benjamin Civiletti declared around this time that an employee's refusal to take an LD test might give rise to an "adverse inference" about his conduct.[5]

Journalist Robert Pear went on to remark that in May, 1980, the FBI adopted guidelines stating that refusal to submit to polygraph testing, by itself, would not be the sole basis for disciplinary action and "all reasonable efforts" had to be made to clear up any allegations without resorting to the use of an LD. During 1979 the FBI conducted about 1,900 polygraph exams, an increase from around 1,100 in 1978. Over two years, from 1977 to 1979, the total of LD exams given by the Army, Navy, Marines, and Air Force increased by 18 percent, from 5,710 to 6,751. Polygraphs, said Pear, were finding a growing market among local and state law enforcement agencies, litigants in civil cases and private retailers. Pear also observed that state courts had increasingly permitted introduction of polygraph test results as evidence because, "with technical improvements, the machine appears to have become more accurate." Although the Justice Department frequently used polygraphs in its investigations, it resolutely opposed the admission of LD evidence in federal criminal trials. Justice had faith in its own polygraph operators but not in the ones in private practice.[6]

A leak to the media in January, 1982, over U.S. Defense Department budget allocation numbers led the administration to attempt to crack down on employees who leaked information. Deputy Secretary of Defense Frank Carlucci gave a number of polygraphs in the Pentagon. As a result of repeated questioning about the new policy on leaks, President Reagan explained that people were taking the LD tests "voluntarily." Contradicting that was an unnamed administration official who told a reporter "There was nothing voluntary about it. If you didn't do it, they presumed you were guilty."[7]

In that January, 1982 Pentagon investigation, after some two dozen senior officials had submitted to the machine, officials concluded that one individual had flunked three separate tests and told him he would be dismissed. Only after that suspect produced sworn denials from everyone he had been accused of leaking information to did the Pentagon change its mind and limit his punishment to a reprimand. Those subjected to the instrument included Navy Secretary John F. Lehman and General David C. Jones, chair of the joint chiefs of staff. Defense Secretary Casper Weinberger said use of the LDs, although necessary, was "very distasteful, very unhappy." One official who took the test described it as "a singularly unpleasant experience."[8]

Around the middle of March, 1983, President Ronald Reagan ordered all government workers in "sensitive" jobs to take a polygraph test if they were asked to do so. It was National Security Directive 84 and was proposed at least in part by the administration's belief there was a widespread problem of information being leaked.[9]

A new congressional study on the value of the polygraph, released in late 1983, concluded that evidence for the device's accuracy was weakest for the kind of dragnet that the Reagan Administration had ordered throughout the government for national security purposes. That study was prepared by the congressional Office of Technology Assessment (OTA) and was a review and analysis of various validity studies of lie detection. One conclusion was that the strongest evidence came from research on criminal investigations where there was a specific crime and a narrow field of suspects. In such cases, said the report, LDs picked liars at a rate better than chance but with a significant number of errors. Correct detection of guilt ranged from 17 to 100 percent. But in cases of general personnel screening, either the screening of job applicants or the periodic testing of employees for unspecified crimes, "there exists no scientific evidence to justify the use of lie detectors," the report concluded. Such screening had become a political issue in the previous several months because of the Reagan Administration's move to significantly expand the use of LDs by all federal agencies.[10]

In the previous year, 1982, the Department of Defense proposed revisions in its polygraph regulations that would permit pre-employment and periodic screening to determine eligibility for high security jobs. Then, in March, 1983, Reagan instructed the directors of all federal agencies to use polygraphs in the investigations of specific leaks. Finally, a few months later, the administration announced that all agencies would be permitted to use LDs to conduct periodic dragnets to catch workers breaking security. It was against that backdrop that the OTA study was released. According to that report, the federal government conducted 22,000 LD tests annually (excluding the CIA for whom data was unavailable). More than 18,000 of those exams were conducted by the Department of Defense, including some 9,000 by the National Security Agency. In response to the administration's actions back in March Representative Jack Brooks (D.–Texas), chair of the House Committee on Government Operations, used an amendment to the defense spending bill to prohibit expanded use of LDs by the Defense Department until April, 1984; In the meantime he requested the OTA validity study. Principal author of that study, Boston University psychologist Leonard Saxe, said "there exists no technology for the detection of lying." Detecting lies, added the report, was a complex psychological process— one that required "that the subject believe in the validity of the test; as a result whether or not the test is successful depends largely on the examiner's skill in psychologically priming the subject for the test." Because people varied both physiologically and psychologically, the polygraph test could be expected to make errors; to identify a certain number of innocent people as guilty and to miss some of the guilty. Saxe added, "the lie detector does work as long as the subject believes it works. A good examiner scares the crap out of you. It's theater."[11]

During the decade prior to the OTA study, wrote journalist Dorothy Samuels, the number of tests done on federal employees had more than tripled. At least one in four of the *Fortune* magazine's list of America's top 500 firms were reported to administer LD tests on a regular basis but "It is difficult to verify that claim because many employers refuse to respond to surveys on the subject." Some one million LD tests were given annually in America, according to estimates but Samuels thought the "true figure is probably twice as high." A survey by the General Accounting Office found that at the time of the OTA study, about 7,000 Defense Department employees and contractors were given polygraph exams in connection with special assignments. Under the proposed regulations (those postponed until April, 1984, at least) the number of individuals who could be required to submit to the machine shot up to approximately 116,000 — the number of Defense Department employees with access to sensitive information. Samuels also reported that Deputy Assistant Attorney General Richard K. Willard candidly told Congress that the test's true potential lay in uncovering damaging information about an employee. Hooked up to the supposedly omniscient machine, "subjects frequently 'confess' highly personal and embarrassing information in a desperate attempt to be judged truthful," explained Willard. It was a phenomenon that could accidentally produce information "that is more useful in terms of the purpose of the examination than the examiner's assessment of the subject's physiological responses." Another hidden dividend, continued

Willard, was that polygraph usage created "a climate of fear — the deterrent effect."[12]

Under the Department of Defense proposal (then still on hold) the agency would begin without notice to test applicants for certain sensitive jobs and to test at random, existing employees with top-level security clearances. For the first time, those who refused the test would risk what was described as "adverse consequences." Finally, in February, 1984, President Reagan backed down and canceled his Orwellian National Security Directive 84 before the period of suspension expired. It was an election year.[13]

At the beginning of 1985, the Pentagon announced the wider use of LDs to assess what retired General Richard Stilwell, Deputy Undersecretary of Defense for Policy, called the "trustworthiness, patriotism and integrity of 3,500 people with access to highly classified information — perhaps as many as 10,000 a year in the future." Stilwell made that announcement even though he admitted he once asked for, and received, a change in a polygraph question when he was being tested, to protect himself from flunking. Accuracy of the device, thought Stilwell, ranged from 75 to 90 percent. Employees of the CIA and the National Security Agency were then already subject to periodic testing. Under a one-year program approved in the previous session of Congress, the Pentagon was set to implement a regular testing program for some 3,500 workers in scores of job categories, or applicants for those posts — both military and civilian Pentagon staff as well as employees from some other agencies and defense contractors. Also, for the first time, people could be barred from keeping, or assuming, a job solely for failing a polygraph exam or for refusing to submit to one. According to the Pentagon, the number of LD tests given by the Pentagon rose from 13,000 in 1980 to over 21,000 in 1984. With regard to employees who failed an LD test, the Pentagon said they could take other jobs at equivalent wages. Representative Jack Brooks dismissed the instrument by saying "a coin toss would be more accurate." Concerned about the idea that people could beat the machine, Allan Adler of the ACLU warned "One of the things you do by relying on this kind of polygraphing is create a false sense of security by clearing people who may in fact be spying."[14]

When he was asked why the new LD policy was needed at the Pentagon, Stilwell replied, "The tests will give us a bit more assurance that we won't lose our most precious secrets." Asked about the possibility that some people could learn how to control their reaction and beat the polygraph he said, "That may happen, but very rarely. We give those tests to employees who work 10 hours or more a day. It's inconceivable that they could also be undergoing vigorous training to control three reactions simultaneously."[15]

In June, 1985, the House of Representatives overwhelmingly endorsed polygraph use when the Representatives voted by a margin of 333 to 71 to increase LD testing of Department of Defense personnel who had access to classified information. Thus, the policy of using the machine on federal employees who had access to classified information reached a total of about 100,000 people, who could potentially be tested. So large was the category that it included Secretary of State George Shultz. When a reporter asked him if he would actually take one Shultz snapped back, "The minute, in this government, I am told that I'm not trusted is the day that I leave." Trying to smooth things over, the White House hurried to explain that Shultz would never be polygraphed under the terms of the policy and the president himself joked to news people that he would not take one either. Shultz had said the device "tends to identify quite a few people who are innocent as guilty, and it misses at least some fraction ... who are guilty of lying." From that Shultz concluded, "So the use of it as a broad-gauged condition of employment seems to me to be questionable."[16]

A few days later, Reagan acknowledged he had more confidence in the usefulness of LD tests than Shultz did but he argued their disagreement was mainly the result of a misunderstanding over how widespread the testing would be. Reagan claimed the tests would be administered only to "a very limited number" of people as an "investigatory tool" in espionage cases. Representative Jack Brooks, chair of the House Government Operations Committee, sharply disagreed with Reagan's description of the directive for increased LD usage, as he tried to mend fences with Shultz. Brooks declared, "I am stunned by the President's denial that his directive would implement a massive, random, polygraph screening program." He added that it was apparent that the President still did not "understand his directive." That November 1, 1985 order signed by Reagan said, "aperiodic, non-life style, counterintelligence-type polygraph examinations" would be given to those with access to sensitive information — well in excess of 100,000 people. "This is not a policy of just testing in the course of an investigation."[17]

Polygraph operators for all federal government agencies, except the CIA, received their training at the U.S. Army Military Police School at Fort McClellan, Alabama. A training manual called the *Polygraph Examiner Training Course* was used there from February, 1984, to November, 1985, when it was suspended after a General Accounting Office survey found that examiners were being taught to ask questions not strictly limited to security matters, as federal law required. Under the heading in the manual "Organizations," subhead "Ethnic organizations" was found the following advice, "The examinee may belong to organizations as a direct result of his ethnic background.... This area should be explored with care, not only because these organizations may have Communist or Fascist motivation, but also because the subject may resent deeply any supposed bias or tactlessness on the part of the examiner." Under the subhead "Racial organizations" was found the observation that many people may have donated their time or their money to racial pressure groups. "Since many of these organizations have been infiltrated by Communists, or are motivated by Fascist principles, participation in such groups should be discussed thoroughly.... Negroes may be expected to have belonged to groups such as the NAACP." Under the subhead "Political organizations" was found the following, "Membership in either of the two major political organizations or affiliated organizations will not be discussed during the interview. Other organizations will be discussed and the degree of activity of the examinee will be determined." And under the heading "Personnel Screening Question Pool" were listed these queries to ask examinees, "Have you ever had a mental breakdown?" and "Have you ever been confined to a rest home?"[18]

That polygraph training school at Fort McClellan opened in 1951 and over the years, agents from the governments of Israel, Venezuela, Taiwan, South Korea, and Canada had been trained there. Over the 35 years the school had been open (through 1986) it had turned out 1,200 alumni and was planning to expand its output from 48 students per year to 108. Ronald Decker, chief of Fort McClellan's polygraph division remarked, about the LD test procedure, "Anybody can sit in that chair and distort and move and make the test inconclusive. The whole procedure requires that the subject cooperate."[19]

Use of the device in the 1980s continued to increase in business. Writing in *Time* in 1980, Bennett Beach declared the LD test had become "big business" with hundreds of thousands of exams given every year and the number rising steadily. When it came to estimating business losses to employee theft, Beach cited the lobby group American Polygraph Association as declaring that as many as three out of four employees handling money and merchandise stole, and they stole a total of $20 billion or more a year.

Linda Voikos, a 22-year-old bookkeeper for S. S. Kresge, reported $150 missing from the previous days' receipts. A few weeks later one of the store's security men took her to a room at the local Holiday Inn. Then another man tried to elicit a confession from Voikos, first with the polygraph, then with persuasion. "Linda, you've tried to deceive me," the examiner said. "You did steal the money." She quit before she was fired. About five years later a Detroit jury ordered the discount chain to pay her $100,000. "The hefty compensation was unprecedented, but there is growing evidence that Voikos's ordeal was not," said Beach. According to Mike Tiner of the United Food and Commercial Workers Union, questions about political, sexual and union matters were "definitely on the increase." At a cost ranging from $35 to $150 per test, the polygraph exam was still much cheaper than a traditional background job check, at an average of $300.[20]

Researcher Trudy Hayden observed that nearly all employers who used polygraphs regarded them as a requirement of employment and that for every job applicant who refused the test another could be found who was willing to submit. She felt "the uncooperative employee can be pressured in many subtle and not so subtle ways." Any notion that tests were taken voluntarily was false in her view and the irony of the supposedly "voluntary" test was only underscored by the insistence of many examiners that their subjects sign a waiver asserting their "voluntary agreement to be tested." Another irony she saw was that most employment polygraph testing was "virtually useless" to the employer. That was because very little day-to-day polygraph practice, especially in pre-employment screening met the standards considered necessary to a valid test: a well-trained, skilled examiner; carefully drawn, objective queries; sufficient time; a calm atmosphere, and a willing, cooperative subject. As a result, the employer did not care whether the operator claimed to have caught the examinee in an outright lie or had simply "induced" him into admissions of misbehavior or character defects, "in daily practice, the latter occurs much more often than the former." Industry critic David Lykken argued that any experienced interrogator could do much better than chance accuracy if he had the opportunity, as did an LD operator, "to study the charges against the suspect that makes him a suspect, to listen to his alibi; and to engage him in a pretest interview to observe his behavior, his demeanor, to administer the polygraph questions and then have subsequent discussions between repetitions of the questions." Hayden reported it appeared to be widespread practice around New York State for employers to insist on polygraph tests after the discovery of a shortage and to fire, or at least severely harass, anyone who refused, anyone who failed, and anyone who was accused by the LD operator. She also said it seemed to be increasingly common for employers, especially in large retail franchises and chains, to implement periodic testing, once or even twice yearly, and to dismiss workers who failed even if there had been no discovered shortage. At a gun import and retail firm, LD tests were given to all applicants for positions as sales clerks and stock room clerks. They would not hire anyone who refused a test, failed a test or whose test results were assessed as inconclusive. Hayden concluded polygraph operators should not be regulated and licensed as that only legitimized "a practice that is by its very nature coercive, intrusive, and conducive to harassment and discrimination." Polygraph tests do not need to be regulated, she added, "they need to be banned."[21]

Hotel chain Days Inn implemented a policy around 1978 that all applicants for management positions had to submit to the machine. Five years later Lawrence W. Talley, vice president of corporate security for the hotel, said he was pleased with the results believing it cut money losses. He added that he could not understand why other major hotel chains "are constantly concerned about their losses," but at the same time, refused to implement the test in their own hiring procedures. Talley claimed that less than one percent of his applicants declined to submit to the machine and that the LD test did not "offend" people. Claiming the polygraph was 96 percent reliable, he said 917 LD tests were administered by Days Inn in 1981 to job applicants and of those 588 (64.1 percent) was recommended for hiring, which meant 35.9 percent of the applicants were rejected on the basis of the LD test results.[22]

H. Ray Ellis was vice president and manager of security and fraud control at the Phoenix-based Arizona Bank. The 1982 policy at this bank, reported Ellis, was that any officer or employee who refused to submit to the machine could be terminated from employment, for that reason alone. Pointing out that the results of any polygraph exam would be kept in "strict confidence" Ellis nevertheless added that "a copy of the examination results and the investigative report will be provided to Human Resources for file and may be submitted to appropriate law enforcement agencies as an investigative aid." Ellis admitted his bank had a three strikes and you're out policy with regard to specific event LD investigations. If an employee failed a polygraph exam the employee was suspended without pay and provided with an opportunity to take up to two additional LD tests. If the employee passed a subsequent exam, and employment was continued, the employee was given back pay. However, if the employee did not pass the additional tests, employment was terminated.[23]

At the Jack Eckerd Corporation, based in Florida, and the largest American drug company, each of the 30,000 employees took an LD test every 12 to 15 months, after each had submitted to the initial pre-employment polygraph. Reportedly there were no exceptions to that rule with even chief executive officer Stewart Turley taking his turn. A condition of employment with the company was a signed agreement to take a polygraph upon request. Reporter Kenneth Englade gave as evidence to support his contention of increasing LD use in business the fact that in the Atlanta Yellow Pages there were only three polygraph firms advertised in 1970; in 1975 there were 20; in 1982 there were 30. Eckerd's had 40 polygraphers on its payroll but still occasionally had to turn to outside independent firms for help when the work load got too heavy. Englade remarked, "A testee doesn't have to be overawed by the machine, but according to the APA, he has to be convinced the test is going to work; to respond properly he has to believe the machine will really catch him if he tries to lie."[24]

Journalist Carolyn Crowley reported the APA had 2,000 members at the end of 1982, and an estimated 6,000 polygraphers were practicing in America. She thought between 500,000 and one million Americans would be given polygraph tests that year.[25]

Exact numbers on how many LD tests were given were unknown because, said New York Times reporter Raymond Bonner, no one, including industry groups, was willing or able to supply exact figures. Still, the New York Civil Liberties Union estimated that each year a half million job applicants and employees nationwide were required to take a polygraph exam. The APA claimed about 30 percent of the Fortune 500 firms used the machine. Among the users were Chase Manhattan Bank, Chemical Bank, and Gimbels department store. In New York state, Attorney General Robert Abrams was strongly backing legislation that would prohibit their use there. Abrams supported similar legislation the previous year, which failed to pass, but now the matter had become more urgent due to a "dramatic increase" in complaints about the device. Timothy Gilles, Abrams's press secretary, said the number of complaints about LDs had doubled in the past six months—now, about four a week—rising to be the most frequent category of complaints received by the Attorney General's Civil Rights bureau, which also dealt with employment discrimination and housing issues.[26]

Most companies were "unwilling to talk about" their use of LDs, said APA president Lynn Marcy. He felt that reticence was because of the "adverse treatment" the issue of LDs had generally received in the press, which he blamed on "unobjective and biased" reporters. Bonner's request to discuss LD usage was declined by Lehigh Oil, Duane Reade, Gimbels, and Alexander's. The latter, a large New York department store chain, was the defendant in numerous complaints filed by the Legal Action Center (a nonprofit New York group) on behalf of workers dismissed by Alexander's after having been given a polygraph. A spokesman for Chase Manhattan Bank, Kenneth Mills, said he could not provide data on the number of people who had not been hired because of the results of LD tests. Harry Johnson, vice president in charge of risk management for the Zale Corp., was asked how reliable the instrument was. "That's a tough one," he replied, adding it was "a lot less reliable in pre-employment screening than in a specific theft situation." Civil libertarians such as Norma Rollins, director of the privacy project for the New York Civil Liberties Union, wanted them banned, as did others. One complaint filed against Zale charged race discrimination in the use of the polygraph. According to the complaint, while Zale had dismissed many employees for having failed an LD test, only one was a white person. In Florida, a man won a $250,000 settlement against the discount department store chain the Zayre Corp. after being fired for failing a polygraph exam. During the trial, evidence was introduced that another employee was guilty of the theft for which David Ivey had been dismissed. That other worker had passed an LD test.[27]

Another person who attacked the business use of polygraphs was John Belt, a former personnel administrator but an assistant professor of personnel management at Wichita State University in 1983 when he wrote his article. First, he mentioned an ancient method used by the Bedouins of Arabia whereby they had the suspect lick a hot iron. The modern polygraph, he said, varied "from its historical predecessors only in its pseudoscientific mechanization and in the greater number and types of measurements monitored." Of all the conditions necessary to the polygraph testing process he identified the most important condition was that "the person being questioned must believe the machine really does detect lies." With regard to the argument that LD testing was a low-cost applicant screening method Belt noted that costs associated with growing lawsuits against the polygraph had to be included, as did employer/employee relations over the long term. That is, it created a climate of distrust and fostered informing on other employees. Another problem Belt identified was that the examinee had "little chance to refute the results of the machine." Even if the LD was proven to be reliable, valid and economical, thought Belt, the ethical question still remained, "and it is this point about polygraphs which generates the most intense feelings."[28]

A survey of Houston, Texas polygraph firms revealed that pre-employment testing accounted for 90 percent of their business. The 45 clients those firms represented gave an average of 2,000 pre-employment LD tests per year. And, said the account, the pre-employment polygraph represented the majority of all LD tests given in the U.S.[29]

Robert Messina reported in 1986 that a growing number of grocers were turning to polygraphs and even paper-and-pencil tests for honesty, because employee theft, which accounted for 65 percent of food retail shrinkage, stood at $40 billion a year. One supermarket chain that used LDs to test applicants was the Lakeland, Florida–based Publix Supermarkets, which had been doing so for about three years. Bud Ruth, Publix vice president of personnel, boasted that Publix had one of the lowest shrinkage rates in the industry, but added, "Of course, that's been the case since the early 1950s." Publix administered around 200 LD tests per week. Ironically, those paper-and-pencil honesty tests were invented by polygrapher John Reid. Major selling points for them included the fact they were legal in all 50 states and cost $4 to $15 per applicant compared to $50 or more for a polygraph exam. An example of a not-very-subtle query found on one of these tests was, "When you read about a successful robbery in the papers, do you feel good?"[30]

A 1987 study conducted by Robert Half International, the world's largest financial, accounting, and data processing recruiters, of 100 of the country's top 1,000 companies disclosed that only 10 percent of those firms used polygraphs. And of those companies that did use the device, only one-third of them requested applicants to submit to the test.[31]

The *Harvard Law Review* brought up the point that businesses in the states that by law restricted LD use suffered no apparent disadvantage when compared to their counterparts in states that allowed unrestricted use of the instrument. As to why they were used at all, this account believed employers might have been relatively unconcerned about false positive errors (assessing innocent people as deceptive) compared to false negative errors (assessing liars as being truthful). Also, employers used the test "principally as a scare tactic to frighten examinees into confessing some past misconduct. This use of polygraph testing is an 'abomination' and offends societal notions of fairness."[32]

In March, 1988, *Business Week* ran a huge article (five full pages with no ads) on privacy in the workplace, encroachment by employers and resistance by workers and unions. The focus was on issues like drug testing, computer surveillance, LD tests, and so forth. In this account, employee theft from employers was estimated at "up to $10 billion annually."

A drugstore employee refused to take an LD test during an investigation of stock shortages at Rite-Aid of Maryland. Although the company violated a state law in ordering the test, it forced the woman to resign. A state appeals court affirmed a $1.3 million court award to the woman.

Business Week estimated that about 30 percent of America's largest firms and more than 50 percent of retail business used the polygraph to some extent.

By 1982 John O'Brien had worked nearly 10 years for Papa Gino's of America, a New England restaurant chain. As an area supervisor he was in charge of 28 restaurants and 500 employees. Then, despite repeated requests from higher-up, he refused to promote an employee who was the son of a company director, maintaining the man was not competent. A few weeks later O'Brien's boss told him that someone — Papa Gino's never identified the person — had seen him take drugs at a party. The company gave him two choices: be fired, or submit to a polygraph test. After he took the test, Papa Gino declared the results proved he lied and fired him. He sued and in 1985 a federal jury found the polygraph investigation to have been "highly offensive" and awarded damages that eventually totaled $595,000. That award was upheld by a federal appeals court.[33]

A November, 1987 survey of 995 human resources managers was conducted by the American Management Association into LD usage. Of those firms, 398 (40 percent) were small companies with sales less than $50 million annually; 367 (36.8 percent) were mid-size companies with sales from $50 million to $500 million; 174 (17.5 percent) were large companies with over $500 million in sales; 466 (46.8 percent) of the firms were service providers; 338 (34 percent) were manufacturers; 188 (18.9 percent) were "other." Eric Greenberg reported the survey found polygraph testing was limited and largely concentrated in the banking and securities industries; some retail companies also used the device. Ten percent of the respondent firms used the device to some extent; 7.6 percent reported using LD tests for existing employees while 4.7 percent said they polygraphed new hires. Overall, newly hired employees most likely to be tested were those applying for positions in security operations, in retail outlets where large amounts of cash were handled, and in bookkeeping operations. According to the survey, "Eighty percent of the respondents do not hire job applicants who fail polygraph tests." Costs of running LD testing programs varied widely in 1987 from a low amount of $50 declared by two respondents up to a high of $700,000 reported by one large conglomerate that tested all applicants and all existing workers, on an ongoing basis.[34]

Going into more detail, Greenberg reported that if a current employee failed a polygraph test in one of the 56 companies that gave tests in that category, action taken was as follows: 51.8 percent were dismissed; 14.3 percent were placed on suspension/probation; 7.1 percent were reassigned; 5.4 percent were given a referral; 21.4 percent resulted in "other" action.[35]

A year later, the American Management Association released the results of a second survey on workplace testing; this one included 1,005 firms. The most dramatic result was the sharp increase in the number of companies using drug testing; 21 percent in 1986, to 37 percent in 1987, to 48 percent in 1988. HIV testing of employees was practiced by 6.1 percent of the respondent concerns in 1987, and 7.5 percent in 1988. On the other hand, polygraph use was declining, from 10.7 percent in 1987 to 8.7 percent in 1988 (a federal ban on the device was just then about to come into effect). Of the companies that drug tested applicants, 96 percent of them would not hire a positive. Of those that drug tested current employees, 25 percent of the companies fired positives, 60 percent referred them for treatment or other counseling, 11 percent administered other discipline such as suspension or probation. Of the 88 firms in the survey that used polygraph testing, 28 tested new hires— 21 selectively by job category, and seven tested all new hires. Some 28 percent of the respondents said their state laws permitted unrestricted LD use. Those 88 companies that did polygraph represented 31.1 percent of the companies operating where testing was legal. Half of the wholesale trade firms in the survey used the machine where state law permitted as did 43 percent of the bank and finance companies, 30 percent of the healthcare providers, and 17 percent of the manufacturers. Highest incidence of polygraph use was among retailers, at 71 percent where states allowed unrestricted use. On average, companies that used LDs had done so for more than 10 years; 13 percent had used the device for more than 20 years. Average expenditure by respondent firms on polygraph testing in 1988 was $14,900 (for drug testing it was $20,100) with one-third of the firms that reported their cost having each spent less than $1,000. Three companies spent over $100,000. Forty-six percent of the LD-using respondents fired current employees who failed the LD exam (worse than with drug testing) and another 27 percent imposed other disciplinary measures such as suspension or probation. Job applicants who failed were not hired by 94 percent of the companies that polygraphed new hires.[36]

As the 1980s ended and the federal LD ban was in place, Robert Deevey, loss prevention director at Turtle's records and tapes and a 30-year veteran in retail loss prevention summed up the situation when he commented, "In my estimation the polygraph caused more problems than it solved. It became a crutch in many companies where, if they had a problem, the solution was to put everybody on polygraph." Peat, Marwick, Main consultant Toby Horowitz remarked, "Some companies were using the polygraph to the point they relied on it as their only program."[37]

One of the more unexpected places to find the device was in the school system. In April, 1986, Polk County (Barstow, Florida) schools halted their five-year-old practice of subjecting students to polygraphs in disciplinary cases after a controversy over the use of the tests. Superintendent of Schools, John Stewart, read a memo to school board members stating the schools were discontinuing the tests in grades seven through twelve. Board member Ted Aggelis remarked, "I'm just flabbergasted.... By discontinuing it, basically the news media and American Civil Liberties Union are making policy for the board."[38]

Throughout its history, the LD remained a uniquely American device. Its use in other nations was very limited. Trying to put the best face on that was LD proponent Carolyn Crowley writing in the trade publication *Security Management* where she declared that law enforcement agencies in Canada, Japan and Israel regularly employed the instrument while "Twenty other nations use the polygraph to a lesser extent." Except for those operators trained at government schools in Japan and Israel, most foreign operators, she explained, had received their training in the U.S., and many were said to belong to the APA. "European courts, legal codes, and commentators have rejected lie detection, not because they question its reliability," she said, but because it has been found "to violate essential dignity, human personality, and the individuality of the citizen." Actually, they had indeed rejected it in Europe, and other foreign areas, at least in part because the LD was neither reliable nor valid.[39]

The United Kingdom trade publication *Personnel Management* did an article on the subject in 1984 wherein it said use of the device in the UK had been "extremely rare, partly perhaps because such evidence is not permissible in court." Polygraphs received some publicity at the time when the UK government floated a proposal (later abandoned) to try the device for an experimental period within a part of the government. Also, a private firm, Polygraph Security Services, was set up around that time to attempt to market a polygraph service — apparently the first such company in the UK. In the wake of that minor flurry of publicity, the Occupational Psychology Section Committee of the British Psychological Society issued a statement on the device. "There is no available research evidence which demonstrates the validity of the polygraph for personnel screening purposes," said the statement. In view of the absence of supportive data on the device's validity for personnel screening and the "substantial amount of 'negative' data available at present, the British Psychological Society considers it should not be used for personnel screening purposes, either for pre-employment or for current employee screening (for fraud or security breaches)." In conclusion, asserted the statement, "The Society deplores the possibility that, despite the evidence, the polygraph might still be used."[40]

A few years later, a study was commissioned by the UK government in connection with its consideration of the recommendation in the Security Commission's report that there should be a pilot study to test the feasibility of polygraph security screening in the intelligence and security agencies (this also did not take place). Conducted by Dr. A. B. Levey, that study was released in 1988. A practical objection to LD use in screening employees raised by Levey was that it was "Well established that counter-measures, i.e. means of producing a misleading result in order to escape detection, can easily be learned … the capability for escaping detection is extremely high." He added that "its accuracy as an instrument of detection is not high enough to meet conventional psychometric standards." That led to a paradox for Levey because the accuracy figures quoted by the industry, including the "responsible leaders of the profession," were much higher than those obtained in the laboratory by objective researchers. "Indeed, they are impossibly high given the known limitations on the reliability of psychophysiological measure," Levey concluded. "There is a strong probability that these inflated values represent a mixture of a high proportion of self-deception and a low proportion of simple chicanery." He found that polygraph screening applied a procedure of limited accuracy biased toward "the erroneous exclusion of suitable applicants and the false accusations of those already in employment…." Polygraph technique, said Levey, had "no scientifically acceptable theory at its base … and it is applied to the detection of low base-rate frequencies in an area — the identification of honesty — which is itself ill understood."[41]

High profile people continued to surface who demanded they be given an LD test, or who challenged someone else to take one, or both, or who were challenged themselves. One thing that emerged from the Jimmy Carter and Ronald Reagan 1980 presidential campaign was that some pur-loined papers from Carter's White House turned up in the hands of Ronald Reagan's campaign aides just before a debate. FBI officials proposed to the Justice Department that as many as a dozen Reagan aides be given poly-graph tests. Reporter Bob Woodward said the FBI wanted to ask CIA Direc-tor William Casey and White House chief of staff James Baker to submit to the machine to resolve conflicts in their stories. White House spokesman Larry Speakes publicly said the president would not object if his senior peo-ple submitted to the polygraph. Privately, the White House was said to be furious at the FBI for raising the specter of high-level staff "being fluttered like common thieves." Backing away the FBI declared they had not sought approval for tests, and the idea was merely under consideration if other investigative measures failed.[42]

Tom Osborne, Nebraska's football coach, challenged Booker Brown, at the end of 1984, to an LD test over the former player's accusations that in 1972 Osborne used rule-breaking inducements to recruit Brown (Osborne was then Nebraska's offensive coordinator). Osborne challenged, "I would invite him to take a polygraph test on this matter, and I'm will-ing to do so myself."[43]

When John DeLorean (a highly visible figure in the 1980s with a failed, namesake automobile company and various charges leveled against him) found himself accused of wrongdoing he went on the offensive by announcing his claim of FBI entrapment had been confirmed by an LD test administered by a well-known polygrapher who reported there was a probability greater than 0.99 that DeLorean's story was truthful. A month later, DeLorean was tested again. That second test was conducted by an FBI examiner who concluded that his story was clearly deceptive.[44]

Keeping with its own growing status, the polygraph got its own television show in the 1980s, albeit briefly. Early 1983 saw the launch of the daily syndicated program "Lie Detector" on which lawyer and host F. Lee Bailey and polygraph operator Ed Gelb, past president of the American Polygraph Association, put guests, some of them accused criminals, to the test while viewers in 80 cities watched at home. One example of the guests on the show was a man who claimed he once gave Howard Hughes a ride in his car and was left a fortune by the reclusive billionaire. Journalist Ted Guest worried that combined with the Reagan order (to drastically increase polygraph usage in the federal government) the television show, "which treats the lie detector with studied reverence, is likely to encourage the spread of polygraph testing in industry."[45]

On the show Bailey urged potential participants "Bring us your questions. We'll give you the truth." Volunteers who wished to affirm or refute some allegation that was important in their own lives were tested right in the studio and then endorsed as truthful or denounced as liars by Bailey after he and Gelb had examined the charts. Bailey declared the program was dedicated to the principle that "every American has the right to prove his innocence." However, that program was quickly canceled due to low ratings, probably in the year of its debut. Appearing on ABC-TV's "Nightline" program in 1985, F. Lee Bailey contended that for every 100 LD tests administered, 96 were correct, three were inconclusive, and one was in error. While there were 4,000 polygraphers in America in 1979, there were an estimated 10,000 by 1985. Florida alone had 27 polygraph training schools in 1983, but only three of them had APA accreditation.[46]

As the federal government made more serious efforts to adopt restrictive polygraph legislation states continued, in some cases, to take their own action. In the area of labor arbitration, Daniel Dennehy argued in 1980 for more acceptance of polygraph evidence in arbitration. To support that opinion in the *Labor Law Journal* he came to some unusual conclusions, such as "Even critics admit that the polygraph technique unquestionably possesses a significant degree of validity and reliability" and "there has been a marked change in acceptance of polygraph testing" in the years since those early court rejections in 1923 and 1934. There was a widespread increase in the use of the LD but that was not the same as acceptance. In the 1930s, the device was accepted in the sense there was next to no criticism of the instrument, but that situation did not last.[47]

Several years later, researchers Herman Theeke and Tina Theeke analyzed labor arbitration cases involving polygraph tests during the period 1958 to 1986. They concluded, "Analyses of cases during the period 1958–1986 indicate that when polygraph evidence is admitted, it is given little weight, and that arbitrators have not become more likely to admit polygraph evidence in recent times." A review of cases in which employees refused to take polygraph tests indicated that a majority of arbitrators upheld the employee's right of refusal. "It is remarkable that use of the polygraph continues in the absence of scientific evidence supporting the validity of such tests," observed the Theekes. They looked at a total of 79 cases (all that were publicly reported in the 1958 to 1986 period); 46 of them dealt with the admissibility of LD evidence, and 33 with employees' refusal to submit. In the group of 46 the arbitrators admitted LD results in 28 cases (60 percent); in 18 cases (40 percent) they did not. Within that 28, the arbitrator gave no weight to that evidence in six cases (21 percent); little weight in seven (25 percent); some weight in three (11 percent); corroborating weight in four (14 percent); amount of weight given not stated in eight cases (29 percent). In those 33 refusal to submit cases, the right to refuse was upheld in 27 cases (82 percent) and denied in six (18 percent).[48]

By 1975, a total of 17 states had enacted legislation that restricted use of the polygraph in some fashion. Ten years later, 26 states and the District of Columbia had enacted statutes restricting the use of LDs in the workplace. However, many of those laws were very weak. In 14 of those states the employer was allowed to "request" that his workers take a polygraph. Also, a majority of those states exempted police and law enforcement agencies and, in a few cases, other government agencies. Both New Jersey and Washington state exempted businesses from their LD law if that business dealt in drugs or controlled, dangerous substances.[49]

New York State Attorney General Robert Abrams wrote a letter to the editor of the *New York Times*, in July, 1986 to correct an earlier article that said New York State had a law restricting polygraph use. Abrams noted the state had a law against use of PSEs only but in New York State employers could legally fire workers and applicants for refusing to take a test. "For five years I have sought legislation to prohibit employers from requiring applicants or employees to subject themselves to these 'heartbreak machines,' as one victim dubbed them," observed Abrams. "Five times that legislation has died in the State Senate." One example he gave was of a job applicant who was told by the polygraph operator that he had lied when he gave his address. He was not hired.[50]

With more than half of the states with restrictive laws forbidding only compulsory testing, the employer was free to use coercive pressure to request or suggest someone take a test. One measure of the ineffectiveness of these state laws could be seen in the fact that in 1985 the 27 state polygraph boards received a total of only 145 complaints from people feeling the law had been violated. Yet the ACLU reported it received over 1,800 complaints regarding polygraph exams.[51]

One of the more interesting experiments, which showed some of the psychological power of the instrument, came in 1982 and involved 21 males serving in the Israeli police. All took what was presented to them as a paper-and-pencil aptitude test that was important to their careers. Finished tests were passed in to the researchers who, unbeknownst to the subjects, removed a specially treated under sheet from the test booklet that recorded all the answers. Then the subjects were given back their test books, the answer sheet, and told to score their own exams. That allowed them to cheat by filling in blanks and changing answers, and so on; seven cheated. After a few days, the subjects were told there was a suspicion that some of them had cheated and they were all offered the chance to take an LD test. Initially, all 21 agreed to take it. Subsequently, one of the guilty seven was a no-show and two (one guilty and one innocent) refused to take it. Three other guilty subjects confessed to cheating before taking the polygraph test. Thus, only 15 took the LD test, of whom, only two had actually cheated. Those tests were evaluated by three polygraphers; one had access to LD charts only; one observed the subjects' behavior, but not the charts; and the third, who conducted the interrogation, had access to both types of information. Assessments of deception based on both behavior observation and on physiological charts were superior to those based on either type of information alone. However evaluations based on the physiological charts alone were not superior to those based on the behavioral observation alone.[52]

Another of those who developed paper-and-pencil instruments, in case the LD was banished, was Carl Klump and his business, the Stanton Corporation. After eight years in the Army, the last three in military intelligence, Klump became fascinated with the polygraph and decided to make it his career. As a result of his experiences he came up with a series of written questions that he developed into the Stanton Survey. "The written test can do just as good a job as the polygraph at weeding out poor employment risks," he said, "but people like machines, and I still get a lot of calls for polygraph tests." Among the several different written tests he sold to companies were ones that purported to measure attitudes toward honesty among existing employees and applicants. From his "wealth of experience" Klump had the following advice for employees shifting through applications, "Be very cautious about hiring people who leave dirty fingerprints on the form, and those who have passed through the education system but make gross spelling errors."[53]

While critics of the polygraph were easy to find, those who defended the instrument and embraced it with an unqualified enthusiasm were very much harder to locate. One supporter was David Devine, manager of polygraph services for the Eckerd Drug company. First he cited the opinions of then CIA director George Bush who declared, "The polygraph is an integral and essential part of security processing to determine the security eligibility of persons for agency employment and for operational purposes." Devine then exclaimed that LD exams had "gained greater acceptance in our society because of the high professionalism of the examiners, because of regulation by state government, and because of public awareness of the reasonable needs this tool can address."[54]

Another true believer was Richard Phannenstill, who wrote in *Security Management* in 1983 that business losses were in the range of $30 billion to $40 billion a year; that the largest percentage of that was attributable to employee theft and "In fact, more than twenty percent of all business failures each year are a direct result of employee theft...." He went on to state that there was little empirical data to support the charge that "properly conducted preemployment polygraph examinations are an invasion of privacy or constituted an offensive screening procedure." To clear that up, Phannenstill cited a survey of some 200 job applicants in Milwaukee who were asked several questions. Among them was, "Do you think the test was unfair in any way?" (89 percent said no); "Did the test or any part of it offend you?" (87 percent said no); "Do you think the test was an invasion of your privacy?" (79 percent said no). As well, he cited five other, similar studies, done by different people wherein the "no" response to the three queries ranged from 77 percent to 100 percent and all but four of the 15 were above 90 percent "no" responses. Of course, those studies had no validity at all. In all cases, the person who asked the questions was the polygraph operator. Those questions were asked before the applicant knew if he had passed the LD test and before the applicant knew whether or not he had gotten the job.[55] George Barlan was president of his own LD firm and in 1985 he said 90 percent of all polygraph work was done for businesses and half of that involved screening job applicants. To industry critics he said "If it were but half as bad as its critics claim, it would have died out decades ago." After asking himself how accurate the polygraph was in pre-employment screening he replied, "Nobody knows for sure." Nevertheless, he went on to declare, "A case can certainly be made that everybody should be screened on the polygraph prior to being hired."[56]

Richard Paterson was a spokesman for the National Wholesale Druggists' Association (NWDA) who defended the device during federal hearings that were held to consider imposing restrictions. Based on a 1985 survey the NWDA found that 80 percent of its member firms used polygraph tests to some extent. The 20 percent who did not were said to be primarily located in sparsely populated rural areas where family-run businesses and close community ties precluded the need for such testing. During 1984, one drug wholesaler administered over 1,500 LD tests to people applying for jobs at its drug distribution operation; one in four was not recommended for hiring, explained Paterson, "based on polygraph examinations in combination with other preemployment screening tools." In pleading against any federal ban he said, "We hope Congress will acknowledge the vital role polygraph examinations can play in protecting American society from drug abusers and diverters." Paterson added that "A ban on polygraph examinations for the drug wholesale industry would undermine the federal government's aggressive campaign against drug addiction and abuse."[57]

Supporters of the device could do little but make unsubstantiated claims about the device; critics rested on more solid ground. Jerome Skolnick, director of the Center for the Study of Law and Society at the University of California at Berkeley, pointed out in 1980 that while the lack of accuracy on the part of the LD was a major point of objection, equally important was the inadequacy of the theory behind lie detection. That is, the act of lying led to conscious conflict; that conflict induced anxiety or fear; those emotional responses were accompanied by measurable and interpretable physiological changes. All those assumptions, said Skolnick, were questionable. Moreover, bodily responses did not vary regularly, either with each other or with emotional states. If they did, he argued, only a unigraph, and not a polygraph, would be required. Four imprecise measurements were not more accurate than one precise measurement. "Since the relations among lying, conflict, emotion and bodily responses are so fuzzy, the accuracy of the lie detector is not comparable to that of, say, blood tests or X-rays." Skolnick stated. "A dozen lie-detector examiners would not consistently reach the same conclusion regarding truth or falsity if they depended on the squiggles produced by a polygraph." Given that his conclusions were correct, he wondered why then was the use of LDs increasing sharply. He felt it was because "An unreliable method can also be an effective social-control instrument." Due to the scientific look of the machine, and so on, the coercive power of the interrogators was heightened. He concluded the machine was not highly accurate but that it was effective in eliciting information from subjects who believed that it was.[58]

Eric Matusewitch was an equal-opportunity employment specialist for the New York Human Rights Commission from 1976 to 1980. In his view, the use of a machine to detect lies was "inappropriate and impractical. More seriously, it violates our society's cherished ideals of individual privacy and civil liberties." Matusewitch cited former Senator Sam Ervin who had remarked in 1974, "If the right to privacy means anything at all in our society, it means that people are entitled to have thoughts, hopes, desires, and dreams that are beyond the grasping reach of a bureaucrat, an employer, or an electronic technician."[59]

One of the industry's most persistent, and cogent, critics was psychologist David Lykken whose 1981 book *A Tremor in the Blood: Uses and Abuses of the Lie Detector* demolished any claims to accuracy that may have then remained to the polygraph. At that time he estimated over one million Americans would be polygraphed in the course of a year. Some people believed in the devices, he felt, because the device looked and sounded like scientific technology and because they were simple and convenient short-cuts to difficult and complicated decisions. LDs, argued Lykken, were especially unreliable for truthful people.[60]

Lykken told *People* magazine, in an interview to publicize his book, that there was only one catch to them; "they don't work." Innocent people would fail them 50 percent of the time. "You'd do as well flipping a coin." Asked why it was that we believed in the polygraph he replied, "I don't know exactly. The lie detector is almost exclusively an American artifact. Many Europeans have never heard of it. Americans are hooked on the mystique of science and technology — an aura exploited by advocates of the devices. There is nothing scientific about them." In conclusion he told *People*, "The lie detector has no more place in the courts or in business than a psychic or tarot cards."[61]

At a 1984 scientific convention, Lykken said it was both curious and disturbing that a technique "based on such implausible assumptions has managed to become entrenched in American mythology." The field of polygraphy, he added, "is shot through with a degree of psychological naiveté that would be funny if it didn't result in so much harm."[62]

Lykken remarked that John Reid, LD pioneer and creator of the control question method, had published a report back in 1945 acknowledging that, through a process of self-stimulation, an examinee could beat the machine, without the operator's awareness. A subject could augment, or increase, his own physiological responses to the control questions (reactions to relevant questions were compared to those of control questions by, for example, pressing down with one's free arm, tensing the muscles of the legs, squeezing the toes, biting the tongue, pushing down on a stone or nail in the shoe. Lykken had also apparently discovered a motto on an office wall at the Pentagon, "In God We Trust: Others We Polygraph."[63]

Researchers Benjamin Kleinmuntz and Julian Szucko also argued there had been no evidence presented in the psychological or polygraphic literature that demonstrated a high correlation between LD results and the "ground truth" of honesty. They cited false positive rates of 40 percent "which seems to be par for most laboratory and field studies." Also pointed out was an additional and more subtly biased factor. "This factor is a motivational one: polygraphers are motivated to serve their paying clients. Since clients have an interest in identifying guilty suspects, the polygraphers must expect to uncover cases of deception." Companies and government agencies that wanted to weed out dishonest people or security risks in their organizations "expect the polygrapher to identify such people."[64]

Writing in *The Progressive*, Francis Flaherty agreed the device was not accurate but said, in one sense, the accuracy question was irrelevant to the polygraph debate since the primary use of the machine was as a "confessional device." Relying on the respondent's belief in the infallibility of the machine, LD operators hoped to "extort a confession rather than rely on a reading of the squiggles on the graph paper." All over the country, the ACLU told Flaherty, their office received up to hundreds of calls each year from people who had been embarrassed, offended and outraged by their experiences in polygraph examinations. "They protest the extreme intrusiveness of many of the questions, the intimidating, sometimes outright bullying behavior of the examiner, and the indignity and humiliation of their subjection to a dehumanizing procedure." It was, in the words of former Senator Sam Ervin, "an invasion of personal rights through economic power." When the New York State Legislature failed, again, in the early 1980s in its perennial attempt to restrict LD usage it was reported that the most recent failure occurred because "the jewelry industry told [New York Governor Hugh] Carey they would leave the state if the bill passed," according to Peter Ramos, assistant professor of criminal justice at the State University of New York at Farmingdale. Walter Davis, an official of the 700,000-member Retail Clerks International Union, estimated that one-fifth of his union's collective bargaining agreements restricted management's use of the LD. But most polygraphy occurred in non-union places. Robert Ellis Smith, publisher of *Privacy Journal* brought up the class issue when he told a Senate hearing, "Let there be no doubt that polygraphing in employment is a matter of class status. Bank tellers take polygraph tests. Bank presidents do not." Yet Flaherty's article was curiously sympathetic to business. "By banning polygraphs, would we be saying to employers ... that they can't take measures to protect themselves?" Part of the reason may have been that he accepted uncritically the numbers tossed around by business as an estimate of their losses from employee crime—put in this account at from $15 billion to $50 billion a year. Still, it was a strange attitude to take in a publication such as *The Progressive.*[65]

Even the unlikely magazine *Parents* published a vigorously harsh attack on LDs, by Lori Andrews, in its March, 1983, issue. Titled "How lie detectors lie" and with a subhead, "Not only do they invade your privacy—they're often dead wrong" Andrews went on to describe the experience of taking an LD test as "the mental equivalent of a strip search." She said "The minute you walk into a polygrapher's office you will feel intimidated. This is by design." Andrews reported the results of a national Louis Harris survey in which it was revealed that 65 percent of workers, 55 percent of employers, and 60 percent of Congressmen felt that LD screening of job applicants should be forbidden."[66]

Psychology Today magazine posed the following question to its readers in 1984: Suppose you applied for a job, submitted a resume, filled out the application, went through the interview and then were told the job was yours if you passed a polygraph. Would you take the LD exam or would you refuse and forfeit the job? Of the readers who responded, 55 percent said they would refuse to submit to the machine. Reasons most commonly cited for refusing were: suspect accuracy of the test, a belief the test was an invasion of privacy, and an unwillingness to work for someone with a fundamental distrust of employees. Reasons given by those who expressed a willingness to take the test could be summed up in five words, "I have nothing to hide."[67]

When *Changing Times* discussed the subject in 1984, the magazine estimated up to four million LD tests were given annually and that internal theft was a major factor in many small business bankruptcies "as many as three in five, according to some estimates." Cited was a statement from a committee of the New York City Bar Association, made in 1981, that said, "There can be little doubt that these tests are conducted in a coercive atmosphere. The consequences of refusing to take the test is nearly always loss of the job."[68]

Researchers Phillip Davis and Pamela McKenzie-Rundle were both former polygraph operators, with one year and ten years experience, respectively. Their approach to the subject was to view LD tests as a "social control convention," with the setting and interaction organized toward two intellectual goals, "to produce 'good charts' and to generate admissions and confessions. These ends in turn are sought by 'selling' the subject on the polygrapher's ability to detect deception, overcoming subjects' 'countermeasures,' and presenting test results to subjects in ways that can induce confessions." Subjects were encouraged to believe they would pass or fail, that they were non-continuous alternatives with no middle-ground. During the pretest interview with the subject, the LD operator employed various strategies designed to convince the subject that the device worked. The most important strategy involved the presentation of the instrument as a piece of scientific hardware with the use and manipulation of the device symbolizing the technical expertise of the examiner. One tactic the researchers mentioned was the use of a 'stimulation' test in the pre-test phase. Telling the subject the stimulation test was to calibrate his machine, he used the old pick-a-card routine. The subject was suitably impressed, and cowed, when the examiner announced the correct card. However, said Davis and McKenzie-Rundle, "On occasion, all cards in the deck actually have the same number so the examiner will be sure to announce the correct number. At other times, the examiner simply notes where the card is replaced in the deck and surreptitiously glances at that spot later."[69]

Davis and McKenzie-Rundle also observed that many clients would not accept inconclusive test results, figuring they had paid for a final resolution of something. Inconclusive test results could create the impression, said the researchers, that the technique was invalid or, even worse, that the examiner was incompetent. Some clients interpreted inconclusive results as de facto indications of deception since the subject did not pass. Another method used by examiners sometimes was to point to nonexistent chart problems in front of the subject hoping to induce a confession. Although such methods were a violation of professional ethics, according to the APA, "some examiners occasionally do so. A few may do so routinely, but are regarded by other examiners as unprofessional." Nevertheless, Davis and McKenzie-Rundle argued that according to a working polygraphic ideology "the discovery of previously concealed information mitigates most such infractions." In conclusion they declared, "the technique's effectiveness hinges more upon the examiner's scientific dramaturgy and interactive skills that upon the procedure's scientific validity and the instrument's accuracy."[70]

One person in the government who opposed the policy change

announced by General Richard Stilwell was John Beary, the acting assistant secretary of Defense for health affairs. Beary sent a note to Stilwell that outlined in some detail the scientific objections to the polygraph. Stilwell's reply to the note skipped over the scientific issues and pointedly asked Beary how he viewed the "utility" of the polygraph process in view of its demonstrated value at the CIA and at the NSA. Not long before he left the Department of Defense, Beary sent Stilwell another memo. "One could reasonably ask at this juncture," he wrote, "why has Washington been bamboozled by the polygraph community for over 20 years? I can only speculate that it may have something to do with the poor state of science education in the United States."[71]

Reporting in an op-ed style piece in *Newsweek* in 1985, Irving Kaler wrote that his 16-year-old son applied for a job as stockboy in the pet department of a local discount store. He failed the LD test he was required to take. Wondering why American society tolerated the device he wrote, "it is absolutely incomprehensible that we rely upon some goofy, Rube Goldberg–type contraption to make sensitive decisions." A federal judge in Macon, Georgia, Wilbur Owens, ruled that it was unconstitutional for certain Georgia municipalities to compel their employees to take LD exams even during investigations into suspected drug use. Owens declared the LD test was "nothing more than the polygraph examiner's personal opinion of the truthful or deceptive manner in which the questioned person responded."[72]

Benjamin Kleinmuntz, professor of psychology at the University of Illinois at Chicago, writing in the *Harvard Business Review* told an anecdote about three guys tested at a brokerage house for the theft of securities. Dealing with one of the three the polygraph operator reportedly pointed to "tracings that show deception" while stating the other two had already confessed and implicated the third (they had not). "Polygraphers intent on 'getting the truth out of the defendant' often use this ploy," said Kleinmuntz, who estimated that two million LD tests were given each year: 98 percent in industry. Of those latter exams, 75 percent were given in pre-employment screening. Some 23 years earlier this publication had examined the effectiveness of LDs and warned, "There is no really effective mechanical technique yet available for screening job applicants or investigating dishonesty." Kleinmuntz added, "that judgment holds true today." From his assessment of research, he concluded that false positives ranged as high as 50 percent while false negatives (liars passing the test) were as high as 36 percent. Thus, if an LD test was 72 percent accurate, and if 80 percent of people were truthful, in a testing of 1,000 subjects, 224 truthful people would be assessed liars while 56 liars would be declared truthful. With higher rates for false positives, compared to false negatives, Kleinmuntz concluded LD operators had a strong bias toward finding truthful subjects to be deceptive rather than the other way around. In the face of no data to support the instrument's accuracy, he felt its popularity within business firms could perhaps be explained by "The fact is that managers, along with many others who need to have a scientific procedure for detecting dishonesty, want to believe that the device works.... No person should be deprived of a job on the basis of such a flawed procedure."[73]

Daniel Jussim in a 1985 piece in *The Nation* argued the device was especially popular among employees who resented federal and state regulations on hiring and firing. The LD's "reputation as a supposedly scientific tool gives them a license to reject or sack whoever they please." Don Blews had once been a manager for a department store chain in the Carolinas. In testimony before a Senate Judiciary subcommittee, he said his district supervisor told him that blacks "just don't work out" and ordered him to dismiss two black women workers. Blews said that when he refused the supervisor remarked, "We'll have to show you how the polygraph test works around here." Those two women were later fired, after their polygraph results indicated "a sign of a possibility of deceit." Also, the supervisor turned down the only two blacks Blews had ever recommended for management training positions, again on the basis of LD test results. Blews also testified that the LD firms used by his company "apparently had a quota of employees they had to fire at every round of testing in order to show that the testing was accomplishing something and that the cost ... was justified." After protesting misuse of the LD, Blews was himself fired, but not before being given a polygraph and being accused of deceptive answers. Jay Harvey, director of legislation for the AFL-CIO's food and allied service trades department remarked that there were two kinds of employers who used the polygraph. One kind, a minority, honestly held the mistaken belief the device worked. "The majority of employers know that the machines is not necessarily reliable, but believe, as Richard Nixon put it, that polygraphs scare the hell out of people." A Chicago court case disclosed blacks may have suffered the adverse consequences of LD errors more than whites. In a discrimination suit brought in U.S. District Court, plaintiffs seeking jobs as prison guards proved to the satisfaction of the court that blacks failed pre-employment polygraph exams more often than whites.[74]

In an op-ed article in the *New York Times* Roy M. Cohn declared, "In my opinion, based on my service as a criminal prosecutor for the Justice Department and later as a defense lawyer, 'lie-detector' tests are not worth a damn." After giving a few examples he added "The tests are just so much malarkey and almost never admitted as evidence in a courtroom."[75]

The 61,000-member American Psychological Association adopted a 1986 resolution that stated the scientific evidence on the effectiveness of the LD was "still unsatisfactory." After more than a year of study, the resolution was unanimously adopted by the group's 115-member council. American Psychological Association executive Arnold Kahn said it was adopted in an effort "to inform the public about the real limitation of polygraph tests."[76]

Wayne Biddle, in a lengthy article in 1986 in *Discover* magazine, had a large type subhead that described the LD as "an unreliable pseudoscience thingamabob." Noting that polygraph exams were performed in few other countries (Israel and Japan, he felt, were the main exceptions) but that U.S. government use of the LD exam had tripled in a decade he concluded that was "startling in light of the fact that the tests are little more than sophisticated carnival tricks." After the OTA report had helped destroy any remaining credibility the instrument may have still retained advocates of the device, said Biddle, switched from arguing the tests had validity to using the argument that the tests had utility. Frank Horvath, an APA director, said "The marketplace, not the scientific community, has decided the need." Former U.S. Ambassador to the United Nations, Jeanne Kirkpatrick (a hardliner on security matters) called the LD "a gross instrument that is probably least effective against the most effective professional spies." Former Oklahoma police polygrapher Douglas Gene Williams, had been conducting a personal campaign against the device since 1979. Calling the machine an "insidious Orwellian instrument of torture," he claimed he had taught thousands of people how to beat the machine. First he taught them how to recognize various types of questions (control versus relevant versus irrelevant) and then how to subtly alter physiological responses to confound the operator. "If you can control your bowels, you can control your test results," said Williams, referring to the strategy of tightening the sphincter muscle for several seconds.[77]

Michael Phillips of the Chicago Medical School did a study to examine the device's predictive power, subjecting the polygraph to the same scrutiny that medical diagnostic tests received. If 1,000 people were tested (assume 76 percent accuracy and 50 percent liars), then the sample had 500 liars and 500 truth tellers. Yet the LD results would have 380 liars testing guilty, 120 liars testing innocent. In a second sample of 1,000 subjects (assume 80 percent accuracy, five percent liars) there were 50 liars and 950 truth tellers. Polygraph results would be: 40 liars tested guilty, 10 liars tested truthful, 190 truth tellers tested as liars, 760 truth tellers tested innocent. Phillips concluded, "If you're truly innocent, never take a lie detector test. But if you're guilty, by all means take one; you might be exonerated."[78]

Writing in *The New Republic* Stephen Dujack argued that the biggest problem with LD screening was "with the large number of innocents who become wrongly accused." He felt the polygraph misidentified truthful persons as liars "perhaps as much as half the time."[79]

The American Medical Association recommended in 1987 that LD testing not be used to screen job applicants. In their view, the effect of polygraph testing to deter theft and fraud associated with employment had never been measured, nor had its impact on employee morale and productivity been assessed. Even under the best of conditions, said the AMA, LDs "wrongly accuse innocent people more than one third of the time. The erosion of employee morale and risk of employer liability may not be worth the possible benefits of uncovering a disloyal employee."[80]

Well-known journalist William Safire attacked the instrument in an opinion piece in the *New York Times* early in 1988 when he observed that two million people a year in America who had done "nothing more criminal than to apply for a job are subjected to the humiliation of being hooked up to a polygraph machine. This inaccurate and fear-inspiring device, the modern equivalent of the hot lights and truncheons of the 'third degree,' measures only nervousness."[81]

While federal legislators had made isolated and ineffective efforts in the past to enact a federal law to restrict polygraphs, pressure to do so became more intense in the 1980s as criticism against LD usage steadily increased and seemingly came from every corner. Polygraph opponents pushed for federal legislation because most of the state regulations then in force were, said journalist Daniel Jussim, "toothless." In response to a proposed ban, the polygraph industry argued for a federal licensing law that would set standards for examiners. That the industry favored such an approach did not surprise Jussim who observed that use of the device was "more widespread in the twenty-six states that have licensing laws than in states having no polygraph statutes." In 1985, more than 160 federal Representatives of Congress were co-sponsors of the so-called Polygraphic Protection Act, a proposal by Representative Pat Williams (D.–Montana) to ban "intrusive and inaccurate" LD testing by business.[82]

Speaking about his bill, Williams said a ban was necessary because it was a question of a worker's right not to be "intimidated." Also, he said he was deeply troubled that each year more and more workers were required to take LD tests. This account estimated that two million tests were given in 1985 and that 75 percent of those were administered in connection with pre-employment screening. Reportedly, that was three times the number of tests given a decade earlier. Asked why a federal law was necessary since many states already restricted LD testing, Williams replied those state laws did not work because businesses in states that restricted polygraphs found it fairly easy to send their employees or prospective employees across state lines to be tested in states that did not restrict the device. "This is one of those problems that requires a national solution," he explained.[83]

During Congressional consideration of this bill, the APA sent a letter to Congressmen in October, 1985, announcing the formation of a pro–lie detector PAC, called the Committee for Integrity in the Workplace, and called on Congress to pass a regulatory bill rather than a ban. That bill under consideration exempted the national security establishment. Journalist Wayne Biddle observed, "House aides concede that the legislation calling for a private sector ban is carefully written so as not to step on the toes of the national security establishment."[84]

In the spring of 1986, the House of Representatives approved legislation (HR 1524) that would prohibit most private firms from giving polygraph tests to current or prospective employees, by a vote of 236 to 173. That came after the House accepted amendments that permitted LD tests to be given to four categories of workers: a) those in day-care centers, b) security guards, c) those in the manufacture of dangerous drugs, d) those involved in the production and transmission of electricity. Also, all federal intelligence agencies were exempted. Representative Jack Brooks called the tests "profoundly un–American because they assume the people are guilty until proven innocent." The Senate companion bill (S 1815 — sponsored by Orrin Hatch, a Republican from Utah, and Edward M. Kennedy, a Massachusetts Democrat) exempted only government use. Federal legislation to restrict polygraph use had then been in the works for a long time with some 40 bills having been introduced in the previous 12 years. However, strong support for such legislation only developed from the time of the release of the OTA report in 1983. At hearings on the bill then under consideration, David Raskin of the University of Utah observed that the vast majority of large successful companies did not use polygraphs. A statement submitted to the hearings by the International Brotherhood of Electrical Workers said that a survey of 33 large electric utilities (a category proposed for exemption), fifteen of which had licensed nuclear plants, revealed that only five used polygraphs.[85]

About 18 months later, the House passed another bill. (The previous one had died, as had all that had gone before it.) That caused *Fortune* magazine to briefly look at the issues and to conclude that "nobody can claim to know how useful the machine is in personnel screening." Because of that, said the staunchly anti-regulation business publication, "a powerful case for legislative action" was presented. Outside of their own industry membership, the polygraph industry had virtually no friends, even in the business community itself.[86]

Finally, a bill that would be enacted began to take shape. A House bill was passed in November, 1987, that exempted security firms and drug makers while a Senate bill, passed in March, 1988, barred most private employers from using the polygraph in the hiring process although it permitted the testing of current employees during investigations of a theft or other incident causing "economic loss or injury." It also exempted security firms and nuclear power plants. That caused *The Economist* to state that two million people were tested annually in the U.S. and "At least 300,000 Americans are falsely branded as liars each year." Businesses like the instrument, thought the UK publication, for the same reason that unions hated it, "it intimidates. It lends a spurious objectivity to the judgment that somebody has lied, which both satisfies the employer that justice has been done and deters the employee from lying, and from thievery."[87]

On May 17, 1988, after conference and compromise a bill was unanimously agreed upon by House and Senate negotiators. Private firms would be allowed to use LDs in cases of "economic loss or injury" (specific theft) under certain conditions. At the end of June that year President Ronald Reagan signed the bill that sharply restricted employers' use of LD tests into law. Becoming effective on December 27, 1988, the new law prohibited pre-employment polygraph screening and random testing of existing employees. Also, it set strict rules about giving the test to workers suspected of a specific theft. Some businesses, including pharmaceutical companies and many firms that provided security guards for operations related to "health and safety" were exempt from the ban. Even though permitted to investigate a specific theft, the employer had to do certain things such as provide the worker with a written statement indicating the purpose of the investigation and the reason why the worker had been selected for the test. Those regulations were imposed so employers could not engage in wholesale fishing expeditions in the case of a theft investigation. Also, the law said a worker could not be fired on the basis on an LD test without other supporting evidence. A survey of some 160 large banks taken 18 months earlier by the Bank Administration Institute at a bank security seminar, disclosed that 78 percent of those banks used LDs. Victor Kaufman, president of the New York–based polygraph firm New York Lie Detection

Laboratories, estimated the new law would "knock out about 98% of our polygraph business." Among backers of the banning bill were the American Medical Association, the American Psychological Association, civil liberties groups, labor unions, and Labor Secretary Ann McLaughlin. Reporter Albert Karr listed only one opponent of the bill (outside of the LD industry and existing users), the Justice Department, which tried to persuade Reagan to veto the bill.[88]

The Employee Polygraph Protection Act of 1988 (EPPA) also exempted the following: federal, state and local governments; testing administered for national defense or security reasons, including the National Security Agency, CIA, the Defense Intelligence Agency and contractors of the FBI, pre-employment testing of security guards and employees who would have direct access to controlled substances, and polygraph testing with respect to specific thefts or other economic loss to an employer's business, under certain conditions. For that last exemption, the company had to have a reasonable suspicion that the employee was involved in the events leading to the loss; the employee must have had access to the property subject to the investigation; the employer had to sign a statement that described the specific incident being investigated and the basis for believing the employee was involved in the loss. That statement had to be given to the employee before testing. Questions regarding religious, political, racial, and union beliefs were all prohibited from use on LD tests, as were queries relating to sexual behavior. The new law entitled workers who were tested in violation of the law to sue for reinstatement, promotion and payment of lost wages and benefits.[89]

Just before the new law took effect, some large retailers such as J. C. Penney and K-Mart said they would not be affected by it because they had already cut back on LD use. Penney spokesman Duncan Muir said "We experimented with it and felt it wasn't particularly useful. We decided it was not worthwhile for us and it wasn't worthwhile for candidates." Many criticized the statute for exempting all three levels of government. Such sentiments were captured in the comments of labor lawyer Peter Pankin who said, "If polygraphs are inaccurate, then it ought to be the same for everybody." Labor lawyer Sheldon Engelhard observed, "The exemptions were purely political, having nothing at all to do with the recognized view that polygraphs aren't reliable."[90]

Attorney David Nagle, who represented management in employment litigation, complained in the trade publication *Personnel Administrator* that the EPPA was passed "due to some cagey political maneuvering by its advocates." Pointing out that few employers would bother to use the polygraph in the case of specific theft because of all the conditions and red tape imposed by the EPPA, Nagle argued employers would "need to consider an alternative" that advocates of the law never envisioned. Bearing in mind no employee could be fired on the basis of an LD result alone — there had to be other corroborative evidence — Nagle said that would raise the question, "is it wiser for an employer to discharge all suspects without ever raising the possibility of polygraph tests ... without even concluding the investigation?"[91]

Writing an advice article in the *Journal of Small Business Management,* Janell Kurtz and Wayne Wells took many pages to explain the meaning and working of the new law before concluding that any small business using or contemplating the use of LDs in employment decisions "should seriously reconsider their decision" in light of the act. So fraught with pitfalls was the bill that a small business would first have to hire a lawyer, before administering any LD tests, thus shooting up their costs. And even then, they might still get sued by the examinees. "Small businesses are advised to avoid this litigation by not administering polygraph tests," they concluded.[92]

Jeffrey Cross looked at opposition to the bill and found it limited to private firms and the Justice Department. The private sector argued the exemptions within the bill itself illustrated the usefulness of the instrument with the government agencies' exemption from the act refuting any claim that LDs were unreliable. The National Retail Merchants Association stated, "By this action, the House apparently overwhelmingly acknowledged the usefulness of the polygraph in protecting our national security." Although the Justice Department stood in opposition, it did not do so because it officially supported the polygraph. Rather, Justice objected to the bill because of federalism. It believed the states should not have been preempted in this issue, where no evidence of an overriding need for national policy uniformity should therefore limit the ability and responsibility of the states generally to govern the affairs of their citizens.[93]

The most important thing that happened to polygraphs in the 1980s was, obviously, the passage of federal legislation imposing severe restrictions on their usage. It had taken a very long time to happen even though critics of the instrument were everywhere and even though the LD had no friends outside the industry itself and its users. It had taken a very long time to happen even though the critics had thoroughly demolished the LD as having any accuracy or validity while the device's proponents could offer nothing in the way of an impartial, objective defense. One might have, therefore, again expected the polygraph to rather rapidly fade away into oblivion. But it did not.

9

The LD Survives; New Ideas
Surface, 1990s to 2002

> *...because they have little more scientific validity than fortune cookies, the results of the [LD] tests can be adjusted to serve whatever purpose their customers desire.*
> — *The Economist,* 1997

> *polygraphy is not about increasing security or catching spies, it is solely abut exercising political control through intimidation.*
> — Society of Professional Scientists
> and Engineers at Lawrence Livermore
> National Laboratory, 2000

> *[The LD] is no more capable of assessing truth telling than were the priests of ancient Rome standing knee-deep in chicken parts.*
> — Alan Zelicoff, 2001

In the years after the passage of the EPPA, court use of LD evidence remained a controversial topic. Some argued that it even became slightly more likely to be admitted into evidence, despite a pervasive prohibition on its use in the private sector. Yet another political use of the device occurred in connection with a death row case. Roger Keith Coleman was executed in Virginia's electric chair on May 20, 1992, for the rape and murder of his sister-in-law. Over the years his case attracted national and international media attention as he and his supporters claimed he was innocent and attention focused on the death penalty in general. Public attention was intense enough as the execution date neared that Virginia Governor Douglas Wilder ordered a polygraph test for Coleman as an unusual response to the attention. Wilder, who had stated two days before the execution date that he would not cancel it, said the LD test that he ordered was proof that the state was willing to do whatever was necessary to make certain that Coleman was fairly treated. After the test was given, Wilder declared he was not surprised by the results that found Coleman was "not truthful on the pertinent questions" relating to the crime.[1]

For the first time, in the 1990s, the U.S. Supreme Court made a direct ruling on polygraph evidence. It was a case that grew out of a military court's conviction of an air force man found guilty of, among other things, using methamphetamine. Although his urine test for the drug was positive, he argued for the admission of a polygraph test result allegedly proving that his statement that he did not use the drug was truthful. Initially his argument was rejected but eventually, in 1996, the highest court in the military justice system reversed the verdict; the defendant, it held, had a constitutional right to present evidence in his defense that could be judged for whatever it was worth. From there, an appeal was launched to the U.S. Supreme Court. While that decision was awaited, some worried that if the highest court in the land agreed with the air force man's argument, the "floodgates" for LD results could be opened wide in every courtroom in America. One account remarked, "Like astrology, polygraphs still retain a certain validity in the public mind; but, because they have little more scientific validity than fortune cookies, the results of the tests can be adjusted to serve whatever purpose their customers desire."[2]

On March 31, 1998 the U.S. Supreme Court ruled that because there was no scientific consensus on the reliability of polygraphs as instruments for establishing the truth, a criminal defendant had no constitutional rights to present evidence at trial of having passed an LD test. The eight to one decision overturned the military court's ruling. In his majority opinion Justice Clarence Thomas said a defendant's right to present evidence had always been subject to reasonable limitations based on considerations of reliability. Excluding polygraph evidence from the courtroom "is a rational and proportional means of advancing the legitimate interest in barring unreliable evidence," declared Thomas. While ruling there was no constitutional right to introduce polygraph evidence the Supreme Court did, however, leave state and lower Federal courts free to relax the barriers against such evidence as a matter of policy. Thomas said individual jurisdictions "may reasonably reach differing conclusions as to whether polygraph evidence should be admitted." New Mexico was then the only state in which polygraph evidence was routinely admitted in criminal trials. That trend to leave it to judges in individual cases had accelerated in the five years since the Supreme Court, in a 1993 case called Daubert v.

Merrell Dow Pharmaceuticals, gave Federal trial judges more discretion in evaluating and admitting scientific evidence.[3]

In the wake of the Daubert decision, which essentially overruled the old, 1923 Frye decision, three of the nation's 11 appeal circuits—the Fifth, Ninth and Tenth Circuits—adopted a similar position. That position was summarized in the words of the Fifth Circuit in 1995 when it stated, "the rationale underlying this circuit's per se rule against admitting polygraph evidence did not survive Daubert." That court limited its ruling somewhat by adding, "We do not hold that polygraph examinations are scientifically valid or that they will always assist the trier of fact.... We merely remove the obstacle of the per se rule against admissibility, which was based on antiquated concepts about the technical ability of the polygraph and legal precepts that have been expressly overruled by the Supreme Court." Writing in the *Hastings Law Journal*, Paul Giannelli noted also that some district courts had admitted polygraph evidence and he believed that a trend appeared to be moving toward admissibility. Giannelli thought the extensive use of the instrument by the government raised a paradox, especially for prosecutors challenging its admissibility. During 1996, the Department of Defense conducted 12,548 LD exams with 7,945 (63 percent) of them being involved in the Counterintelligence-Scope Polygraph (CSP) Program. Other categories included 2,696 (21.5 percent) tests given in criminal investigations, 579 (4.6 percent) exculpatory, and 1,328 (10.6 percent) miscellaneous. Giannelli argued that after the Frye decision, the polygraph faded into the background where it remained until it moved to the forefront in the 1970s and 1980s and in the post–Daubert period. From Frye until the 1970s, the courts overwhelmingly rejected polygraph evidence. Then, in 1972, several trial courts departed from almost 50 years of precedent and admitted the results of some unstipulated LD tests. New Mexico's Supreme Court held in 1975 that such evidence was admissible, as did both Ohio and New York trial courts in 1979. Yet there was no great rush to admissibility. By the end of the 1970s, courts could be divided into three groups: a) those courts that held to the traditional position, declaring polygraph evidence per se inadmissible; b) those that admitted LD evidence on stipulation; c) a few jurisdictions entrusted the admissibility question to the discretion of the trial court. During the 1980s there were a few more examples of admission, and a few set backs.[4]

When David Gallai looked at the effects of the Daubert decision on LDs he concluded, in 1999, it had not made any great change in the admissibility of polygraph evidence, nor had the Supreme Court decision written by Thomas. Gallai argued the results of LD tests "should not be admissible in federal courts." They were simply not reliable enough, "they still are not accurate enough to be brought into the courtroom as evidence." To place such material in front of a jury under the guise of scientific evidence was, he felt, "not appropriate." He warned, "The dangers of admitting polygraph evidence are great. The benefits of admitting the same evidence are few, if any."[5]

Governmental use of the device continued through the 1990s as all levels of government were exempt from the EPPA prohibition. However, some states did have laws that barred some government agencies from using the device. A Federal district court in Texas in 1990 ruled that polygraph tests given to job applicants by the City of Houston violated the applicants' privacy rights under the United States and Texas Constitutions. As a result, the court prohibited the city from continuing to use the offensive parts of the tests, awarded nearly $500,000 in damages, attorneys' fees, and costs, and allowed individuals who had failed the test to reapply. Plaintiffs were three men, each of whom applied for a job with a different Houston agency — police department, fire department, and airport police department. Specifically, the court order banned the city from inquiring into applicants' sexual activity, religious practices, membership in organizations, criminal activities, marijuana and certain other drug use, and confidential medical information. One commentator remarked that this case showed that even in instances where the Federal EPPA did not apply, "the ability of a public employer to administer such tests is not without limits."[6]

Sarah joined the CIA in 1987 and, like all the other new hires, she took a pre-entry LD test. They asked her questions about her sex life, said journalist Daniel Jeffreys. After the embarrassment of the Aldrich Ames scandal in 1994, when the CIA discovered that one of its agents had sold America's most sensitive secrets undetected for almost a decade, it was decided that all agency staff members would have to take a polygraph at least once every five years. Case officers— spies such as Sarah — had to submit to the machine more frequently. She described her LD exam in July, 1996, as an exercise in abuse and intimidation. "They kept coming back to my sex life," said Sarah. "They asked how many times we have sex in a month, what kind of sex we have, what kind of positions." During an 18-month period in 1995 and 1996, the CIA lost about 20 percent more case officers than the average over the previous ten years because, remarked Jeffreys, "protests from active officers about the lie-detector tests are having a marked negative impact, and CIA recruiters are finding it hard to meet their targets."[7]

Michael Kelly, a former CIA intelligence officer declared, "The polygraph test is undermining morale throughout the agency. Good people are leaving rather than face an annual ritual of humiliation ... they insist on probing the more personal details, and that has made many officers angry." Jeffreys reported that case officer Mary was also asked about her sex life with the examiner taking her "through a list of the most perverse sexual acts, asking her if she ever practiced them with her new boyfriend." Rather than face similar tests every year or so, Mary quit. In 1995, Jane fell in love while on a posting in Asia. When she reported the relationship, as CIA regulations demanded, she was subjected to repeated polygraphs of "a most intimate nature." Then Jane decided to get married. The agency told her the fiancé had to take an LD test. When he failed, Jane was given the choice of dumping the man or leaving the agency. She quit.[8]

Edward Curran, the CIA's chief spy hunter, recalled that in the aftermath of the CIA crackdown in the wake of the Ames scandal, routine polygraphs became grueling interrogation sessions. Polygraph operators treated their colleagues "like criminals," he said. "This might be great in a prison but not with civil servants. As many as 100 people—including some of America's top spies—found their careers paralyzed as they lost transfers, or were pushed into dead end jobs, and so on. Former CIA officials remembered U.S. Representative Norman Dicks, a member of the House Intelligence Committee, ordering at the time "If they can't pass a CIA polygraph, fire them." One station chief remembered being interrogated for six hours a day for five days.[9]

Los Alamos National Laboratory began using polygraph tests in the summer of 1999 to screen all of its nuclear weapons scientists. Those tests were ordered by Energy Secretary Bill Richardson after allegations that China had obtained critical design information concerning America's most advanced nuclear weapons. The object of it all was said to be to convince Congress that strong measures were being taken to protect America's weapons secrets. Yet "It's a sham.... Overreliance on polygraph screening can lead labs to shortchange traditional security checks," said Robert Park, physics professor at the University of Maryland, in an op-ed piece in the *New York Times*. He recalled that notorious CIA turncoat Aldrich Ames had taken "scores" of LD tests and passed them all. Although he was arriving at work intoxicated and living on a scale usually reserved for the very wealthy nobody thought to investigate the source of his sudden wealth. Interviewed in prison by a reporter, Ames said his Russian handlers had laughed at his worries about LD tests. "Just relax and cooperate with the examiner they told him, because lie detectors don't work. And they didn't." Park also mentioned the 1986 case of Larry Wu-Tai Chin, a career CIA analyst who was a spy for China. "He also fooled the polygraph repeatedly." Indeed, argued Park, the thousands of LD screening exams administered by the CIA, the FBI, and the National Security Agency "have yet to uncover a single spy." How could the weapons lab expect to attract and retain talented scientists when careers could be jeopardized at the whim of a polygraph exam, he wondered. A group leader at Los Alamos "could not find one scientist at the lab who believes that the polygraph works. Most are furious." One scientist joked that the LD testing would make it easy to pick out the spies five years down the road because "There won't be anyone else still working here."[10]

Journalist Tim Beardsley claimed that the testing begun at Los Alamos marked the first time civilian scientists had been required to pass polygraph exams en masse to gain, or to retain, access to secret information. Beardsley also observed that "Aldrich Ames passed routine polygraph exams as an employee of the Central Intelligence Agency, as did another former CIA employee and convicted spy, Harold J. Nicholson."[11]

Later in the summer of 1999, the Department of Energy (DOE) moved closer to subjecting up to 5,000 researchers and other employees at its three nuclear weapons laboratories (Los Alamos, Lawrence Livermore and Sandia) by publishing its proposal for polygraph testing — time had to be allowed for comment and for public meetings on the proposal. The DOE's proposal stated the LD exams were voluntary, but that those who refused to submit to them could face "consequences," including loss of their security clearance and possible transfer to a less sensitive position. Acknowledging that some people considered polygraph tests to be generally unreliable, the DOE nevertheless contended that there were "no scientific studies" that cast doubt on their value "as an investigative tool."[12]

A Congressional report by the House Permanent Select Committee on Intelligence on the new security program implemented by DOE at its three nuclear labs was released in June, 2000. It concluded that the plan was not accompanied by a strong effort by department officials to "sell" the changes and, as a result, there had been "open rebellion" against that plan. Lab employees had worn buttons to work that bore slogans like "Just say no to the polygraph." According to the report, attitudes toward LDs at the laboratories ran the gamut "from cautiously and rationally negative to emotionally and irrationally negative." Also, since the polygraph was a highly visible part of the overall counterintelligence effort, the entire counterintelligence program "has been negatively affected by this development." Efforts by the DOE to explain to the employees the need for LD tests were described by the report as "ineffectual." While the report noted that resistance to the instrument had in some cases been "unreasonable," DOE's response had been "dictatorial and pre-emptory."[13]

Senior research analyst at the Federation of American Scientists,

Steven Aftergood, also opposed DOE's program, noting that polygraph testing had never operated to apprehend anyone leaking information nor did it function to even deter such leaks. It had all been an overreaction in 1999 when Congressional legislators enacted a provision in the National Defense Authorization Act requiring a counterintelligence polygraph exam for certain DOE employees (those with access to secrets). One of the best critical studies done on LD tests, recalled Aftergood, was performed in 1983 by the Congressional OTA. That office was abolished by the new Republican-majority Congress in 1995. According to the Society of Professional Scientists and Engineers, an employee organization at Lawrence Livermore National Laboratory, "polygraphy is not about increasing security or catching spies, it is solely about exercising political control through intimidation." Aftergood felt it was that perception of an arbitrary exercise of power that offended people so deeply. He observed that in the past, and at the current time, there were no objections at the labs to requirements for background investigations, security clearances, or nondisclosure agreements, and so on, all long accepted as reasonable precautions. "But the polygraph, with its evanescent empirical foundation, symbolizes the defeat of reason by the national security state," Aftergood concluded.[14]

Alan P. Zelicoff was Senior Scientist at the Center for National Security and Arms Control at Sandia National Laboratories, Albuquerque, New Mexico. He was one of the employees critical of the DOE LD program and declared the polygraph "is no more capable of assessing truth telling than were the priests of ancient Rome standing knee-deep in chicken parts." Continuing on he added, "The truth is this: The polygraph is a ruse, carefully constructed as a tool of intimidation, and used as an excuse to conduct an illegal inquisition under psychologically and physically unpleasant circumstances. Spies know how to beat it, and no court in the land permits submission of polygraphs, even to exonerate the accused." Zelicoff further argued that money spent on LDs took dollars away from other, sensible security measures, that use of the device demoralized staff, did not find any spies, and created a false sense of security. However, during official hearings, charged Zelicoff, neither DOE nor Congress paid any attention to the concerns of the scientists. Since the majority of Sandia engineers and scientists who serviced nuclear weapons had refused to submit to the machine, "the DOE is suddenly without authorized staff to deal with a nuclear weapons emergency." During those public hearings, polygraphers admitted there was no scientific evidence that medical conditions, such as diabetes, high blood pressure, or heart disease, affected the outcome of the polygraph. Yet, said Zelicoff, they still insisted that each subject provide a list of all prescription medications and a complete history of medical conditions. David Renzelman, chief of the DOE polygraph program said, "We need to know about medications so we can adjust our machine and our readings." Zelicoff concluded, "It is time to relegate the polygraph — the fanciful creation of a comic book writer — to the ash heap of bad ideas and misplaced belief."[15]

Reporter Jim Wilson said Zelicoff was perhaps the most vocal opponent against DOE's LD tests but scientists at all three labs complained. After pushing quietly for reform from within the DOE, Zelicoff decided, after getting nowhere, to go public. He published his piece in the *Skeptical Inquirer*, the official journal of the Committee for the Scientific Investigation of Claims of the Paranormal (CSICOP). For some 25 years it had earned a reputation as a formidable debunker of junk science. In response the DOE portrayed Zelicoff as a lone voice in the wilderness, but it was not true.[16]

Zelicoff's article drew a number of letters to the editor of the *Skeptical Inquirer*. One was a handwritten letter mailed to the editor from Allenwood federal penitentiary in White Deer, Pennsylvania, from an inmate who knew a little something about LDs— Aldrich Ames. A 31-year CIA employee, Ames had volunteered his services to the Russian KGB in 1985. During the following nine years until his arrest in February, 1994, he compromised more than 100 intelligence operations against the Soviet Union. Ames wrote that in his experience with the polygraph as user and subject, its "junk science" did provide an important but "discreditable" service for "lazy and timid national security managers." Decisions about personnel suitability for sensitive jobs could be difficult to make for the usual and obvious reasons and they could be risky for the careers of the decision makers. And that was where the LD came into it since it offered an "attractive refuge from responsibility." Ames concluded that "Like handing fate to the stars, or entrails on the rock, bureaucrats can abandon their duties and responsibilities to junk scientists and interrogators masquerading as technicians."[17]

LDs continued to make little or no progress in foreign nations, with one exception — China. A 2001 debt dispute in Beijing's Changping District Court had little hard evidence and with the two sides wrangling the judge finally asked for a polygraph and later gave his verdict based on that test result. Polygraph evidence was gradually being introduced into judicial practice there. Research on LDs first began in China in the 1960s but was stopped when the LD technique was dismissed as "mentalism." Research resumed in the 1980s after an inspection team, sent to Japan by the Ministry of Public Security, confirmed that lie detection was indeed "scientific." In 1991 China's first LD was manufactured and put into use.

Then, in January, 2001, the Scientific and Technological Commission of the Ministry of Public Security issued an evaluation report on that domestically-made polygraph that declared results from the device had been "encouraging." Deng Zibin, a doctoral student from the Law School of Peking University, argued the LD should not be used "since the lie detector, though under the cloak of science, actually just provides a means for inquisition by spiritual torture, as against physical torture." Comments from several other people were all in favor of using LDs in China. Nowhere in the article was there a mention made of accuracy.[18]

In the area of celebrities, New York Yankees relief pitcher Steve Howe was arrested on cocaine-related charges near the end of 1991. Early the next month he took, at his own request, a polygraph test from a federal drug agent in Helena, Montana. One of his attorneys, Steve Nardi, said, "It's a way of helping everyone in the government understand who he is. He's showing his good faith efforts."[19]

When six-year-old JonBenet Ramsey was murdered in December, 1996, the case attracted national and international media attention that lasted for years. In May, 2000, the parents, John and Patsy Ramsey, released results of LDs they had taken and which they said should remove any suspicion that they were involved in the killing of their daughter. The polygraph operator declared no deception was registered in those exams.[20]

Lawyer F. Lee Bailey testified in 2000 that days after O. J. Simpson's former wife and a friend were stabbed to death, Simpson took a polygraph test that Bailey stopped because it was not going well. He revealed that information while in court in Florida where his license to practice law was being challenged. Bailey related that shortly after the murders of Nicole Brown Simpson and Ronald C. Goldman in June, 1994, he received a phone call from Robert Shapiro, a Los Angeles defense lawyer. Shapiro had wanted advice about an LD test of Simpson then in progress that was not going well. Bailey described himself as an expect on polygraph tests. The test was going badly, Bailey told Shapiro, because it was being given at an emotional time for Simpson and he told Shapiro to halt the test. Later, Bailey became part of Simpson's legal team. According to Bailey, Shapiro took the results from that abruptly-ended LD test and no one had seen them since. Reportedly, Shapiro did not then have the results. Simpson had said that he never took a polygraph test. In the civil case against Simpson, lawyers for the Goldman family contended that Simpson had failed a polygraph shortly after the murders. Simpson was acquitted of criminal charges, but a civil jury found him liable for the crimes and ordered him to pay $33.5 million in damages to the victims' families.[21]

Some 10 weeks after the disappearance in Washington, D.C., of intern

Chandra Levy, the Washington police said they wanted U.S. Representative Gary A. Condit (D.–California), who had by then admitted to having a relationship with Levy, to take a polygraph test as part of their investigation into the disappearance of the young woman. A few days later, on July 13, 2001, Abbe Lowell, Condit's lawyer, announced that a privately administered LD test showed that his client was not deceptive. An official of the Metropolitan Police Department called the exam, which was given by an expert selected by Condit's lawyer and done without police involvement, "a bit self-serving." Assistant Police Chief Terrance Gainer said the police and Lowell had been in discussion for around a week about a time for the police to give Condit a polygraph and that Lowell's unilateral action caught the police somewhat by surprise. Billy Martin, lawyer for the Levy family, called on Condit to submit to an LD test administered by the police or by the CIA. Calling the Condit polygraph "meaningless" because police officials were not present during the exam, the Washington police, nevertheless, did ask the FBI to analyze the results. On July 20, the FBI dismissed that test as "useless" because, said the bureau, there was "no way to verify" the results of the test since no one was there except the private examiner.[22]

Researchers Lois Recascino and Steven Charvat took a look in 1990 at the status of state legislation with respect to polygraph use in the public sector. Although the federal EPPA exempted all levels of government from its LD prohibition states were free to adopt more stringent measures. A total of 24 states had no written law on polygraphs; 26 had a written law but just four of those states (Michigan, Minnesota, Wisconsin and New York) imposed a complete ban. Thirteen of the states made exemptions for police agencies; four exempted police and narcotics handlers; ten exempted state and local government. Recascino and Charvat found two trends; one was a geographic pattern and the other was a trend toward greater regulation. Partial or complete bans in state polygraph use were in effect in almost all of the eastern states, the northern portion of the Midwest and the north Pacific states. On the other hand, in the central, plains, southern and southwestern states, there were few restrictions against LD testing. Also, states that limited the use of polygraphs also had relatively high levels of work force unionization. Of the 26 states whose level of unionization was above the medium rate, only six did not restrict polygraph testing. Of the 20 states with the lowest rates of work force unionization just three of them restricted polygraph usage. The very first state law was passed in Massachusetts in 1959; fourteen states restricted testing during the 1980s.[23]

The U.S. Labor Department's Wage and Hour Division charged the operator of Wendy's Restaurants in Kansas City, Missouri, in 1991, with unlawfully forcing employees to take LD tests. It proposed fining the franchise $314,000, the largest proposed penalty assessed under the EPPA to that date. An investigation by the Labor Department was said to have showed violations at 26 of the franchise's 30 restaurants operating in the Kansas City metro area, which had illegally tested 143 of its 950 employees. Those tests were administered between December, 1988, when the EPPA took effect, and June, 1990. One employee was fired based on the results of one of those unlawful polygraph tests.[24]

Kenneth Kovach, professor of human resource management at George Mason University in Fairfax, Virginia, looked at the aftermath of the EPPA, in 1995. After outlining the EPPA and how it worked in great detail he declared that the administration of LD tests to applicants or present employees was "a practice fraught with dangers for both employees and employers." He further concluded that in view of all the factors, "most employers today should reach the conclusion that except in extreme circumstances the use of polygraphs in employment situations is simply not a good policy." Expressing sympathy with employer groups that decried that state of affairs Kovach warned that, however, as society became increasingly dependent on technology and technological innovation, "a constant vigil must be kept to protect civil liberties and personal privacy. The Employee Polygraph Protection Act has struck the proper balance."[25]

Effects of countermeasures on the control-question polygraph test were examined in a 1994 experiment with 120 subjects recruited from the general community. Twenty subjects were innocent and of the 100 guilty subjects, 80 were trained in the use of a physical countermeasure (biting the tongue or pressing the toes to the floor, or both) or a mental countermeasure (counting backward by seven) to be applied while control questions were being asked during their exams. Although the polygraph examiner correctly classified 72.5 percent of the innocent control and the guilty control subjects (with 12.5 percent inconclusive and 15 percent incorrect outcomes), he correctly classified only 41.2 percent of the 80 countermeasure subjects (50 percent was the chance level) with 11.3 percent assessed as inconclusive and 47.5 percent classified incorrectly. Also, said the researchers, the countermeasures when employed "were difficult to detect either instrumentally or through observation." It was yet another example of how easy it was to beat the machine. A conclusion drawn by the researchers was that it was prudent "to limit rather than expand the use of polygraph techniques in government security screening programs."[26]

David Lykken and W. G. Iacono, both at the University of Minnesota, conducted mail surveys to obtain the opinions on polygraphs from two groups of scientists from relevant disciplines; 195 members of the Society for Psychophysiological Research (SPR — 91 percent of questionnaires returned from 214 mailed out) and 168 Fellows of the American Psychological Association's Division 1, General Psychology (74 percent of questionnaires returned from 226 mailed out). Made clear by the survey was that the question referred to the conventional LD using the Control Question Technique. Only 36 percent of the SPR respondents considered the LD to be based on principles that were "scientifically sound;" 75 percent disagreed with the statement that the instrument was accurate 85 percent of the time; 9 percent accepted the idea the LD could be beaten by a subject augmenting his responses to the control questions. From the second survey, it was discovered that the Fellows estimated the accuracy of the polygraph at around 60 percent for both innocent and guilty subjects. Some 74 percent of the SPR members and 78 percent of the Fellows said they opposed the use of polygraph evidence in court. "Most of the respondents believed that polygraphic lie detection is not theoretically sound, claims of high validity for these procedures cannot be sustained," Lykken and Iacono concluded from their surveys. And "the lie test can be beaten by easily learned countermeasures, and polygraph test results should not be admitted into evidence in courts of law."[27]

In February, 2001, the National Academy of Sciences began an academic study of polygraphs — at the request of the Department of Energy, who funded them with $860,000. It was the first major government-sponsored LD study since the one by the OTA in 1983 and was expected to take up to two years to complete.[28]

As usage of the standard LD withered away, a host of new inventions were cited, each of which had supposedly found a new way to detect lies. Never before had so many new ways of pinpointing liars been announced at around the same time with the last few years of the 1990s and the first couple of the new millennium being especially fruitful. An inexpensive new LD test that could be used over the phone and required only a personal computer with a CD-ROM drive was announced at the start of 1998. Makh-Shevet, a small Israeli high-tech company insisted that its $149 software could detect whether a subject was under stress or lying outright. The company insisted their computer program, which measured changes in voice frequency was "85 percent accurate in identifying stress that is indicative of a lie." Called Truster, the machine had reportedly been created for the Israeli military to use in stopping terrorists at border checkpoints in that country. A military version was then said to be six months away but the consumer version was then for sale and had already sold some

2,200 copies. Makh-Shevet advised potential buyers to first obtain legal advice before purchasing the product. While it was illegal to tape a phone conversation without permission, this system did not make a tape. Company president Tamir Segal said he decided to sell the software for $150, rather than $50, to ensure only serious users would purchase it. "We could have charged less," he explained, "but we don't think this should be treated as a gimmick." Of course, this was nothing more than the 1970s PSE, added to a computer.[29]

Remarkably similar-sounding was the product offered in 1999 from a new company, Digital Robotics of Westmont, Illinois, headed by B. Francis Camis. This company offered an LD program designed to work on any PC equipped with a microphone. Said to analyze the stress levels in a person's voice to determine whether or not they were telling the truth, the device was called the Fortress Personal Lie Detector. Camis said he was initially aiming the Fortress at home users for "personal experimentations." Hoping to avoid legal problems Camis stressed that anyone using Fortress had to get the written consent of the person whose voice was being analyzed; it sold for $29.95.[30]

Around the same time, scientists at the Salk Institute in La Jolla, California, reported they had developed a computer system that had learned to read the rapidly changing expressions in a human face and might one day be able to draw conclusions about the emotions lying behind them. It was touted that one day the system could be a working LD, "one that would be far more reliable and much less intrusive than existing polygraphs." A subhead of the article explained that a real smile was usually characterized by crinkly eyes and a generally relaxed expression while a lying smile "reveals itself in subtle ways, notably eye wrinkles that are more crow's feet than laugh lines. The computer can spot this easily."[31]

When the National Academy of Sciences announced it was undertaking a new polygraph study the Department of Defense was then reviewing outside proposals received in response to a broad solicitation for new ways to study lie detection. Technology being explored included research on thermal imaging, in which the temperature changes caused by variations in facial blood flow during lying was detected with an infra-red camera; the use of lasers to pick up muscular, circulatory and other bodily changes in a process called "laser Doppler vibrometry"; use of a new voice stress analyzer known as the Vericator; and the monitoring of brain waves.[32]

Monitoring brain waves to detect liars received more attention than did other new methods. As early as 1993 a new LD technology that used brain wave analysis drew interest from both the CIA and the FBI. The

Farwell Multifaceted Electroencephalographic Response Analysis System, was the invention of scientist Lawrence Farwell who enthused, "For the first time we can get access to the one place where a thorough record of the crime is stored — in the brain of the perpetrator." Electrodes were attached to a subject's head to measure the brain's electrophysiological reactions to specific stimuli such as words, phrases or pictures. Ron Ferguson, who oversaw the FBI's polygraph unit said the bureau was "cautiously optimistic" about Farwell's work but not ready to commit to it. CIA spokesman Peter Earnest said Farwell's results looked "promising" to the agency, which was funding some of the work. However, he noted, "there's considerable research to be done" before it was proven.[33]

Reporter Jim Wilson was tremendously enthusiastic about this technique (which he called Brain Fingerprinting) in 2001 when he predicted in the future people subjected to deception detection would not be asked if they had unauthorized contact with an agent of a foreign government. Rather, with Brain Fingerprinting, the examiner would simply flash pictures of enemy agents on a screen. "Brain Fingerprinting is not yet admissible as evidence," said Wilson. "But it seems to us, its eventual acceptance is only a matter of time." Although the early part of Wilson's article was highly critical of the polygraph, the latter part was enthusiastic and uncritically accepting of the brain technique; the same attitude that 1930s articles displayed toward the polygraph.[34]

From 1993 onward, one of the points Farwell argued was that terrorist operations could be investigated through careful monitoring of the brain waves emitted by suspects during interrogation. In the wake of the World Trade Center and Pentagon attacks of September 11, 2001, he was pressing that point more intently. Reporter Barnaby Feder thought that one of the reasons people were interested in Farwell's work was "that the most widely used lie detectors, known as polygraphs, have long been considered an embarrassment by many scientists." Speaking of polygraphs Dr. Drew Richardson said, "The diagnostic value of this type of testing is of no more value than that of astrology or tea-leaf reading." He was a psychologist who once headed the FBI's research lab at Quantico, Virginia. Recently he left the FBI to join Human Brain Science, a company in Fairfield, Iowa, founded by Farwell, who began researching brain waves in the mid–1980s as a graduate student at the University of Illinois. Farwell worked with three types of stimuli — targets, probes and irrelevants. Targets were sights, sounds or other stimuli the subject already knew or had been trained to recognize — for example, a picture of the White House shown to an American. Probes were stimuli only a guilty subject would be likely to know — for example, the living room where a murder took place.

Irrelevants were stimuli unlikely to be recognized. Based on some 1991 research, Farwell claimed his brain analysis was 87 percent accurate in detecting lies. However, Dr. J. Peter Rosenfeld, a brain wave researcher at Northwestern University said that a 1993 effort by Japanese researchers to replicate Farwell's findings produced an accuracy of only 48 percent — no better than the chance level of 50 percent. Feder concluded his article by stating, "A number of brain-wave researchers say they are nervous about how aggressively Dr. Farwell and his company are pushing the technology."[35]

By November, 2001, it was reported that the CIA had funded Farwell's research in brain fingerprinting to a total of more than $1 million to that date.[36]

Early in 2002, Farwell declared that anyone wanting to live in or visit the U.S. should have to take a brain fingerprinting test that could consist of a series of images of terrorist training camps or training manuals in Arabic. "With that, we can identify someone who's perpetrated a crime and we can also identify a person who has specific information — for example, a trained terrorist," said Farwell. Emanuel Donchin, one of Farwell's mentors and an early collaborator (He was co-researcher on the 1991 study.) was then a critic. Farwell had also irritated the scientific community with claims that his real world tests of his system had yet to produce an error. Reporter David Akin said, "So far, he has done brain fingerprinting on about 120 people, and he says the tests have produced a 100-percent accuracy rate."[37] Rob Sutherland, director of the Canadian Center for Behavioral Neuroscience at the University of Lethbridge in Alberta, stated, "Antennae should go up when someone's claiming to have a perfect technology based on lie detection. It's implausible but not impossible."

10

-\/-\/-

Conclusion

The search for truth, and its separation from lies, has been one of humankind's preoccupations since time began. For most of recorded history, that search has been rooted in superstition and religion. A test of some kind was administered and a supreme being intervened to declare the suspect, through the test result, to be a liar or a truth teller. Often the methods were nothing more than torture designed to elicit a confession either to take the place of a test result or to reinforce that test result. None of these methods worked, of course, in the supposed intended manner of separating truth from lies. They likely did work as one facet of social control used within societies to maintain order and to allow the world to unfold to serve the needs of the ruling classes. For truth itself was never the object. When it was suggested that the Earth was not flat or that it revolved around the sun, these were truths not sought and not accepted, at least initially. In the era of slavery when someone suggested that blacks were human beings equal in all respects to whites, and so forth, these were truths not sought and not accepted. Throughout history and up to the current time, the search for truth has never been the search for truth. Rather, it has been, and remains, the search for methods of control, coercion, and intimidation and the verification and validation of society's conventional wisdom and ideas accepted as true.

Late in the 1800s, the old methods of lie detection had mostly faded away. As religious influences decreased in North America, the secular religion of science became more and more important as it supplanted religion in many ways. People working in academic settings began to experiment with deception detection. They adopted various existing medical instruments and they refined and improved those early efforts to produce the lie

183

detector, or polygraph, which began to be used in America in the 1920s. During that same period, the responsibility for social control was in the process of being passed to professional police forces. Police brutality was a regular feature of the era up to and including the beating of suspects to extract confessions with everything short of a beating — the so-called third degree with its harassments, deprivations, and so on — also used to the same end. As such behavior was exposed in the media, and cries for reform surfaced, the police were happy to embrace the new truth machine — the polygraph. It promised to deliver a painless third degree.

With science generally held in high public esteem, early media articles on the LD were full of uncritical praise for the device. Undoubtedly they helped to establish a myth of infallibility that came to surround the device. A cycle was established wherein people confessed when confronted by the instrument, which increased its usage and reputation, which led to even more confessions, and so on. However, police usage of the LD stalled early on because the courts, seeing the device as inaccurate, ruled LD results to be inadmissible since they had no scientific validity. During the period through the 1930s, the polygraph was promoted, and operated, by mostly academic people. That, too, helped it to achieve and maintain a degree of credibility it might not otherwise have had.

After Word War II, that promotion and operation of the instrument passed to private companies and businessmen. Use of the device by business and by government increased substantially in this period as the paranoia of the Cold War settled in over America. It was an era in which Americans were expected to show their patriotism and to show they were more American than the next guy. The polygraph seemed appropriate. Had it not been for this period in American history, the LD might very well have faded into obscurity — especially since it was not accepted by the courts nor was there a single piece of objective research to show it to be accurate. Ironically, the Cold War era, which was fueled by a plethora of lies — Senator McCarthy's, for example — was likely instrumental in launching the LD into becoming a bigger part of the American scene. Outside of the USA, the polygraph was little used anywhere, and even unknown in many countries. The reason for that may have been because no other country experienced the paranoia of the Cold War in the way America did. There were no wholesale demands for displays of patriotism; no pervasive loyalty oath programs. It was common in this period for someone to publicly demand that so-and-so take a lie detector test. Paradoxically, it was a demand sometimes made by people who did not even believe in the machine.

Also in this period, critical voices began to grow louder and to become more numerous. For the first time, opponents of the device began to point out the many and obvious faults of the instrument. Partly the growing critical storm was a result of media exposure of the extent of LD use in government and business, especially in the former. Complaints that the instrument violated the right of privacy and the right to not self-incriminate were made as civil rights became an issue. Still, use of the device continued to spread in the 1960s, 1970s, and 1980s in the face of a mounting barrage of criticism and even in the face of study after study (that is, objective ones where the researchers had no vested interest in the outcome), which condemned the device. Even some business publications that were normally anti-regulation and which usually favored business positions whatever they were, started to argue against the instrument. The polygraph industry found itself with virtually no friends or supporters, outside of its own members and users of the device (always a minority of businesses). Still, despite the fact the polygraph industry was a relatively small lobby group, it succeeded in holding off effective regulation until 1988 when the federal government passed legislation that effectively severely restricted business use of the polygraph.

Bizarrely, the federal government continued to use the polygraph after that date, mainly within its national security establishment. It did so even though the LD had never exposed a single spy and even though many spies (exposed by other means) had taken and passed polygraph tests, some for years on end. The unanswerable question was often raised; If the LD was not accurate for business, as determined by objective research, some of it federal, why was it accurate when used by agencies like the Department of Defense? But in that case, of course, the quest was not for the truth. Allowing one part of the federal government to continue using the device was a political decision, nothing more.

Currently, people are working on new and improved truth machines. One of those may or may become the new polygraph of the future. But even if one does, the search will not really be for the truth. The history of the polygraph was the story of a device which never did have any objective evidence to support its claims. What was unusual was that something so devoid of merit as the LD gained as large a hold on American society as it did. One thing it offered was the same thing the ancient methods offered — a resolution to a situation. If it did not and could not find the person who committed the crime, then it did and could find a victim. If it did not find the real pilfering employee, then it did find a sacrifice. If it was not a panacea, then it could intimidate and coerce and control. Operating under the guise of science and under the guise of seeking the truth gave the LD a noble and honorable look, on the surface. Underneath, the reality was quite different.

Notes

Chapter 1

1. Raphael Demos. "Liars and lying." *The Yale Review* 10 (January, 1921): 380.
2. A. A. Lewis. "Looking for an honest man." *The Scientific Monthly* 49 (September, 1939): 267.
3. Benjamin Kleinmuntz and Julian J. Szucko. "Lie detection in ancient and modern times." *American Psychologist* 39 (July, 1984): 766.
4. Paul V. Trovillo. "A history of lie detection." *Journal of Criminal Law & Criminology* 29 (March/April, 1939): 849–850.
5. Richard H. Underwood. "Truth verifiers: from the hot iron to the lie detector." *Kentucky Law Journal* 84 (Spring 1995/1996): 603.
6. *Ibid.*, p. 604; Paul V. Trovillo. Op. cit., p. 852.
7. Richard H. Underwood. Op. cit., p. 606.
8. Paul V. Trovillo. Op. cit., pp. 850–851; Richard H. Underwood. Op. cit., p. 606.
9. Paul V. Trovillo. Op. cit., p. 851.
10. Richard H. Underwood. Op. cit., p. 612.
11. *Ibid.*, p. 616.
12. H. Ray Ellis. "Polygraph." *The Magazine of Bank Administration* 58 (September, 1982): 28; Richard H. Underwood. Op. cit., p. 617.
13. H. Ray Ellis. Op. cit., p. 28.
14. Paul V. Trovillo. Op. cit., pp. 853–855.
15. Richard H. Underwood. Op. cit., p. 619.
16. *Ibid.*, pp. 603–604.
17. *Ibid.*, p. 627.

Chapter 2

1. Paul V. Trovillo. "A history of lie detection." *Journal of Criminal Law & Criminology* 29 (March/April, 1939): 858; Anton Rose. "Psychophysical tests for falsehood." *Scientific American* 110 (June 20, 1914): 502.
2. "Crime at Columbia solved by science." *New York Times*, September 20, 1930, p. 5.
3. Henry Morton Robinson. "Science gets the confession." *Forum and Century* 93 (January, 1935): 17.
4. Paul V. Trovillo. Op. cit., pp. 858, 860.
5. *Ibid.*, p. 863; "The lie detector." *Literary Digest* 111 (December 26, 1931): 35; Wayne Biddle. "The deception of detection." *Discover* 7 (March, 1986): 29.
6. Paul V. Trovillo. "A history of lie detection, part 2." *Journal of Crimi-*

187

nal Law & Criminology 30 (May/June, 1939): 104–105.

7. Dwight Macdonald. "The lie-detector era." *The Reporter* 10 (June 8, 1954): 11; Christian A. Ruckmick. "The truth about the lie detector." *Journal of Applied Psychology* 22 (February, 1938): 51.

8. Fred E. Inbau. "The first polygraph." *Journal of Criminal Law & Criminology* 43 (January/February, 1953): 679–681.

9. A. A. Lewis. "Looking for an honest man." *The Scientific Monthly* 49 (September, 1939): 269.

10. "Science devises a painless '3rd degree.'" *Current Opinion* 76 (April, 1924): 474–475.

11. Eugene E. Levitt. "Scientific evaluation of the lie detector. *Iowa Law Review* 40 (Spring, 1955): 441

12. Anton Rose. Op. cit.

13. Paul V. Trovillo. "A history of lie detection." Op. cit., p. 870.

14. Geoffrey C. Bunn. "The lie detector, 'Wonder Woman' and liberty: the life and work of William Moulton Marston." *History of the Human Sciences* 10 (February, 1997): 92, 95.

15. Thomas Hayes Jaycox. "Scientific detection of lies." *Scientific American* 156 (June, 1937): 371; "Lie detector." *Newsweek* 9 (March 13, 1937): 34; Eugene E. Levitt. Op. cit., p. 441.

16. Dwight Macdonald. Op. cit., p. 11; William Moulton Marston. "Problems in living." *Forum and Century* 100 (July, 1938): 32.

17. Geoffrey C. Bunn. Op. cit., pp. 95–96.

18. *Ibid.*, pp. 92, 98–99.

19. Phillip W. Davis and Pamela McKenzie-Rundle. "The social organization of lie-detector tests." *Urban Life* 13 (July/October, 1984): 201–202; Geoffrey C. Bunn. Op. cit., p. 96; William Moulton Marston. Op. cit., p. 32.

20. Paul V. Trovillo. "A history of lie detection." Op. cit., p. 871; Dwight Macdonald. Op. cit., p. 11; Alva Johnston. "The magic lie detector, pt. 2." *Saturday Evening Post* 216 (April 22, 1944): 27, 63.

21. "Science devises a painless '3rd degree.'" *Current Opinion* 76 (April, 1924): 474.

22. J. A. Larson. "Present police and legal methods for the determination of the innocence or guilt of the Suspect." *Journal of Criminal Law & Criminology* 16 (August, 1925): 252–253.

23. *Ibid.*, pp. 254–255, 259, 271.

24. "Breathing test fails to discover lying." *New York Times*, August 30, 1925, sec. 7, p. 8; Eugene E Levitt. Op. cit., p. 443.

25. Paul V. Trovillo. "A history of lie detection." Op. cit., p. 875; Eugene E Levitt. Op. cit., p. 444.

Chapter 3

1. John A. Larson. *Lying and its Detection*. Montclair, NJ: Patterson Smith, 1969, pp. 95–168.

2. "Lie detector traps Philadelphia youth." *New York Times*, July 7, 1931, p. 6.

3. "Lie detector gets $10 from 2 boys." *New York Times*, June 8, 1937, p. 27.

4. "Lie detector clears Winkler." *New York Times*, November 26, 1931, p. 56.

5. "Lie tracer is honored." *New York Times*, January 21, 1933, p. 7.

6. "Lie detector used in Maine." *New York Times*, October 12, 1935, p. 3; "Lie detector test proves bloodhounds are liars." *New York Times*, November 11, 1935, p. 6.

7. "New lie detector was used on Green." *New York Times*, January 15, 1937, p. 3.

8. "Psychologists hold session at Vassar." *New York Times*, April 4, 1937, sec. 2, p. 10.

9. Thomas Hayes Jaycox. "Scientific detection of lies." *Scientific American* 156 (June, 1937): 370–372; "Wichita's use of the lie detector." *American City* 51 (December, 1936): 91.

10. Thomas Hayes Jaycox. "Lies—

truths." *Scientific American* 161 (July, 1939): 8–9.

11. "Spurn lie detector, detectives demoted." *New York Times*, July 13, 1938, p. 4.

12. "Lie detector pays." *American City* 54 (October, 1939): 15.

13. Leonarde Keeler. "The lie-detector proves its usefulness." *Public Management* 22 (June, 1940): 163–166.

14. Richard H. Underwood. "Truth verifiers: from the hot iron to the lie detector." *Kentucky Law Journal* 84 (Spring 1995/1996): 628.

15. Fred E. Inbau. "The lie-detector." *The Scientific Monthly* 40 (January, 1935): 86–87.

16. "Guilty by lie detector." *New York Times*, May 24, 1930, p. 2.

17. "Lie-detector test asked by prisoner." *New York Times*, January 6, 1935, sec. 4, p. 7.

18. "Catching criminals with lie-detector." *Literary Digest* 119 (February 23, 1935): 17.

19. "Lie test is given in auto graft case." *New York Times*, November 17, 1937, p. 48; "Lie-detector casts doubt on constable." *New York Times*, November 18, 1937, p. 19.

20. "Lie detector raises fine $75." *New York Times*, February 3, 1938, p. 26.

21. "Lie detector case ends in acquittal." *New York Times*, March 30, 1938, p. 23.

22. "Law." *Newsweek* 11 (April 11, 1938): 26.

23. "Court bars proof by lie detector." *New York Times*, November 30, 1938, p. 25.

24. "Notes and legislation." *Harvard Law Review* 53 (December, 1939): 293–294.

25. "Lie detector seals doom of murderer." *New York Times*, March 2, 1937, p. 44.

26. "Lie-detector." *News-week* 9 (March 13, 1937): 34; "Polygraph proof." *Literary Digest* 123 (March 13, 1937): 9–10; "The liars." *New Statesman and Nation* 13 (March 6, 1937): 362–363.

27. "Lie detector drafter in compensation case." *New York Times*, August 18, 1935, sec. 2, p. 1; "Admits lie detector in compensation case." *New York Times*, August 20, 1935, p. 5.

28. Fred E. Inbau. "Scientific evidence in criminal cases." *Journal of Criminal Law & Criminology* 24 (March, 1934): 1144–145.

29. *Ibid.*, p. 1145.

30. Fred E. Inbau. "The lie-detector." *The Scientific Monthly* 40 (January, 1935): 84–85.

31. "Principal wrecks his lie detector." *New York Times*, September 25, 1936, p. 26.

32. William Moulton Marston. "Problems in living." *Forum and Century* 100 (July, 1938): 32; William Moulton Marston. "Problems in living." *Forum and Century* 100 (October, 1938): 168–169.

33. "State bar to fight for civil liberties." *New York Times*, January 27, 1939, p. 7.

34. J. P. McEvoy. "The lie detector goes into business." *Reader's Digest* 38 (February, 1941): 69.

35. *Ibid.*, p. 70.

36. *Ibid.*, pp. 71–72.

37. "Lie detector tried on bomb suspects." *New York Times*, July 25, 1931, p. 15.

38. "Couples 'I do' is verified by lie detector at wedding." *New York Times*, June 1, 1932, p. 18.

39. "Hauptman pleads for a truth test." *New York Times*, December 17, 1935, p. 3; "Gov. Hoffman urges lie-detector test." *New York Times*, January 24, 1936, p. 40; Wayne Biddle. "The deception of detection." *Discover* 7 (March, 1986): 29.

40. "Coogan and fiancée robbed in Chicago." *New York Times*, February 13, 1936, p. 25.

41. "Police heads hear hit-run solution." *New York Times*, August 30, 1938, p. 2.

42. "Love used as the key in lie detector test." *New York Times*, February 26, 1939, p. 38.

43. William Moulton Marston.

"Problems in living." *Forum and Century* 100 (October, 1938): 168–169.

44. William Moulton Marston. "Problems in living." *Forum and Century* 100 (July, 1938): 30–31.

45. *Ibid.*, p. 32.

46. "Would you are take these tests?" *Look*, December 6, 1938, pp. 16–17.

47. "Lie detector 'tells all.'" *Life*, November 21, 1938, p. 65.

48. Henry Morton Robinson. "Science gets the confession." *Forum and Century* 93 (January, 1935): 18; Fred E. Inbau. "Scientific..." op. cit., p. 1154.

49. "Lie detectors that don't work." *Literary Digest* 114 (November 19, 1932): 24.

50. Gilbert Geis. "In scopolamine veritas." *Journal of Criminal Law & Criminology* 50 (November/December, 1959): 349–356.

51. "Truth-serum frees two." *New York Times*, March 10, 1935, p. 16; "Cleared by truth serum." *New York Times*, November 29, 1935, p. 3.

52. Fred E. Inbau. "Scientific..." op. cit., p. 1157.

53. Henry Morton Robinson. Op. cit., p. 17.

54. Fred E. Inbau. "Scientific..." op. cit., pp. 1140–1147; Paul V. Trovillo. "A history of lie detection." *Journal of Criminal Law & Criminology* 29 (March/April, 1939): 878.

55. Alva Johnston. "The magic lie detector, pt. 2." *Saturday Evening Post* 216 (April 22, 1944): 27.

56. Waldemar Kaempffert. "The week in science: detecting lies of criminals." *New York Times*, January 13, 1935, sec. 8, p. 4.

57. Fred E. Inbau. "The lie-detector." Op. cit., p. 82.

58. "Psychogalvanometer." *Time* 28 (October 12, 1936): 44.

59. Henry Pringle. "How 'good' is any lie?" *Reader's Digest* 29 (November, 1936): 75–76.

60. "Lie-detector." *News-week* 9 (March 13, 1937): 34.

61. "Lie detector useful only in ex- pert hands." *Scientific American* 156 (June, 1937): 390, 392.

62. "New lie detector traces eye moves." *New York Times*, September 7, 1940, p. 13.

63. J. P. McEvoy. Op. cit., p. 72.

64. "The lie-detector." *Literary Digest* 111 (December 26, 1931): 35.

65. "Detecting liars." *Literary Digest* 114 (October 22, 1932): 22.

66. George N. Coad. "Modern detective turning to science." *New York Times*, November 20, 1932, sec. 2, p. 6.

67. Henry Morton Robinson. "Science gets the confession." *Forum and Century* 93 (January, 1935): 15–16.

68. "Catching criminals with lie-detector." *Literary Digest* 119 (February 23, 1935): 17.

69. Louther S. Horne. "Lie detector gains in use." *New York Times*, July 28, 1935, sec. 4, p. 11.

70. Kenneth Murray. "Two simple ways to make a lie detector." *Popular Science* 128 (May, 1936): 63, 98.

71. Julius Steinberg. "Electric lie detector." *Popular Science* 136 (April, 1940): 144–145.

72. "The lie-detector." *New Statesman and Nation* 1 (March 14, 1931): 100–101.

73. "Our rostrum." *Forum and Century* 93 (March, 1935): sup. 17, 19; "Minimizes lie detector." *New York Times*, February 18, 1937, p. 3.

74. "Lie detectors." *Journal of the American Medical Association*, January 29, 1939, p. 3540.

75. Eugene E. Levitt. "Scientific evaluation of the lie detector." *Iowa Law Review* 40 (Spring, 1955): 445.

76. "From the research laboratories." *New York Times*, March 27, 1938, sec. 2, p. 5; Richard H. Underwood. Op. cit., p. 629.

Chapter 4

1. Hartley Barclay. "Mass production on atom defense." *New York Times*, September 14, 1948, p. 46.

2. "Guards to take lie test." *New York Times*, March 7, 1952, p. 6.

3. Dwight Macdonald. "The lie-detector era." *The Reporter* 10 (June 8, 1954): 10.

4. Charles A. McInerney. "Routine screening of criminal suspects by the polygraph (lie-detector) technique." *Journal of Criminal Law & Criminology* 45 (March/April, 1955): 736–738.

5. "Philadelphia lie detector." *New York Times*, July 17, 1955, p. 48.

6. "The lie-detector vs. civil rights." *Senior Scholastic* (Teacher's ed.) 59 (January 23, 1953): 5.

7. M. E. Bitterman and F. L. Marcuse. "Minor studies from the psychological laboratory of Cornell University." *American Journal of Psychology* 60 (July, 1947): 407–412.

8. "Lie detector frees man in policy case." *New York Times*, February 27, 1944, p. 38.

9. Waldemar Kaempffert. "Science in review." *New York Times*, February 27, 1944, sec. 4, p. 9.

10. "Lie detector verdict reversed." *New York Times*, May 20, 1949, p. 18.

11. Richard O. Arther and John E. Reid. "Utilizing the lie detector technique to determine the truth in disputed paternity cases." *Journal of Criminal Law & Criminology* 45 (July/August, 1954): 214–215.

12. "Slayer's 'saviors' fail." *New York Times*, May 7, 1950, p. 53.

13. Dwight Macdonald. Op. cit., p. 16.

14. "Lie detector tested in atom bomb plant." *New York Times*, March 14, 1946, p. 12.

15. Dwight Macdonald. op. cit., pp. 16–17.

16. *Ibid.*, p. 17.

17. *Ibid.*

18. "Notes on science." *New York Times*, April 12, 1953, p. 11.

19. Anthony Leviero. "U.S. tests staffs by lie detectors." *New York Times*, December 20, 1951, p. 1.

20. *Ibid.*, p. 20.

21. Anthony Leviero. "Morse denounces lie detector use." *New York Times*, January 18, 1952, p. 9.

22. "Lie detector still used." *New York Times*, February 17, 1952, sec. 5, p. 8.

23. Dwight Macdonald. "The lie-detector era, pt. 2." *The Reporter* 10 (June 22, 1954): 23.

24. *Ibid.*, pp. 23–24.

25. *Ibid.*, p. 25.

26. *Ibid.*, p. 26.

27. William M. Carlile. "City uses polygraph to screen applicants." *Public Management* 41 (October, 1959): 237–238.

28. Hartley Barclay. "Mass production on atom defense." *New York Times*, September 14, 1948, p. 46.

29. "Lie-detector tests on workers." *Business Week*, April 28, 1951, p. 24.

30. *Ibid.*

31. Marilyn French. "Oh, my employees are all honest." *American Business* 21 (August, 1951): 18–19, 49.

32. "Balk at lie detector tests." *Business Week*, February 11, 1956, p. 148.

33. William E. Lissy. "Labor law." *Supervision* 21 (June, 1959): 15.

34. William Leonard. "How the lie detector works." *Science Digest* 46 (July, 1959): 5.

35. Alva Johnston. "The magic lie detector, pt. 3." *Saturday Evening Post* 216 (April 29, 1944): 20.

36. C. P. Trussell. "Hiss bars lie-detector test." *New York Times*, August 20, 1948, pp. 1, 8.

37. "The reporter's notes." *The Reporter* 8 (June 9, 1953): 1–2.

38. "A witness in Capital." *New York Times*, May 14, 1949, p. 5; "Reprieves continued for 6 Malmedy Nazis." *New York Times*, May 21, 1949, p. 3.

39. Dwight Macdonald. "The lie-detector era." Op. cit., p. 16.

40. "Lie detector tests urged by McCarthy." *New York times*, December 22, 1951, p. 5.

41. "What the lie detector really detects." *New York Times*, March 29, 1953,

sec. 4, p. 13; "The reporter's notes." *The Reporter* 8 (June 9, 1953): 1–2

42. W. H. Lawrence. "McCarthy proposes lie detector test him and Army witnesses." *New York Times*, March 22, 1954, pp. 1, 19.

43. W. H. Lawrence. "Welch questions the authenticity of McCarthy data." *New York Times*, June 2, 1954, pp. 1, 19.

44. Alva Johnston. "The magic lie detector." *Saturday Evening Post* 216 (April 15, 1944): 9–11+; Alva Johnston. "The magic lie detector, pt. 2." *Saturday Evening Post* 216 (April 22, 1944): 26–27, 63; Alva Johnston. "The magic lie detector, pt. 3." *Saturday Evening Post* 216 (April 29, 1944): 20+.

45. Alva Johnston. "The magic lie detector." Op. cit., pp. 11, 62.

46. Alva Johnston. "The magic lie detector, pt. 2." Op. cit., pp. 26–27.

47. Joseph F. Kubis. "Electronic detection of deception." *Electronics* 18 (April, 1945): 192.

48. *Ibid.*, pp. 192, 196.

49. Joseph F. Kubis. "Instrumental, chemical and psychological aids in the interrogation of witnesses." *Journal of Social Issues* 13 no. 2 (1957): 43.

50. F. K. Berrien. "Lie trap." *Maclean's Magazine* 58 (September 1, 1945): 19–20, 22,

51. "Fangs and polygraphs." *New Yorker* 24 (September 4, 1948): 18.

52. William Leonard. "How the lie detector works." *Science Digest* 46 (July, 1959): 2, 4.

53. William E. Lissy. Op. cit.

54. "Truth wanted." *Time* 43 (January 10, 1944): 60.

55. "Against lie detectors." *New York Times*, June 25, 1944, sec. 4, p. 9.

56. "Lie detector doesn't." *Science News Letter* 49 (March 30, 1946): 207.

57. Anthony Leviero. "The truth machine." *New York Times Magazine*, February 10, 1952, pp. 40–41.

58. "What the lie detector really detects." *New York Times*, March 29, 1953, sec. 4, p. 13.

59. "Lie gadgets." *Scientific American* 188 (June, 1953): 46, 48.

60. Dwight Macdonald. "The lie-detector era." Op. cit., pp. 10–18; Dwight Macdonald. "The lie-detector era, pt. 2. op. cit., 22–29.

61. Dwight Macdonald. "The lie-detector era." Op. cit., p. 12.

62. *Ibid.*, p. 13.

63. *Ibid.*, pp. 13–14.

64. *Ibid.*, p. 14.

65. *Ibid.*, p. 15.

66. Dwight Macdonald. "The lie-detector era, pt. 2." Op. cit., p. 24.

67. "The lie detector." *New York Times*, August, 1954, sec. 4, p. 8.

68. Arnold Cortesi. "Use of lie detector assailed by Pontiff." *New York Times*, April 11, 1958, pp. 1, 12.

Chapter 5

1. Colonel Maurice Levin. "Lie detectors can lie!" *Labor Law Journal* 15 (November, 1964): 710, 712.

2. *Ibid.*, pp. 713–716.

3. "Decision barring lie-test upheld." *New York Times*, December 12, 1969, p. 88.

4. Colonel Maurice Levin. Op. cit., p. 710.

5. William E. Lissy. "Labor law." *Supervision* 27 (October, 1965): 15.

6. George Washnis. "Polygraphs aid in choosing policemen and firemen." *Public Management* 43 (June, 1961): 134.

7. "Senator scores tax unit inquiry." *New York Times*, February 23, 1960, pp. 1, 16.

8. Ben A. Franklin. "Ex-homosexual got U.S. job back." *New York Times*, October 18, 1964, p. 34.

9. "Lie-detector study in U.S. agencies set." *New York Times*, June 9, 1963, p. 48.

10. "Lie-detector use by U.S. disclosed." *New York Times*, February 23, 1964, p. 40; "House unit queries lie detector's use." *New York Times*, April 5, 1964, p. 77.

11. "Federal lie-detectors." *New York Times*, February 29, 1964, p. 20.

12. John D. Morris. "House unit opens polygraph study." *New York Times*, April 8, 1964, p. 17.

13. John D. Morris. "Services tell of monitoring lie-detection tests." *New York Times*, April 11, 1964, p. 6.

14. "Pentagon curbs lie detector use." *New York Times*, April 30, 1964, p. 24.

15. Elinor Langer. "Lie detectors: sleuthing by polygraph increasingly popular; claims of accuracy are unproved." *Science* 144 (April 24, 1964): 396–397.

16. Robert Burkhardt. "How to lie successfully to the lie detector." *The New Republic* 150 (May 6, 1964): 6–7.

17. Jack Raymond. "U.S. study hostile to lie detectors." *New York Times*, June 18, 1964, p. 21.

18. "The lie detector investigated." *Scientific American* 212 (May, 1965): 50; "House panel scores lie detectors' use." *New York Times*, March 21, 1965, p. 76.

19. "What is truth." *Newsweek* 64 (December 7, 1964): 27; "C.I.A. lie detector said to outwit itself." *New York Times*, November 24, 1964, pp. 1, 14.

20. "Pentagon curtails polygraphs." *New York Times*, July 21, 1965, p. 21.

21. "President creates U.S. policy panel on lie detection." *New York Times*, December 14, 1965, p. 35.

22. "Business uses the lie detector." *Business Week*, June 18, 1960, p. 98.

23. *Ibid.*, p. 105.

24. *Ibid.*

25. *Ibid.*, pp. 105–106.

26. *Ibid.*, p. 106.

27. William M. Carley. "To tell the truth." *Wall Street Journal*, October 17, 1961, pp. 1, 14.

28. "Theft control through lie detection." *Restaurant Management* 90 (March, 1962): 50, 90.

29. *Ibid.*, pp. 90–91.

30. Alex Lee Gregory. "Why workers steal." *Saturday Evening Post* 235 (November 10, 1962): 68–69.

31. Richard A. Sternbach, Lawrence A. Gustafson and Ronald L. Colier. "Don't trust the lie detector." *Harvard Business Review* 40 (November, 1962): 127

32. *Ibid.*, pp. 128–129.

33. *Ibid.*, pp. 129–130.

34. *Ibid.*, pp. 130–134.

35. Philip Shabecoff. "Thievery rising in U.S. industry." *New York Times*, June 16, 1963, sec. 3, pp. 1, 9.

36. "The dangerous polygraph." *Scientific American* 209 (July, 1963): 66–67.

37. "How the lie detector is used in business." *The Office* 59 (April, 1964): 72–73.

38. John A. Grimes. "Lie box battle." *Wall Street Journal*, April 8, 1965, p. 20.

39. Bruce Gunn. "Polygraph hoax or panacea?" *Business Topics* 14 (Autumn, 1966): 46–47.

40. *Ibid.*, pp. 48–51.

41. *Ibid.*, p. 54.

42. "7 begin in lie detection." *New York Times*, April 13, 1960, p. 19.

43. Bruce Gunn. Op. cit., pp. 55–57.

44. C. Glenn Walters and Bruce Gunn. "Appraising retailers' use of the polygraph." *Journal of Retailing* 43 no. 4. (Winter, 1968): 12–13.

45. *Ibid.*, pp. 13–17.

46. *Ibid.*, pp. 18–21.

47. Bruce H. Frisch. "The great lie-detector hoax." *Science Digest* 54 (August, 1963): 28–29.

48. Elinor Langer. Op. cit., p. 396.

49. Damon Stetson. "Drive on lie tests started by labor." *New York Times*, February 26, 1965, p. 20.

50. John A. Grimes. "Lie box battle." *Wall Street Journal*, April 8, 1965, pp. 1, 20.

51. *Ibid.*

52. Douglas Dales. "Curb on lie test voted in Albany." *New York Times*, March 15, 1961, p. 41.

53. *Ibid.*

54. Gene Currivan. "Schools' drivers face screening." *New York Times*, March 18, 1961, p. 14.

55. Warren Weaver Jr. "Anti-usury bill is voted by Assembly." *New York Times*, May 25, 1965, p. 33; "Lie detector tests." *New York Times*, June 28, 1966, p. 90; "Rockefeller signs moonlight bill." *New York Times*, May 4, 1967, p. 27.

56. Felix Belair Jr. "G.E. official denies role in price-fixing." *New York Times*, April 28, 1961, pp. 1, 19.

57. "Butts of Georgia passes a lie test." *New York Times*, March 21, 1963, p. 15.

58. "Uproar over news leak and lie detectors." *U.S. News & World Report* 54 (April 15, 1963): 8.

59. "The polygraph-happy Pentagon." *Saturday Evening Post* 236 (May 4, 1963): 82.

60. Donald Janson. "Ruby is examined by psychiatrists." *New York Times*, December 22, 1963, p. 22; John A. Grimes. Op. cit. p. 20.

61. John Kifner. "State's Attorney in Chicago makes photographs of Black Panther apartment available to newspaper." *New York Times*, December 12, 1969, p. 46.

62. Richard O. Arther. "The lie-detector — is it of any value." *Federal Probation* 24 (December, 1960): 36–39.

63. James V. Bennett. "A penal administrator views the polygraph." *Federal Probation* 24 (December, 1960): 41.

64. "The lying machine." *Newsweek* 61 (April 29, 1963): 82–83.

65. Elinor Langer. Op. cit., p. 396; Bruce H. Frisch. Op. cit., p. 29.

66. Stewart Alsop. "It's none of your lousy business." *Saturday Evening Post* 237 (June 13, 1964): 12.

67. Stanley Meisler. "Trial by gadget." *The Nation* 199 (September 28, 1964): 160–162, 176.

68. Walter Goodman. "Lie detectors don't lie, but –." *New York Times Magazine*, January 24, 1965, pp. 12, 68, 70.

69. "Criminal justice." *Time* 88 (November 4, 1966): 70.

70. Burke M. Smith. "The polygraph." *Scientific American* 216 (January, 1967): 27.

71. Lee M. Burkey. "Privacy, property and the polygraph." *Labor Law Journal* 18 (February, 1967): 79,

72. *Ibid.*, pp. 80–81.

73. *Ibid.*, pp. 85–86.

74. *Ibid.*, pp. 87–88.

Chapter 6

1. Berkeley Rice. "The new truth machines." *Psychology Today* 12 (June, 1978): 63–64.

2. Fred P. Graham. "New voice lie detector device stirs controversy after gaining acceptance." *New York Times*, June 5, 1972, p. 30.

3. "Big brother is listening." *Time* 99 (June 19, 1972): 91–92; "New trap for lies." *Newsweek* 79 (June 19, 1972): 103.

4. "The stress test — who's lying." *Newsweek* 82 (July 23, 1973): 19.

5. James Lincoln Collier. "Again, the truth machine." *New York Times Magazine*, November 25, 1973, p. 116.

6. "The PSE could prove your innocence." *Saturday Evening Post* 247 (July/August, 1975): 38–44.

7. Constance Holden. "Lie detectors: PSE gains audience despite critics' doubts." *Science* 190 (October 24, 1975): 359–360.

8. *Ibid.*, pp. 360, 362.

9. Berkeley Rice. Op. cit., p. 64.

10. *Ibid.*

11. *Ibid.*, p. 67.

12. *Ibid.*, pp. 67, 72, 74, 77.

13. *Ibid.*, p. 77.

14. Malcolm W. Browne. "Voice lie detectors decried as unscientific." *New York Times*, November 13, 1979, pp. C1, C2.

15. *Ibid.*

16. Robert B. Peters. "A hard look at some voice lie detectors. *Security Management* 24 (October, 1980): 1, 23.

17. Barnaby J. Feder. "Court test for voice analyzer." *New York Times*, January 5, 1982, pp. D1, D6.

18. Howard W. Timm. "The efficacy of the psychological stress evaluator in

detecting deception." *Journal of Police Science and Administration* 11 (March, 1983): 62, 66–67.
19. *Ibid.*, p. 67.

Chapter 7

1. C. R. Lewart. "Electronic lie detector tells it like it is." *Popular Science* 202 (May, 1973): 118–119.
2. "Cops vs. lie detectors." *Newsweek* 81 (February 26, 1973): 52.
3. William F. Buckley Jr. "On the right." *National Review* 26 (August 16, 1974): 942–943.
4. "The polygraph as a truth detector." *The Office* 72 (August, 1970): 39–41.
5. Virginia Lee Warren. "No fibbers wanted." *New York Times*, December 4, 1970, p. 52.
6. Laurie Johnston. "Bonwit Teller tests use of lie detectors." *New York Times*, July 27, 1971, p. 35.
7. "Bonwit Teller ends lie-detector tests of store employees." *New York Times*, August 4, 1971, p. 35.
8. Ben A. Franklin. "Lie detector's use by industry rises; rights peril feared." *New York Times*, November 22, 1971, pp. 1, 45.
9. *Ibid.*
10. Stanley Klein. "The truth about lie-detectors in business.." *New York Times*, October 29, 1972, sec. 3, p. 3.
11. *Ibid.*
12. "Corporate lie detectors come under fire." *Business Week*, January 13, 1973, pp. 88, 90.
13. *Ibid.*
14. *Ibid.*
15. "Truth or consequences." *Time* 101 (March 19, 1973): 73–74.
16. James Lincoln Collier. "Again, the truth machine." *New York Times Magazine*, November 25, 1973, pp. 108, 110.
17. "W.Va. pharmacists rebel against polygraph testing." *American Druggist* 169 (June 15, 1974): 38.

18. Frye Gaillard. "Polygraphs and privacy." *The Progressive* 38 (September, 1974): 44.
19. "Yes to lie detector tests for private employees." *Nation's Business* 63 (August, 1975): 16.
20. "Now a furor over lie detectors in business." *U.S. News & World Report* 80 (March 8, 1976): 68–70.
21. Ray W. Chambers. "An argument against anti-polygraph legislation." *Security Management* 21 (July, 1977): 21.
22. *Ibid.*, pp. 22–23.
23. *Ibid.*, pp. 23–24.
24. Anna Quindlen. "Polygraph tests for jobs: truth and consequences." *New York Times*, August 19, 1977, p. B1.
25. "Bitter beercott." *Time* 110 (December 26, 1977): 15.
26. "Business buys the lie detector." *Business Week*, February 6, 1978, p. 100.
27. *Ibid.*, p. 101.
28. *Ibid.*, p. 104.
29. John A. Belt and Peter B. Holden. "Polygraph usage among major U.S. corporations." *Personnel Journal* 57 (February, 1978): 80–86.
30. *Ibid.*, pp. 82–83.
31. *Ibid.*, pp. 83, 86.
32. "Lie detectors." *Business Week*, September 4, 1978, pp. 85–86.
33. "Employee theft: plugging the leaks." *Drug Topics* 123 (April 6, 1979): 57–60.
34. Philip G. Benson and Paul S. Krois. "The polygraph in employment: some unresolved issues." *Personnel Journal* 58 (September, 1979): 616–621.
35. "Don't use polygraph test for employee witch hunt." *Supermarketing* 34 (September, 1979): 46.
36. Martin Markson. "A reexamination of the role of lie detectors in labor relations." *Labor Law Journal* 22 (July, 1971): 394–400.
37. John Janssen. "Deterring employee theft." *The Office* 80 (August, 1974): 58.
38. Berkeley Rice. "The new truth machines." *Psychology Today* 12 (June, 1978): 78.

39. Frye Gaillard. Op. cit., pp. 44–45.

40. "Rights unit seeks end to lie tests." *New York Times*, April 11, 1976, p. 38.

41. "Outlaw lie-detector tests?" *U.S. News & World Report* 84 (January 30, 1978): 45–46.

42. Peter Carlyle-Gordge. "The truth shall not be free." *Maclean's* 92 (April 23, 1979): 27–28.

43. "N.F.L. owners get lie detector test." *New York Times*, January 3, 1972, p. 36.

44. "U.S. aide says 3 took C.I.A. lie tests." *New York Times*, May 23, 1973, p. 29.

45. James Lincoln Collier. Op. cit., p. 35.

46. *Ibid.*, p. 107.

47. "Rizzo is baffled at lie-test result." *New York Times*, August 15, 1973, p. 15.

48. William F. Buckley Jr. Op. cit.

49. James Lincoln Collier. Op. cit., pp. 35, 104.

50. Stephen C. Carlson, Michael S. Pasano and Jeffrey A. Jannuzzo. "The effect of lie detector evidence on jury deliberations: an empirical study." *Journal of Police Science & Administration* 5 (June, 1977): 148–149.

51. "Unions score use of lie detectors." *New York Times*, February 15, 1970, p. 76.

52. Patricia D. Beard. "Truth or consequences." *Harper's Bazaar* 105 (October, 1972): 44, 46.

53. David T. Lykken. "Psychology and the lie detector industry." *American Psychologist* 29 (October, 1974): 734–738.

54. "Rights unit seeks end to lie tests." *New York Times*, April 11, 1976, p. 38; Linda Charlton. "Subjects of a survey are found to value privacy on the job." *New York Times*, February 12, 1978, p. 33.

55. Jonathan Kwitny. "X plus Y equals Z." *Wall Street Journal*, May 4, 1977, p. 22; Jonathan Kwitny. "The dirty little secret of lie detectors." *Esquire* 89 (January, 1978): 73–76, 142.

56. Berkeley Rice. "Lie detection." *Psychology Today* 12 (July, 1978): 107.

57. Richard H. Underwood. "Truth verifiers: from the hot iron to the lie detector." *Kentucky Law Journal* 84 (Spring 1995/1996): 628.

Chapter 8

1. Nancy Faller. "A second assault." *The Progressive* 45 (July, 1981): 29.

2. David T. Lykken. "Detecting deception." *Society* 22 (September/October, 1985): 34.

3. Victor S. Alpher and Richard L. Blanton. "The accuracy of lie detection: why lie tests based on the polygraph should not be admitted into evidence today." *Law & Psychology Review* 9 (Spring, 1985): 68, 74.

4. "Lie detectors in the workplace: the need for civil action against employees." *Harvard Law Review* 101 (February, 1988): 807.

5. Robert Pear. "As use of polygraph grows, suspects and lawyers sweat." *New York Times*, July 13, 1980, sec. 4, p. 2.

6. *Ibid.*

7. "To tell the truth." *The Nation* 234 (February 6, 1982): 132.

8. Philip M. Boffey. "Can lie detectors be trusted?" *New York Times*, July 20, 1982, pp. C1, C6; Francis J. Flaherty. "Truth technology." *The Progressive* 46 (June, 1982): 30.

9. "Liar dice." *The Economist* 286 (March 26, 1983): 65.

10. W. Herbert. "Study disputes Reagan lie detector policy." *Science News* 124 (November 5, 1983): 292.

11. *Ibid.*; Wayne Biddle. "The deception of detection." *Discover* 7 (March, 1986): 26.

12. Dorothy J. Samuels. "What if the lie detector lies?" *The Nation* 237 (December 3, 1983): 566, 568.

13. Christopher Joyce. "Lie detector." *Psychology Today* 18 (February, 1984): 6–7; "Canceled order." *Time* 123 (February 27, 1984): 86.

14. "Fluttering the Pentagon." *Newsweek* 105 (January 14, 1985): 31.

15. "Use lie detectors on defense workers?" *U.S. News & World Report* 98 (February 25, 1985): 44.

16. "It's a lie." *Nation's Business* 73 (December, 1985): 12; "Schultz: a-flutter." *Newsweek* 106 (December 30, 1985): 20.

17. David E. Rosenbaum. "Reagan insists budget cuts are way to reduce budget deficit." *New York Times*, January 8, 1986, p. B7; David Burnham. "Reagan disputed by Rep. Brooks on polygraph directive's meaning." *New York Times*, January 9, 1986, p. A14.

18. "Have you ever owed a bar bill?" *Harper's Magazine* 272 (March, 1986): 14–15, 17.

19. Wayne Biddle. Op. cit., pp. 28, 32.

20. Bennett H. Beach. "Blood, sweat and fears." *Time* 116 (September 8, 1980): 44.

21. Trudy Hayden. "Employers who use lie detector tests." *Business and Society Review* no. 41 (Spring, 1982): 16–21.

22. Paul Frumkin. "Days Inn cuts employee theft with lie detector tests for all." *Hotel & Motel Management* 198 (January, 1983): 17, 29.

23. II. Ray Ellis. "Polygraph." *The Magazine of Bank Administration* 58 (September, 1982): 34.

24. Kenneth F. Englade. "The business of the polygraph." *Across the Board* 19 (October, 1982): 20–21, 24.

25. Carolyn H. Crowley. "The truth about polygraph." *Security Management* 26 (December, 1982): 30.

26. Raymond Bonner. "Lie detectors as corporate tools." *New York Times*, February 13, 1983, sec. 3, p. 4.

27. *Ibid.*

28. John A. Belt. "The polygraph: a questionable personnel tool." *Personnel Administrator* 28 (August, 1983): 66, 69, 91.

29. Kemit S. Grafton. "The laws that apply to honesty testing." *Security Management* 29 (August, 1985): 33.

30. Robert Messina. "Honesty tests: the best policing for supers?" *Progressive Grocer* 65 (September, 1986): 163–165.

31. Lisa Westbrook. "Polygraph update." *Security Management* 31 (July, 1987): 51.

32. "Lie detectors in the workplace: the need for civil actions against employers." *Harvard Law Review* 101 (February, 1988): 812.

33. "Privacy." *Business Week*, March 28, 1988, pp. 61–63.

34. Eric Rolfe Greenberg. "Workplace testing: results of a new AMA survey." *Personnel*, April, 1988, pp. 36, 38.

35. *Ibid.*, pp. 38, 40.

36. Eric Rolfe Greenberg. "Workplace testing: who's testing whom?" *Personnel*, May, 1989, pp. 39–43.

37. "Life after polygraph? How are responses from LP executives." *Stores* 71 (June, 1989): 64, 66.

38. "Florida schools end use of polygraph tests." *New York Times*, April 23, 1986, p. A10.

39. Carolyn H. Crowley. Op. cit., p. 31.

40. "The polygraph." *Personnel Management* (UK) 16 (September, 1984): 70–71.

41. A. B. Levey. *Polygraphy: An Evaluative Review*. London: HMSO, 1988, pp. viii, 20, 70.

42. "Truth tests." *Time* 122 (August 29, 1983): 17; "Debategate: fluttering the President's men?" *Newsweek* 102 (August 29, 1983): 21.

43. "Osborne's challenge." *New York Times*, December 28, 1984, p. A26.

44. David T. Lykken. "Detecting deception." *Society* 22 (September/October, 1985): 34.

45. "Liar dice." The Economist 286 (March 26, 1983): 65; Ted Guest. "When employers turn to lie detectors." *U.S. News & World Report* 94 (April 4, 1983): 78.

46. David T. Lykken. "Detecting deception in 1984." *American Behavioral Scientist* 27 (March/April, 1984): 482; David T. Lykken. "Detecting deception."

Society 22 (September/October, 1985): 34.

47. Daniel T. Dennehy. "The status of lie detector tests in labor arbitration" *Labor Law Journal* 31 (July, 1980): 432–433.

48. Herman A. Theeke and Tina M. Theeke. "The truth about arbitrators' treatment of polygraph tests." *Arbitration Journal* 42 (December, 1987): 23–28.

49. Thomas L. Bright and Charles J. Hollow. "State regulation of polygraph tests at the workplace." *Personnel* 62 (February, 1985): 50.

50. "Unfortunately, New York State doesn't ban use of polygraph." *New York Times*, July 9, 1986, p. A26.

51. "Lie detectors in the workplace: the need for civil actions against employers." *Harvard Law Review* 101 (February, 1988): 815.

52. Avital Ginton. "A method for evaluating the use of polygraph in a real-life situation." *Journal of Applied Psychology* 67 (April, 1982): 131–133.

53. "Neo-Diogenes uses tests, not lantern." *Nation's Business* 69 (June, 1981): 91.

54. "Polygraph: should they be used in business?" *Drug Topics* 124 (December 12, 1980): 12, 14.

55. Richard J. Phannenstill. "The polygraph passes the test." *Security Management* 27 (August, 1983): 52, 59–60.

56. Gordon H. Barland. "The case for the polygraph in employment screening." *Personnel Administrator* 30 (September, 1985): 58, 61, 64.

57. Richard D. Paterson. "In favor of the polygraph." *Security Management* 29 (November, 1985): 47–52.

58. "The lie detector as an instrument of social control." *New York Times*, August 3, 1980, sec. 4, p. 18.

59. Eric P. Matusewitch. "Fear of lying: polygraph in employment." *Technology Review* 83 (January, 1981): 10–11.

60. "Lie detector tests untrustworthy." *USA Today* 109 (February, 1981): 16.

61. Linda Witt. "The truth about lie detectors, says David Lykken, is that they can't detect a lie." *People* 15 (May 11, 1981): 75–76, 79.

62. R. Jeffrey Smith. "Dubious validity." *Science* 224 (June 15, 1984): 1217.

63. David T. Lykken. "Detecting deception in 1984." *American Behavioral Scientist* 27 (March/April, 1984): 481, 494.

64. Benjamin Kleinmuntz and Julian J. Szucko. "On the fallibility of lie detection." *Law & Society Review* 17 no. 1 (1982): 86–98.

65. Francis J. Flaherty. "Truth technology." *The Progressive* 46 (June, 1982): 31, 33–35.

66. Lori B. Andrews. "How lie detectors like." *Parents* 58 (March, 1983): 26, 28, 31.

67. Nick Jordan. "Polygraph interview: blood sweat and fears." *Psychology Today* 18 (June, 1984): 76.

68. "If you're asked to take a lie-detector test…" *Changing Times* 38 (July, 1984): 66–70.

69. Philip W. Davis and Pamela McKenzie-Rundle. "The social organization of lie-detector tests." *Urban Life* 13 (July/October, 1984): 177, 190–193.

70. *Ibid.*, pp. 198–200, 203.

71. Stephen Budiansky. "Lie detectors. *Atlantic* 254 (October, 1984): 44.

72. Irving K. Kaler. "A mole among the gerbils?" *Newsweek* 105 (March 11, 1985): 14–15.

73. Benjamin Kleinmuntz. "Lie detectors fail the truth test." *Harvard Business Review* 63 (July/August, 1985): 36, 42.

74. Daniel Jussim. "Lies, damn lies — and polygraphs." *The Nation* 241 (December 21, 1985): 665, 682–683.

75. Roy M. Cohn. "Lie detectors can't be trusted." *New York Times*, December 29, 1985, sec. 4, p. 15.

76. David Burnham. "Psychologists' association says polygraphs are unreliable." *New York Times*, February 9, 1986, p. 26.

77. Wayne Biddle. "The deception of detection." *Discover* 7 (March, 1986): 25–26, 31–32.

78. "Lie detectors can make a liar of you." *Discover* 7 (June, 1986): 7.

79. Stephen Dujack. "Polygraph fever." *The New Republic* 195 (August 4, 1986): 10–11.

80. Lisa Westbrook. "Polygraph update." *Security Management* 31 (July, 1987): 49–51.

81. William Safire. "The sweat merchants." *New York Times*, February 29, 1988, p. A19.

82. Daniel Jussim. Op. cit., p. 684; "It's a lie." *Nation's Business* 73 (December, 1985): 12–13.

83. Steven Greenhouse. "Machines that try to read minds." *New York Times*, January 26, 1986, sec. 4, p. 4; "Bar lie-detector use by private firms?" *U.S. News & World Report* 100 (February 3, 1986): 81.

84. Wayne Biddle. Op. cit., p. 32.

85. David Burnham. "House vote limits use of polygraph." *New York Times*, March 13, 1986, p. D4; "Days may be numbered for polygraphs in the private sector." *Science* 232 (May 9, 1986): 705.

86. "Keeping up." *Fortune* 116 (December 7, 1987): 188.

87. "Bearers of false witness." *The Economist* 306 (March 12, 1988): 31–32.

88. Albert R. Karr. "Law limiting use of lie detectors is seen having widespread affect." *Wall Street Journal*, July 1, 1988, p. 19.

89. "Federal polygraph law enacted." *Personnel Journal* 67 (August, 1988): 26.

90. Stephen Labaton. "Business and the law." *New York Times*, November 28, 1988, p. D2.

91. David E. Nagle. "The polygraph shield." *Personnel Administrator* 34 (February, 1989): 18–19, 23.

92. Janell M. Kurtz and Wayne R. Wells. "The Employee Polygraph Protections Act: the end of lie detector use in employment decisions?" *Journal of Small Business Management* 27 (October, 1989): 76, 80.

93. Jeffrey L. Cross. The Employee Polygraph Protection Act of 1988: background and implications." *Labor Law Journal* 40 (October, 1989): 667–668.

Chapter 9

1. Peter Applebome. "Virginia executes inmate despite claim of innocence." *New York Times*, May 21, 1992, p. A20.

2. "The colour of lying." *The Economist* 345 (December 6, 1997): 29.

3. Linda Greenhouse. "Justices find no inherent right to use lie-test evidence in trial." *New York Times*, April 1, 1998, p. A18.

4. Paul C. Giannelli. "Polygraph evidence: post–Daubert." *Hastings Law Journal* 49 (April, 1998): 896–902.

5. David Gallai. "Polygraph evidence in federal courts: should it be admissible?" *American Criminal Law Review* 36 no. 1 (Winter, 1999): 88, 115–116.

6. "Polygraph tests." *Monthly Labor Review* 113 (August, 1990): 39–40.

7. Daniel Jeffreys. "Getting down on 'The Farm.'" *World Press Review* 44 (March, 1997): 30–31.

8. *Ibid.*

9. Kevin Whitelaw and David E. Kaplan. "To tell the truth." *U.S. News & World Report* 130 (June 11, 2001): 18–20.

10. Robert L. Park. "Liars never break a sweat." *New York Times*, July 12, 1999, p. A15.

11. Tim Beardsley. "Truth or consequences." *Scientific American* 281 (October, 1999): 21, 24.

12. David Malakoff. "DOE polygraph plan draw fire." *Science* 285 (September 3, 1999): 1467.

13. James Risen. "Report faults Energy Dept. as failing to gain lab staff's support for tighter security." *New York Times*, June 28, 2000, p. A22.

14. Steven Aftergood. "Polygraph testing and the DOE national laboratories." *Science* 290 (November 3, 2000): 939–940.

15. Alan P. Zelicoff. "Polygraphs

and the national labs: dangerous use undermines national security." *Skeptical Inquirer* 25 (July/August, 2001): 21–23.

16. Jim Wilson. "Truth, lies and polygraphs." *Popular Mechanics* 178 (October, 2001): 42.

17. Aldrich Ames. "The polygraph controversy." *Skeptical Inquirer* 25 (November/December, 2001): 72–73.

18. "Should we use lie detectors?" *Beijing Review* 44 (September 6, 2001): 23–24.

19. "Lie detector for Howe." *New York Times*, January 9, 1992, p. B15.

20. "Ramseys release results of polygraph tests." *New York Times*, May 25, 200, p. A23.

21. "Bailey says he halted polygraph test of Simpson." *New York Times*, June 5, 2000, p. A25.

22. Raymond Bonner. "A private lie detector test clears Condit, lawyer says." *New York Times*, July 14, 2001, p. A11; James Risen and Raymond Bonner. "F.B.I. dismisses Condit polygraph results." *New York Times*, July 21, 2001, p. A10.

23. Lois Recascino Wise and Steven J. Charvat. "Polygraph testing in the public sector: the status of state legislation." *Public Personnel Management* 19 (Winter, 1990): 384–385, 389.

24. "Federal agency enforcement activities." *Personnel Journal* 70 (August, 1991): 20.

25. Kenneth A. Kovach. "The truth about employers' use of lie detectors." *Business and Society Review* 93 (Spring, 1995): 65, 69.

26. Charles R. Honts, David C. Raskin and John Kircher. "Mental and physical countermeasures reduce the accuracy of polygraph tests." *Journal of Applied Psychology* 79 (April, 1994): 252, 255, 257.

27. W. G. Iacono and D. T. Lykken. "The validity of the lie detector: two surveys of scientific opinion." *Journal of Applied Psychology* 82 (June, 1997): 426–432.

28. Constance Holden. "Panel seeks truth in lie detector debate." *Science* 291 (February 9, 2001): 967.

29. Matt Richtel. "Some doubts on lie detection by phone." *New York Times*, January 26, 1998, p. D4.

30. Laurie J. Flynn. "Software turns computers into desktop lie detectors." *New York Times*, March 8, 1999, p. C4.

31. Frederic Golden. "Lying faces unmasked." *Time* 153 (April 5, 1999): 52–53.

32. Constance Holden. Op. cit.

33. "The hunt for a better lie detector." *U.S. News & World Report* 114 (June 14, 1993): 49.

34. Jim Wilson. Op. cit., p. 44.

35. Barnaby J. Feder. "Truth and justice, by the blip of a brain wave." *New York Times*, October 9, 2001, p. F3.

36. Sarah Sturmon Dale. "The brain scientist." *Time* 158 (November 26, 2001): 81.

37. David Akin. "Brain's telltale chart." *World Press Review* 49 (February, 2002): 36–37.

Bibliography

"Admits lie detector in compensation case." *New York Times*, August 20, 1935, p. 5.

Aftergood, Steven. "Polygraph testing and the DOE national laboratories." *Science* 290 (November 3, 2000): 939–940.

"Against lie detectors." *New York Times*, June 25, 1944, sec. 4, p. 9.

Akin, David. "Brain's telltale chart." *World Press Review* 49 (February, 2002): 36–37

Alpher, Victor S. and Richard L. Blanton. "The accuracy of lie detection: why lie tests based on the polygraph should not be admitted into evidence today." *Law & Psychology Review* 9 (Spring, 1985): 67–75.

Alsop, Stewart. "It's none of your lousy business." *Saturday Evening Post* 237 (June 13, 1964): 12.

Ames, Aldrich. "The polygraph controversy." *Skeptical Inquirer* 25 (November/December, 2001): 72–74.

Andrews, Lori B. "How lie detectors lie." *Parents* 58 (March, 1983): 26+

Applebome, Peter. "Virginia executes inmate despite claim of innocence." *New York Times*, May 21, 1992, p. A20.

Arther, Richard O. "The lie detector — is it of any value." *Federal Probation* 24 (December, 1960): 36–39.

Arther, Richard O. and John E. Reid. "Utilizing the lie detector technique to determine the truth in disputed paternity cases." *Journal of Criminal Law & Criminology* 45 (July/August, 1954): 213–221.

"Bailey says he halted polygraph test of Simpson." *New York Times*, June 5, 2000, p. A25.

"Balk at lie detector tests." *Business Week*, February 11, 1956, p. 148.

"Bar lie-detector use by private firms?" *U.S. News & World Report* 100 (February 3, 1986): 81.

Barclay, Hartley. "Mass production on atom defense." *New York Times*, September 14, 1948, p. 46.

Barland, Gordon H. "The case for the polygraph in employment screening." *Personnel Administrator* 30 (September, 1985): 58+

Beach, Bennett H. "Blood, sweat and fears." *Time* 116 (September 8, 1980): 44.

Beard, Patricia A. "Truth or consequences." *Harper's Bazaar* 105 (October, 1972): 44, 46.

Beardsley, Tim. "Truth or consequences." *Scientific American* 281 (October, 1999): 21, 24.

"Bearers of false witness." *The Economist* 306 (March 12, 1988): 31–32.

Belair, Felix Jr. "G. E. official denies role in price-fixing." *New York Times*, April 28, 1961, pp. 1, 19.

Belt, John A. "The polygraph: a questionable personnel tool." *Personnel Administrator* 28 (August, 1983): 65–66+.

Belt, John A., and Peter B. Holden. "Polygraph usage among major U.S. corporations." *Personnel Journal* 57 (February, 1978): 80–86.

Bennett, James V. "A penal administrator views the polygraph." *Federal Probation* 24 (December, 1960); 40–44.

Benson, Philip G. and Paul S. Krois. "The polygraph in employment: some unresolved issues." *Personnel Journal* 58 (September, 1979): 616–621.

Berrien, F. K. "Lie trap." *Maclean's Magazine* 58 (September 1, 1945): 19–20, 22.

Biddle, Wayne. "The deception of detection." *Discover* 7 (March, 1986): 24–26+

"Big brother is listening." *Time* 99 (June 19, 1972): 91–92.

"Bitter beercott." *Time* 110 (December 26,1977): 15.

Bitterman, M. E., and F. L. Marcuse. "Minor studies from the psychological laboratory of Cornell University." *American Journal of Psychology* 60 (July, 1947): 407–412.

Boffey, Philip M. "Can lie detectors be trusted." *New York Times*, July 20, 1982, pp. C1, C6.

Bonner, Raymond. "A private lie detector test clears Condit, lawyer says." *New York Times*, July 14, 2001, p. A11.

Bonner, Raymond. "Lie detectors as corporate tools." *New York Times*, February 13, 1983, sec. 3, p. 4.

"Bonwit Teller ends lie-detector tests of store employees." *New York Times*, August 4, 1971, p. 35.

"Breathing test fails to discover lying." *New York Times*, August 30, 1925, sec. 7, p. 8.

Bright, Thomas L., and Charles J. Hollon. "State regulation of polygraph tests at the workplace." *Personnel* 62 (February, 1985): 50–56.

Browne, Malcolm W. "Voice lie detectors decried as unscientific." *New York Times*, November 13, 1979, pp. C1–C2.

Buckley, William F., Jr. "On the right." *National Review* 26 (August 16, 1974): 942–943.

Budiansky, Stephen. "Lie detectors." *Atlantic* 254 (October, 1984): 40+

Bunn, Geoffrey C. "The lie detector, 'Wonder Woman' and liberty: the life and work of William Moulton Marston." *History of the Human Sciences* 10 (February 1997): 91–119.

Burkey, Lee M. "Privacy, property and the polygraph." *Labor Law Journal* 18 (February, 1967): 79–89.

Burkhardt, Robert. "How to lie successfully to the lie detector." *The New Republic* 150 (May 6, 1964): 6–7.

Burnham, David. "House vote limits use of polygraph." *New York Times*, March 13, 1986, p. D4.

Burnham, David. "Psychologists' association says polygraphs are unreliable." *New York Times*, February 9, 1986, p. 26.

Burnham, David. "Reagan disputed by Rep. Brooks on polygraph directive's meaning." *New York Times*, January 9, 1986, p. A14.

"Business buys the lie detector." *Business Week*, February 6, 1978, pp. 100–101, 104.

"Business uses the lie detector." *Business Week*, June 18m 1960, pp. 98, 105–106.

"Butts of Georgia passes a lie test." *New York Times*, March 21, 1963, p. 15.

"Canceled order." *Time* 123 (February 27, 1984): 86.

Carley, William M. "To tell the truth." *Wall Street Journal*, October 17, 1961, pp. 1, 14.

Carlile, William M. "City uses polygraph to screen applicants." *Public Management* 41 (October, 1959): 237–238.

Carlson, Stephen C., Michael S. Pasano and Jeffrey A. Jannuzzo. "The effect of lie detector evidence on jury deliberations; an empirical study." *Journal of Police Science & Administration* 5 (June, 1977): 148–154.

Carlyle-Gordge, Peter. "The truth shall not be free." *Maclean's* 92 (April 23, 1979): 27–28.

"Catching criminals with lie-detector." *Literary Digest* 119 (February 23, 1935): 17.

Chambers, Ray W. "An argument against anti-polygraph legislation." *Security Management* 21 (July, 1977): 21–24.

Charlton, Linda. "Subjects of a survey are found to value privacy on the job." *New York Times*, February 12, 1978, p. 33.

"C.I.A. lie detector said to outwit itself." *New York Times*, November 24, 1964, pp. 1, 14.

"Cleared by truth serum." *New York Times*, November 29, 1935, p. 3.

Coad, George N. "Modern detective turning to science." *New York Times*, November 20, 1932, sec. 2, p. 6.

Cohn, Roy M. "Lie detectors can't be trusted." *New York Times*, December 29, 1985, sec. 4, p. 15.

Collier, James Lincoln. "Again, the truth machine." *New York Times*, November 25, 1973, p. 35+.

"The colour of lying." *The Economist* 345 (December 6, 1997): 29.

"Coogan and fiancée robbed in Chicago." *New York Times*, February 13, 1936, p. 25.

"Cops vs. lie detectors." *Newsweek* 81 (February 26, 1973): 52.

"Corporate lie detectors come under fire." *Business Week*, January 13, 1973, pp. 88, 90.

Cortesi, Arnaldo. "Use of lie detector assailed by Pontiff." *New York Times*, April 11, 1958, pp. 1, 12.

"Couple's 'I do' is verified by lie detector at wedding." *New York Times*, June 1, 1932, p. 18.

"Court bars 'proof' by lie detector." *New York Times*, November 30, 1938, p. 25.

"Crime at Columbia solved by science." *New York Times*, September 20, 1930, p. 5.

"Criminal justice." *Time* 88 (November 4, 1966): 70.

Cross, Jeffrey L. "The Employee Polygraph Protection Act of 1988: background and implications." *Labor Law Journal* 40 (October, 1989): 663–671.

Crowley, Carolyn H. "The truth about polygraph." *Security Management* 26 (December, 1982): 29–35.

Currivan, Gene. "Schools' drivers face screening." *New York Times*, March 18, 1961, p. 14.

Dale, Sarah Sturmon. "The brain scientist." *Time* 158 (November 26, 2001): 81.

Dales, Douglas. "Curb on lie test voted in Albany." *New York Times*, March 15, 1961, p. 41.

"The dangerous polygraph." *Scientific American* 209 (July, 1963): 66–67.

Davis, Philip W., and Pamela McKenzie-Rundle. "The social organization of lie-detector tests." *Urban Life* 13 (July/October, 1984): 177–205.

"Days may be numbered for polygraphs in the private sector." *Science* 232 (May 9, 1986): 705.

"Debategate: fluttering the President's men?" *Newsweek* 102 (August 29, 1983): 21.

"Decision barring lie-test upheld." *New York Times*, December 12, 1969, p. 88.

Demos, Raphael. "Lies and liars." *The Yale Review* 10 (January, 1921): 373–383.

Dennehy, Daniel T. "The status of lie detector tests in labor arbitration." *Labor Law Journal* 31 (July, 1980): 430–440.

"Detecting liars." *Literary Digest* 114 (October 22, 1932): 22.

"Don't use polygraph test for employee witch hunt." *Supermarketing* 34 (September, 1979): 46.

Dujack, Stephen R. "Polygraph fever." *The New Republic* 195 (August 4, 1986): 10–11.

Ellis, H. Ray. "Polygraph." *The Magazine of Bank Administration* 58 (September, 1982): 28+.

"Employee theft: plugging the leaks." *Drug Topics* 123 (April 6, 1979): 57–60+

Englade, Kenneth F. "The business of the polygraph." *Across the Board* 19 (October, 1982): 20–27.

Faller, Nancy. "A second assault." *The Progressive* 45 (July, 1981): 29.

"Fangs and polygraphs." *New Yorker* 24 (September 4, 1948): 18.

Feder, Barnaby J. "Court test for voice analyzer." *New York Times*, January 5, 1982, pp. D1, D6.

Feder, Barnaby J. "Truth and justice, by the blip of a brain wave." *New York Times*, October 9, 2001, p. F3.

"Federal agency enforcement activities." *Personnel Journal* 70 (August, 1991): 20.

"Federal lie-detectors." *New York Times*, February 29, 1964, p. 20.

"Federal polygraph law enacted." *Personnel Journal* 67 (August, 1988): 26.

Flaherty, Francis J. "Truth technology." *The Progressive* 46 (June, 1982): 30–35.

"Florida schools end use of polygraph tests." *New York Times*, April 23, 1986, p. A10.

"Fluttering the Pentagon." *Newsweek* 105 (January 14, 1985): 31.

Flynn, Laurie J. "Software turns computers into desktop lie detectors." *New York Times*, March 8, 1999, p. C4.

Franklin, Ben A. "Ex-homosexual got U.S. job back." *New York Times*, October 18,1964, p. 34.

Franklin, Ben A. "Lie detector's use by industry rises; rights peril feared." *New York Times*, November 22, 1971, pp. 1, 45.

French, Marilyn. "Oh, my employees are all honest." *American Business* 21 (August, 1951): 18–19, 49.

Frisch, Bruce H. "The great lie-detector hoax." *Science Digest* 54 (August, 1963): 23–29.

Frumkin, Paul. "Days Inn cuts employee theft with lie detector tests for all." *Hotel & Motel Management* 198 (January, 1983): 17, 29.

Gaillard, Frye. "Polygraphs and privacy." *The Progressive* 38 (September, 1974): 43–46.

Gallai, David. "Polygraph evidence in federal courts: should it be admissible?" *American Criminal Law Review* 36 no. 1 (Winter, 1999): 87–116.

Geis, Gilbert. "In scopolamine veritas." *Journal of Criminal Law & Criminology* 50 November/December, 1959): 347–357.

Giannelli, Paul G. "Polygraph evidence: post–Daubert." *Hastings Law Journal* 49 (April, 1998): 895–924.

Ginton, Avital. "A method for evaluating the use of polygraph in a real-life situation." *Journal of Applied Psychology* 67 (April, 1982): 131–137.

Golden, Frederic. "Lying faces unmasked." *Time* 153 (April 5, 1999): 52–53.

Goodman, Walter. "Lie detectors don't lie, but — ." *New York Times Magazine*, January 24, 1965, pp. 12–13+.

"Gov Hoffman urges lie-detector test." *New York Times*, January 24, 1936, p. 40.

Grafton, Kemit S. "The laws that apply to honesty testing." *Security Management* 29 (August, 1985): 33–36.

Graham, Fred P. "New voice lie detector device stirs controversy after gaining acceptance." *New York Times*, June 5, 1972, p. 30.

Greenberg, Eric Rolfe. "Workplace testing: results of a new AMA survey." *Personnel*, April, 1988, pp. 36–38+.

Greenhouse, Linda. "Justices find no inherent right to use lie-test evidence in trial." *New York Times*, April 1, 1998, p. A18.

Greenhouse, Steven. "Machines that try to read minds." *New York Times*, January 26, 1986, sec. 4, p. 4.

Gregory, Alex Lee. "Why workers steal." *Saturday Evening Post* 235 (November 10, 1962): 68–69, 71.

Grimes, John A. "Lie box battle." *Wall Street Journal*, April 18, 1965, pp. 1, 20.

"Guards to take lie test." *New York Times*, March 7, 1952, p. 6.

Guest, Ted. "When employers turn to lie detectors." *U.S. News & World Report* 94 (April 4, 1983): 78.

"Guilty by lie detector." *New York Times*, May 24, 1930, p. 2.

Gunn, Bruce. "Polygraph: hoax or panacea?" *Business Topics* 14 (Autumn, 1966): 46–57.

"Hauptman pleads for a truth test." *New York Times*, December 17, 1935, p. 3.

"Have you ever owed a bar bill?" *Harper's Magazine* 272 (March, 1986): 14–15, 17.

Hayden, Trudy. "Employers who use lie detector tests." *Business and Society Review* no. 41 (Spring, 1982): 16–21.

Herbert, W. "Study disputes Reagan lie detector policy." *Science News* 124 (November 5, 1983): 292.

Holden, Constance. "Lie detectors: PSE gains audience despite critics' doubt." *Science* 190 (October 24, 1975): 359–362.

Holden, Constance. "Panel seeks truth in lie detector debate." *Science* 291 (February 9, 2001): 967.

Honts, Charles R., David C. Raskin and John Kircher. "Mental and physical counter-measures reduce the accuracy of polygraph tests." *Journal of Applied Psychology* 79 (April, 1994): 252–259.

Horne, Louther S. "Lie detector gains in use." *New York Times*, July 28, 1935, sec. 4, p. 11.

"House panel scores lie detectors' use." *New York Times*, March 21, 1965, p. 76.

"House unit queries lie detector's use." *New York Times*, April 5, 1964, p. 77.

"How the lie detector is used in business." *The Office* 59 (April, 1964): 71–73+.

"The hunt for a better lie detector." *U.S. News & World Report* 114 (June 14, 1993): 49.

Iacono, W. G., and D. T. Lykken. "The validity of the lie detector: two surveys of scientific opinion." *Journal of Applied Psychology*. 82 (June, 1997): 426–433.

Inbau, Fred E. "Scientific evidence in criminal cases." *Journal of Criminal Law & Criminology* 24 (March, 1934): 1140–1158.

Inbau, Fred E. "The first polygraph." *Journal of Criminal Law & Criminology* 43 (January/February, 1953): 679–681.

Inbau, Fred E. "The lie-detector." *The Scientific Monthly* 40 (January, 1935): 81–87.

"It's a lie." *Nation's Business* 73 (December, 1985): 12–13.

"If you're asked to take a lie-detector test..." *Changing Times* 38 (July, 1984): 66–70.

Janson, Donald. "Ruby is examined by psychiatrists." *New York Times*, December 22, 1963, p. 22.

Janssen, John. "Deterring employee theft." *The Office* 80 (August, 1974): 58.

Jaycox, Thomas Hayes. "Lies—truths." *Scientific American* 161 (July, 1939): 8–9.

Jaycox, Thomas Hayes. "Scientific detection of lies." *Scientific American* 156 (June, 1937): 370–373.

Jeffreys, Daniel. "Getting down on 'The Farm.'" *World Press Review* 44 (March, 1997): 30–31.

Johnston, Alva. "The magic lie detector." *Saturday Evening Post* 216 (April 15, 1944): 9–11+.

Johnston, Alva. "The magic lie detector, pt. 2." *Saturday Evening Post* 216 (April 22, 1944): 26–27, 63.

Johnston, Alva. "The magic lie detector, pt. 3." *Saturday Evening Post* 216 (April 29, 1944): 20+.

Johnston, Laurie. "Bonwit Teller tests use of lie detectors." *New York Times*, July 27, 1971, p. 35.

Jordan, Nick. "Polygraph interview: blood, sweat and fears." *Psychology Today* 18 (June, 1984): 76.

Joyce, Christopher. "Lie detector." *Psychology Today* 18 (February, 1984): 6–8.

Jussim, Daniel. "Lies, damn lies—and polygraphs." *The Nation* 241 (December 21, 1985): 665+.

Kaempffert, Waldemar. "Science in review." *New York Times*, February 27, 1944, sec. 4, p. 9.

Kaempffert, Waldemar. "The week in science: detecting lies of criminals." *New York Times*, January 13, 1935, sec. 8, p. 4.

Kaler, Irving K. "A mole among the gerbils?" *Newsweek* 105 (March 11, 1985): 14–15.

Karr, Albert R. "Law limiting use of lie detectors is seen having widespread effect." *Wall Street Journal*, July 1, 1988, p. 19.

Keeler, Leonarde. "The lie-detector proves its usefulness." *Public Management* 22 (June, 1940): 163–166.

"Keeping up." *Fortune* 116 (December 7, 1987): 188.

Kifner, John. "State's attorney in Chicago makes photographs of Black Panther apartment available to newspaper." *New York Times*, December 12, 1969, p. 46.

Klein, Stanley. "The truth about lie-detectors in business." *New York Times*, October 29, 1972, sec. 3, p. 3.

Kleinmuntz, Benjamin, "Lie detectors fail the truth test." *Harvard Business Review* 63 (July/August, 1985): 36–37+.

Kleinmuntz, Benjamin, and Julian J. Szucko. "Lie detection in ancient and modern times." *American Psychologist* 39 (July, 1984): 766–776.

Kleinmuntz, Benjamin, and Julian J. Szucko. "On the fallibility of lie detection." *Law & Society Review* 17 no. 1 (1982): 85–104.

Kovach, Kenneth A. "The truth about employers' use of lie detectors." *Business and Society Review* 93 (Spring, 1995): 65–69.

Kubis, Joseph F. "Electronic detection of deception." *Electronics* 18 (April, 1945): 192+.

Kubis, Joseph F. "Instrumental, chemical, and psychological aids in the interrogation of witnesses." *Journal of Social Issues* 13 no. 2 (1957): 40–49.

Kurtz, Danell M. and Wayne R. Wells. "The Employee Polygraph Protection Act: the end of lie detector use in employment decisions?" *Journal of Small Business Management* 27 (October, 1989): 76–80.

Kwitny, Jonathan. "The dirty little secret of lie detectors." *Esquire* 89 (January, 1978): 73–76+.

Kwitny, Jonathan. "X plus Y equals Z." *Wall Street Journal*, May 4, 1977, p. 22.

Labaton, Stephen. "Business and the law." *New York Times*, November 28, 1988, p. D2.

Langer, Elinor. "Lie detectors: sleuthing by polygraph increasingly popular; claims of accuracy are unproved." *Science* 144 (April 24, 1964): 395–397+.

Larson, John A. *Lying and its Detection*. Montclair, NJ: Patterson Smith, 1969.

Larson, J. A. "Present police and legal methods for the determination of the innocence or guilt of the suspect." *Journal of Criminal Law & Criminology* 16 (August, 1925): 219–271.

"Law." *Newsweek* 11 (April 11, 1938): 26.

Lawrence, W. H. "McCarthy proposes lie detector test him and Army witnesses." *New York Times*, March 22, 1954, pp. 1, 19.

Lawrence, W. H. "Welch questions the authenticity of McCarthy data." *New York Times*, June 2, 1954, pp. 1, 19.

Leonard, William. "How the lie detector works." *Science Digest* 46 (July, 1959): 1–5.

Levey, A. B. *Polygraphy: An Evaluative Review.* London: HMSO, 1988.

Leviero, Anthony. "Morse denounces lie detector use." *New York Times,* January 18, 1952, p. 9.

Leviero, Anthony. "The truth machine." *New York Times Magazine,* February 10, 1952, pp. 40–41.

Leviero, Anthony. "U.S. tests staffs by lie detectors." *New York Times,* December 20, 1951, pp. 1, 20.

Levin, Colonel Maurice. "Lie detectors can lie!" *Labor Law Journal* 15 (November, 1964): 708–716.

Lewart, C. R. "Electronic lie detector tells it like it is." *Popular Science* 202 (May, 1973): 118–119.

Levitt, Eugene E. "Scientific evaluation of the lie detector." *Iowa Law Review* 40 (Spring, 1955): 440–458.

Lewis, A. A. "Looking for an honest man." *The Scientific Monthly* 49 (September, 1939): 267–275.

"Liar dice." *The Economist* 286 (March 26, 1983): 65.

"The liars." *New Statesman and Nation* 13 (March 6, 1937): 362–363.

"The lie-detector." *New Statesman and Nation* 1 (March 14, 1931): 100–101.

"The lie-detector." *Literary Digest* 111 (December 26, 1931): 35.

"Lie detector." *News-Week* 9 (March 13, 1937): 34.

"The lie detector." *New York Times,* August 8, 1954, sec. 4, p. 8.

"The lie detector as an instrument of social control." *New York Times,* August 3, 1980, sec. 4, p. 18.

"Lie-detector casts doubt on constable." *New York Times,* November 18, 1937, p. 19.

"Lie detector 'clears' Winkler." *New York Times,* November 26, 1931, p. 56.

"Lie detector doesn't." *Science News Letter* 49 (March 30, 1946): 207.

"Lie detector drafted in compensation case." *New York Times,* August 18, 1935, sec. 2, p. 1.

"Lie detector for Howe." *New York Times,* January 9, 1992, p. B15.

"Lie detector frees man in policy case." *New York Times,* February 27, 1944, p. 38.

"Lie detector gets $10 from 2 boys." *New York Times,* June 8, 1937, p. 27.

"The lie detector investigated." *Scientific American* 212 (May, 1965): 50.

"Lie detector pays." *American City* 54 (October, 1939): 15.

"Lie detector raises fine $75." *New York Times,* February 3, 1938, p. 26.

"Lie detector seals doom of murderer." *New York Times,* March 2, 1937, p. 44.

"Lie detector still used." *New York Times,* February 17, 1952, sec. 5, p. 8.

"Lie detector study in U.S. agencies set." *New York Times,* June 9, 1963, p. 48.

"Lie detector tells all." *Life,* November 21, 1938, p. 65.

"Lie detector test asked by prisoner." *New York Times,* January 6, 1935, sec. 4, p. 7.

"Lie detector test proves bloodhounds are liars." *New York Times,* November 11, 1935, p. 6.

"Lie detector tested in atom bomb plant." *New York Times,* March 14, 1946, p. 12.

"Lie detector tests." *New York Times,* June 28, 1966, p. 90.

"Lie detector tests on workers." *Business Week,* April 28, 1951, p. 24.

"Lie detector tests untrustworthy." *USA Today* 109 (February, 1981): 16.

"Lie detector tests urged by McCarthy." *New York Times,* December 22, 1951, p. 5.

"Lie –detector traps Philadelphia youth." *New York Times,* July 7, 1931, p. 6.

"Lie detector tried on bomb suspects." *New York Times,* July 25, 1931, p. 15.

"Lie detector use by U.S. disclosed." *New York Times,* February 23, 1964, p. 40.

"Lie detector used in Maine." *New York Times,* October 12, 1935, p. 3.

"Lie detector useful only in expert hands." *Scientific American* 156 (June, 1937): 390, 392.

"Lie detector verdict reversed." *New York Times*, May 20, 1949, p. 18.

"The lie-detector vs. civil rights." *Senior Scholastic* (Teacher's ed.) 59 (January 23, 1953): 5–7.

"Lie detectors." *Journal of the American Medical Association*, January 29, 1939, p. 3540.

"Lie detectors." *Business Week*, September 4, 1978, pp. 85–86.

"Lie detectors can make a liar of you." *Discover* 7 (June, 1986): 7.

"Lie detectors in the workplace: the need for civil actions against employers." *Harvard Law Review* 101 (February, 1988): 806–825.

"Lie detectors that don't work." *Literary Digest* 114 (November 19, 1932): 24.

"Lie gadgets." *Scientific American* 188 (June, 1953): 46, 48.

"Lie test is given in auto graft case." *New York Times*, November 17, 1937, p. 48.

"Lie tracer is honored." *New York Times*, January 21, 1933, p. 7.

"Life after polygraph? Here are responses from LP executives." *Stores* 71 (June, 1989): 64, 66.

Lissy, William E. "Labor law." *Supervision* 21 (June, 1959): 15.

Lissy, William E. "Labor law." *Supervision* 27 (October, 1965): 15.

"Love used as the key in lie detector test." *New York Times*, February 26, 1939, p. 38.

"The lying machine." *Newsweek* 61 (April 29, 1963): 82–83.

Lykken, David T. "Detecting deception." *Society* 22 (September/October, 1985): 34–39.

Lykken, David. "Detecting deception in 1984." *American Behavioral Scientist* 27 (March/April, 1984): 481–499.

Lykken, David T. "Psychology and the lie detector industry." *American Psychologist* 29 (October, 1974): 725–739.

Macdonald, Dwight. "The lie-detector era." *The Reporter* 10 (June 8, 1954): 10–18.

Macdonald, Dwight. "The lie-detector era, pt. 2." *The Reporter* 10 (June 22, 1954): 22–29.

Malakoff, David. "DOE polygraph plan draws fire." *Science* 285 (September 3, 1999): 1467.

Markson, Martin. "A reexamination of the role of lie detectors in labor relations." *Labor Law Journal* 22 (July, 1971): 394–407.

Marston, William Moulton. "Problems in living." *The Forum and Century* 100 (July, 1938): 30–32.

Marston, William Moulton. "Problems in living." *The Forum and Century* 100 (October, 1938): 168–169.

Matusewitch, Eric P. "Fear of lying: polygraphs in employment." *Technology Review* 83 (January, 1981): 10–11.

McEvoy, J. P. "The lie detector goes into business." *Reader's Digest* 38 (February, 1941): 69–72.

McInerney, Charles A. "Routine screening of criminal suspects by the polygraph (lie-detector) technique." *Journal of Criminal Law & Criminology* 45 (March/April, 1955): 736–742.

Meisler, Stanley. "Trial by gadget." *The Nation* 199 (September 28, 1964): 159–162+.

Messina, Robert. "Honesty tests: the best policy for supers?" *Progressive Grocer* 65 (September, 1986): 162–163+.

"Minimizes lie detector." *New York Times*, February 18, 1937, p. 3.

Morris, John D. "House unit opens polygraph study." *New York Times*, April 8, 1964, p. 17.

Morris, John D. "Services tell of monitoring lie-detector tests." *New York Times*, April 11, 1964, p. 6.

Murray, Kenneth. "Two simple ways to make a lie detector." *Popular Science* 128 (May, 1936): 63, 98.

Nagle, David E. "The polygraph shield." *Personnel Administrator* 34 (February, 1989): 18–19+.

"Neo-Diogenes uses tests, not lantern." *Nation's Business* 69 (June, 1981): 91.

"New lie detector traces eye moves." *New York Times*, September 7, 1940, p. 13.

"New lie detector was used on Green." *New York Times*, January 15, 1937, p. 3.

"New trap for liars." *Newsweek* 79 (June 19, 1972): 103.

"N.F.L. owners get lie detector test." *New York Times*, January 3, 1972, p. 36.

"Notes and legislation." *Harvard Law Review* 53 (December, 1939): 292–294.

"Notes on science." *New York Times*, April 12, 1953, sec. 4, p. 11.

"Now a furor over lie detectors in business." *U.S. News & World Report* 80 (March 8, 1976): 68–70.

"Osborne's challenge.: *New York Times*, December 28, 1984, p. A26.

"Our rostrum." *Forum and Century* 93 (March, 1935): sup. 17, 19.

"Outlaw lie-detector tests?" *U.S. News & World Report* 84 (January 30, 1978): 45–46.

Park, Robert L. "Liars never break a sweat." *New York Times*, July 12, 1999, p. A15.

Paterson, Richard D. "In favor of the polygraph." *Security Management* 29 (November, 1985): 47–52.

Pear, Robert. "As use of polygraph grows, suspects and lawyers sweat." *New York Times*, July 13, 1980, sec. 4, p. 2.

"Pentagon curbs lie detector use." *New York Times*, April 30, 1964, p. 24.

"Pentagon curtails polygraphs." *New York Times*, July 21, 1965, p. 21.

Peters, Robert B. "A hard look at voice lie detectors." *Security Management* 24 (October, 1980): 21, 23.

Phannenstein, Richard J. "The polygraph passes the test." *Security Management* 27 (August, 1983): 52, 59–60.

"Philadelphia's lie detector." *New York Times*, July 17, 1955, p. 48.

"Police heads hear hit-run solution." *New York Times*, August 30, 1938, p. 2.

"The polygraph." *Personnel Management* (UK) 16 (September, 1984): 70–71.

"The polygraph as a truth detector." *The Office* 72 (August, 1970): 39–41.

"The polygraph-happy Pentagon." *Saturday Evening Post* 236 (May 4, 1963): 82.

"Polygraph proof." *Literary Digest* 123 (March 13, 1937): 9–10.

"Polygraph tests." *Monthly Labor Review* 113 (August, 1990): 39–40.

"Polygraphs: should they be used in business?" *Drug Topics* 124 (December 12, 1980): 12, 14, 16.

"President creates U.S. policy panel on lie detector." *New York Times*, December 14, 1965, p. 35.

"Principal wrecks his lie detector." *New York Times*, September 25, 1936, p. 26.

Pringle, Henry. "How 'good' is any lie?" *Reader's Digest* 29 (November, 1936): 75–78.

"Privacy." *Business Week*, March 28, 1988, pp. 61–65.

"The PSE could prove your innocence." *Saturday Evening Post* 247 (July/August, 1975): 38–45.

"Psychogalvanometer." *Time* 28 (October 12, 1936): 44.

"Psychologists hold session at Vassar." *New York Times*, April 4, 1937, sec.2, p. 10.

Quindlen, Anna. "Polygraph tests for jobs: truth and consequences." *New York Times*, August 19, 1977, p. B1.

"Ramseys release results of polygraph tests." *New York Times*, May 25, 2000, p. A23.

Raymond, Jack. "U.S. study hostile to lie detectors." *New York Times*, June 18, 1964, p. 21.

"The reporter's notes." *The Reporter* 8 (June 9, 1953): 1–2.

"Reprieves continued for 6 Malmedy Nazis." *New York Times*, May 21, 1949, p. 3.

Rice, Berkeley. "Lie detection." *Psychology Today* 12 (July, 1978): 107.

Rice, Berkeley. "The new truth machines." *Psychology Today* 12 (June, 1978): 61–64+.

Richtel, Matt. "Some doubts on lie detection by phone." *New York Times*, January 26, 1998, p. D4.

"Rights unit seeks end to lie tests." *New York Times*, April 11, 1976, p. 38.

Risen, James. "Report faults Energy Dept. as failing to gain lab staff's support for tighter security." *New York Times*, June 28, 2000, p. A22.

Risen, James and Raymond Bonner. "F.B.I. dismisses Condit polygraph results." *New York Times*, July 21, 2001, p. A10.

"Rizzo is baffled at lie-test result." *New York Times*, August 15, 1973, p. 15.

Robinson, Henry Morton. "Science gets the confession." *Forum and Century* 93 (January, 1935): 15–18.

"Rockefeller signs moonlight bill." *New York Times*, May 4, 1967, p. 27.

Rose, Anton. "Psychophysical tests for falsehood." *Scientific American* 110 (June 20, 1914): 502.

Rosenbaum, David E. "Reagan insists budget cuts are way to reduce deficit." *New York Times*, January 8, 1986, p. B7.

Safire, William. "The sweat merchants." *New York Times*, February 29, 1988, p. A19.

Samuels, Dorothy J. "What if the lie detector lies?" *The Nation* 237 (December 3, 1983): 566, 568.

"Schultz: a-flutter." *Newsweek* 106 (December 30, 1985): 20.

"Science devises a painless '3rd degree.'" *Current Opinion* 76 (April, 1924): 474–475.

"Senator scores tax unit inquiry." *New York Times*, February 23, 1960, pp. 1, 16.

"7 begin in lie detection." *New York Times*, April 13, 1960, p. 19.

Shabecoff, Philip. "Thievery rising in U.S. industry." *New York Times*, June 16, 1963, sec. 3, pp. 1, 9.

"Should we use lie detectors?" *Beijing Review* 44 (September 6, 2001): 23–25.

"Slayer's 'saviors' fail." *New York Times*, May 7, 1950, p. 53.

Smith, Burke M. "The polygraph." *Scientific American* 216 (January, 1967): 25–31.

Smith, R. Jeffrey. "Dubious validity." *Science* 224 (June 15, 1984): 1217.

"Spurn lie detector, detectives demoted." *New York Times*, July 13, 1938, p. 4.

"State bar to fight for civil liberties." *New York Times*, January 27, 1939, p. 7.

Steinberg, Julius. "Electric lie detector." *Popular Science* 136 (April, 1940): 144–145.

Sternbach, Richard A, Lawrence A. Gustafson and Ronald L. Colier. "Don't trust the lie detector." *Harvard Business Review* 40 (November, 1962): 127–134.

Stetson, Daman. "Drive on lie tests started by labor." *New York Times*, February 26, 1965, p. 20.

"The stress test — who's lying." *Newsweek* 82 (July 23, 1973): 19.

Theeke, Herman A. and Tina M. Theeke. "The truth about arbitrators' treatment of polygraph tests." *Arbitration Journal* 42 (December, 1987): 23–32.

"Theft control through lie detection." *Restaurant Management* 90 (March, 1962): 46–47+.

Timm, Howard W. "The efficacy of the psychological stress evaluator in detecting deception." *Journal of Police Science and Administration* 11 (March, 1983): 62–68.

"To tell the truth." *The Nation* 234 (February 6, 1982): 132.

Trovillo, Paul V. "A history of lie detection." *Journal of Criminal Law & Criminology* 29 (March/April, 1939): 848–881.

Trovillo, Paul V. "A history of lie detection, part 2." *Journal of Criminal Law & Criminology* 30 (May/June, 1939): 104–119.

Trussell, C. P. "Hiss bars lie-detector test." *New York Times*, August 20, 1948, pp. 1, 8.

"Truth or consequences." *Time* 101 (March 19, 1973): 73–74.

"Truth-serum frees two." *New York Times*, March 10, 1935, p. 16.

"Truth tests." *Time* 122 (August 29, 1983): 17.

"Truth wanted." *Time* 43 (January 10, 1944): 60.

"Unfortunately, New York State doesn't ban use of polygraphs." *New York Times*, July 9, 1986, p. A26.

"Unions score use of lie detector." *New York Times*, February 15, 1970, p. 76.

"Uproar over news leak and lie detectors." *U.S. News & World Report* 54 (April 15, 1963): 8.

"U.S. aide says 3 took C.I.A. lie tests." *New York Times*, May 23, 1973, p. 29.

"Use lie detectors on defense workers?" *U.S. News & World Report* 98 (February 25, 1985): 44.

"W. Va. pharmacists rebel against polygraph testing." *American Druggist* 169 (June 15, 1974): 38.

Walters, C. Glenn, and Bruce Gunn. "Appraising retailers' use of the polygraph." *Journal of Retailing* 43 no. 4 (Winter, 1968): 10–21.

Warren, Virginia Lee. "No fibbers wanted." *New York Times*, December 4, 1970, p. 52.

Washnis, George J. "Polygraph aid in choosing policemen and firemen." *Public Management* 43 (June, 1961): 134.

Weaver, Warren Jr. "Anti-usury bill is voted by Assembly." *New York Times*, May 25, 1965, p. 33.

Westbrook, Lisa. "Polygraph update." *Security Management* 31 (July, 1987): 49–51.

"What is truth." *Newsweek* 64 (December 7, 1964): 27.

"What the lie detector really detects." *New York Times*, March 29, 1953, sec. 4, p. 13.

Whitelaw, Kevin and David E. Kaplan. "To tell the truth." *U.S. News & World Report* 130 (June 11, 2001): 18–22.

"Wichita's use of the lie detector." *American City* 51 (December, 1936): 91.

Wilson, Jim. "Truth, lies and polygraphs." *Popular Mechanics* 178 (October, 2001): 42, 44.

Wise, Recascino Lois, and Steven J. Charvat. "Polygraph testing in the public sector: the status of state legislation." *Public Personnel Management* 19 (Winter, 1990): 381–390.

"A witness in Capital." *New York Times*, May 14, 1949, p. 5.

Witt, Linda. "The truth about lie detectors, says David Lykken, is that they can't detect a lie." *People* 15 (May 11, 1981): 75–76, 79.

"Would you dare take these tests?" *Look*, December 6, 1938, pp. 16–17.

"Yes to lie detector tests for private employees." *Nation's Business* 63 (August, 1975): 16.

Zelicoff, Alan P. "Polygraph and the national labs: dangerous ruse undermines national security." *Skeptical Inquirer* 25 (July/August, 2001): 21–23.

Index

Abrams, Robert 144, 152–153
Academy for Scientific Interrogation 57
accuracy 15, 39, 42, 43, 65, 77, 81, 85, 89, 96, 104, 113, 125, 131, 137, 151, 153, 155, 174
Africa 5
Aftergood, Steven 174
Agnew, Spiro 129
Air Force, U.S. 94–95
Akin, David 182
Akron, Ohio 92
Albert, Daniel G. 92
Allen, R. E. 25
Alpher, Victor S. 135
Alsop, Stewart 97
American Civil Liberties Union (ACLU) 115, 132, 157
American Federation of Labor (AFL-CIO) 91, 92, 131
American Medical Association 163
American Polygraph Association 105
American Psychological Assoc. 162, 179
Ames, Aldrich 172–173, 175
Andrews, Bert 61
Andrews, Lori 158
arbitration, labor 59, 74–75, 127, 151–152
Arizona Bank 143
Army, U.S. 77, 101–102

Arther, Richard 89, 95–96, 117, 132
Associated Research Inc. 57
Astor, Saul 115, 119
Atomic Energy Commission 52–54, 78
automobile insurance claims 122
Aylesworth, M. H. 60

Backster, Cleve 89, 93
Bailey, F. Lee 151, 176
Baker, James 150
Baker, Jerry 132
bankruptcy 122
banks 31–33, 165
Barefoot, J. Kirk 92, 102, 116
Barlan, George 154
Bayh, Birch 128
Beach, Bennett 141
Beard, Patricia 131
Beardsley, Tim 173
Beary, John 160
Bell, Allan 102–105
Belli, Melvin M. 95
Belt, John 123–124, 145
Bennett, James 96
Bennett, Rick 107
Benson, Philip 125–126
Benussi, Vittorio 14
Berger, Harriet 34
Biddle, Wayne 162, 164
biofeedback 133
Black Panthers 95–96
Blanton, Richard L. 135
Blews, Don 161

blood pressure 12, 17–18; systolic 15
Boccaccio 6–7
body odor 101
Bohlen, Charles 62
Bonwit Teller 113–114
brain wave monitoring 180–182
Bramson, Leo 82
Braude, J. M. 28
Brennan, Michael 25
Brink's robbery 49
brokerage firms 118
Brooks, Jack 128, 140
Brooks, Jay 164
Brotherhood of Electrical Workers 164
Brown, Booker 150
Browne, Malcolm 107–108
Bryant, Paul (Bear) 94
Buck, Frank 60
Buckley, William F. 130
Burger King 117
Burkey, Lee 75, 98–99, 114–115
Burnett, George 94
Burtt, Harold 15
bus drivers, school 93
Bush, George 154
business losses 33, 57, 81, 85, 88, 114, 116, 141, 154
business usage 32–34, 57–60, 80–91, 111–126, 141–149
Butts, Wallace 94

Camiel, Peter 130
Camis, B. Francis 180

Canada 66, 149
Cannon, Bill R. 122–123
Caputo, Rudolph 118, 130
Carley, William 83
Carlile, William 56
Carlucci, Frank 136
Carroll, Phillip 130
Casey, William 150
Central Intelligence
  Agency (CIA) 54, 55,
  115, 128, 171–172, 181,
  182
challenges, public 60–63,
  93–94, 150–151
Chambers, Ray 120–121
Chambers, Whittaker 60–
  61
character reform 36
Chatham, Russell 52, 56
cheating, tests of 64
Chicago 70
Chicago Junior Assoc. of
  Commerce 22–23
Chicago Municipal Court
  51
Chicago Police Depart-
  ment 40
China 6, 175–176
civil rights 75, 156
Civil Service Commission
  54
civil service usage 26
civil suits against 100, 108
Civiletti, Benjamin 136
Coad, George N. 43
Coghlan, John 96
Cohn, Roy M. 62, 161–162
Cold War era 51–57
Colden, Charles S. 29
Coleman, Roger Keith
  168–169
Colgan, Edward J. 23
Collier, James 118
color, psychology of 39
Communism 60–61, 67
computer software, de-
  ception 179–180
Condit, Gary 17
Coogan, Jackie 35
Coors, William 122
Coors brewery 121–122
Coppage, Allen 121
Cornell University 50
counseling 32, 35–36
court acceptance 17, 27,
  28–30, 44, 50–51, 73–74,
  99–100, 103, 135, 169–171

criminal case usage 23
critics 19, 34, 46
Crosland, H. R. 11
Cross, Jeffrey 167
Crowley, Carolyn 144, 149
Curran, Edward 172

Dark Ages 7
Davis, Phillip 159
Davis, Walter 157–158
Day, Clayton 118–119
Days Inn 143
Dearman, H. B. 87
death row 30, 34–35, 51,
  168–169
Deception Tests Associ-
  ates 57–58
Deevey, Robert 148
Defense Department, U.S.
  137–140
Defoe, Daniel 8
Dektor Counterintelli-
  gence and Security
  102–105, 109–110
Delorean, John 151
Demos, Raphael 3
Dennehy, Daniel 151–152
deterrent effect 125
Detroit Police Depart-
  ment 134
Devine, David 154
Dicks, Norman 172
Di Lillo, Alfonse 50
Diogenes 3–4
disarmament treaty 79
Donahue, Charles 22
Donchin, Emanuel 182
donkey tail test 7
Douglas, Joseph 113
drug distributors 82, 92,
  155
drug stores 125
drug testing 147–148
drugs to detect deception
  37–39
dry mouth 6
Dujack, Stephen 163
Dunham, B. 118

Eames, E. Clayton 23
Earnest, Peter 181
effectiveness studies 53,
  106
electrical manufacturers
  price fixing 93
Ellis, H. Ray 143
employee control 54, 90

Employee Polygraph Pro-
  tection Act (EPPA)
  165–167, 178
employee screening: fed-
  eral 52–54; periodic
  81–85
employee terminations
  31, 74–75, 81–82, 86, 92,
  124, 135, 143, 146, 147
employee theft, tests for
  119–120
Energy Department, U.S.
  173
Engelhard, Sheldon 166
Englade, Kenneth 144
Erasistratus 4
error rates 137, 157, 160,
  162–163, 165
Ervin, Sam, Jr. 98, 116,
  127–128
Europe 149
evaluation of 15–16
Evanston, Illinois 75–76

Faller, Nancy 134
Farwell, Lawrence 181–
  182
fear 12
Feder, Barnaby 181
Federal Aviation Agency
  76
Federal Bureau of Investigation (FBI) 27, 49, 79,
  136, 150, 177, 181
federal government 51–
  57, 76–80, 136–141, 171–
  175
Ferguson, Ron 181
Ferris, Walter A. 25
Fine, William 113–114
fire ordeals 5–6
Flaherty, Francis 157
food ordeals 6–7
food retailers 145–146
football owners 129
football players 129
foreign nations usage 70,
  149–150, 156, 175
Forte, Vincent 29
Franklin, Ben 114
Franklin, Robert Walker
  38
Fremgen, Charles 28
French, Marilyn 58–59
Fries, Beall & Sharp 57
Frisch, Bruce 97
Fuller, Fred 102, 105

Gaillard, Frye 119
Gallagher, Cornelius 76–77
Gallai, David 170–171
Galton, Francis 10
galvanic skin response 12, 14, 20, 41
galvanometer 23, 65–66
Geis, Gilbert 38
Gelb, Ed 151
geography 177
Germann, John D., Jr. 23
Gianneli, Paul 170
Gilles, Timothy 144
Gilpatric, Roswell 94
Goddard, Calvin 34
Goodman, Walter 98
Grable, Betty 35
Graham, Fred 102
Greenberg, Eric 147
Gregory, Alex L. 57, 84
Grimes, John 91–92
Gunn, Bruce 88–89

Hanrahan, Edward 95
Harrison, Jack 70
Hart, William L. 134
Harvey, Jay 161
Hatch, Orrin 164
Hauptmann, Bruno Richard 34–35
Hayden, Trudy 121, 142
Heavy, Edward 112
Heisse, John 107
high school usage 49
Hinduism 4
Hiss, Alger 60–61
HIV testing 147–148
Hoffman, Harold 34–35
Holden, Constance 104
Holden, Peter 123–124
Holmes, Ray 48–49
Home, George K. 19
homosexuality 76, 112
Hoover, J. Edgar 27, 62, 95, 129
Horne, Louther 44–45
Horner, Henry 28, 30
Horowitz, Toby 148
Horvath, Frank 162
House, Robert Ernest 37–38
House Committee on Government Operations 76–78, 128
Houston, Texas 171
Hovath, Frank 106

Hoving, Walter 113
Howe, Steve 176
Hund, Vaclaw 34
hype 16, 23, 43, 65, 67–68, 106–107, 109
hypnotism 39

Iacono, W. G. 178–179
Illinois Retail Merchants Association 88–89
Inbau, Fred 27–28, 31, 77–78
infallibility 7, 16, 34, 44, 58–59, 64, 86, 96, 99, 114, 128, 132, 157
innocent people 26, 84, 88–89
Institute for Defense Analysis 79
insurance premiums 33
Internal Revenue Service (IRS) 76
iron, hot 5–6
Irving, Clifford 130
Israel 149

Jack Eckerd Corporation 143–144
Janssen, John 127
Japan 149
Jasen, Matthew 74
Jaspan, Norman 88
Jaycox, Thomas 24, 25
Jeffreys, Daniel 171
jewelry companies 121
jewelry industry 157
John E. Reid and Associates 58, 125
Johnson, Harry 145
Johnson, Lyndon 80
Johnston, Alva 63–65
Johnston, Philip H. 38
Jones, David C. 137
Jones, Edgar A., Jr. 125
Journal of the American Medical Association 46
Jung, C. G. 12
Juska, Edward 28
Jussim, Daniel 161, 163
Justice Department, U.S. 136, 167

Kaempffert, Waldemar 40
Kahn, Arnold 162
Kaler, Irving 160
Kaufman, Victor 165–166
Keeler, Leonarde 18–20,

22–23, 25–26, 27–28, 30, 35, 46–47, 51–52, 60
Keener, Lee R. 83
Kefauver, Estes 94
Kelly, Michael 171–172
Kemper Corporation 122
Kennedy, Edward M. 164
Kennedy, John F. 94
Kenny, Raymond 28–29
Kentucky 91
KGB (Russian) 97
King, John 129
King Solomon 4
Kirkpatrick, Jeanne 162
Klein, Stanley 115
Kleinmuntz, Benjamin 157, 160–161
Klump, Carl 153–154
Knight, J. Edward 28
Korth, Fred 94–95
Kovach, Kenneth 178
Kradz, Michael 107
Krogh, Egil, Jr. 129
Krois, Paul 125–126
Krupa, William 123
Kubis, Joseph 50, 65, 78, 97, 104
Kupec, Edward 105
Kwitny, Jonathan 132

labor agreements 157–158
Labor Department, U.S. 178
Lacey, John 97
Landis, Carney 19
Langer, Elinor 91, 96–97
Larson, John 17–19, 21–22, 43, 46–47
Laverne, Thomas 92
laws, federal 127–128, 163–167
laws, state, licensing operators 82, 89–90, 91, 115, 117, 120, 123
laws, state, regulation of usage 91, 100, 115, 117, 120, 123, 177
Leckey, Prescott 11
Leedy, Charles B. 38–39
Lehman, John F. 137
Leonard, William 66
Levey, A. B. 149–150
Leviero, Anthony 53–55, 67–68
Levin, Colonel Maurice 73–74

Levy, Chandra 177
liars, demeanor of 4
Li'l General Stores 120–121
Lilly, John C. 57
Lindberg, George 78
Lindbergh, Charles 34–35
Linder, George 87
Lissy, William 59
Lloyd's of London 33
lobbying, by users of 92–93, 127, 157, 164
Lombroso, Cesare 11–12
Los Alamos National Laboratory 172–174
Lovett, Robert A. 54–55
Lowell, Abbe 177
Lowell, Leonard 86
loyalty investigations 53
lying and physiological responses 14–15, 17, 35, 155
lying, physical manifestations of 8–9
lying, place in society 3, 36
Lykken, David 106, 119, 131–132, 142, 156–157, 178–179

Macdonald, Dwight 52, 68–69
Mackenzie, James 13
Magruder, Jeb Stuart 129
Manitoba Chamber of Commerce 129
Manitoba Human Rights Commission 128–129
Marcy, Lynn 144
Markson, Martin 127
marriage ceremony 34
Marsh, Howard W. 119
Marston, William Moulton 15–17, 32, 34–37, 47
Mastersen, John 50
Mathews, J. H. 35
Matusewich, Eric 156
McCarthy, Joseph 61–63
McClure, Theodore, R. 51
McClure, William 83
McDonald's 117
McEvoy, J. P. 32–34
McInerney, Charles A. 49
McKenzie-Rundle, Pamela 159
Meany, George 91
media presentation 11, 18,

32–34, 42–45, 53–54, 63–66, 67–68, 88–89, 97–99, 103–104
medical histories 174–175
Meisler, Stanley 97
Messina, Robert 145–146
Middle Ages 7
military usage 78–80, 136
Mills, Kenneth 144–145
Moffett, James A. 60
moral issues 68–69
Moreland, Gray 32
Morse, Wayne 54–55
Moss, John E. 77–80
Mosso, A. 11–12
motion pictures 60
Muir, Duncan 166
Mulrooney, Edward P. 45–46
municipal governments 56–57, 75–76, 171
Munsterberg, Hugo 12–13
murder cases 17, 23, 29, 30, 34–35, 51, 168–169
muscle tensing 69

Nagle, David 166–167
Nardi, Steve 176
NASA 78–79
National Academy of Sciences 179
National Research Council 15
National Retail Merchants Assoc. 167
National Security Agency (NSA) 55–56, 106, 128, 138
National Training Center of Lie Detection 89
Nebraska Supreme Court 50–51
New Mexico 91
New York City 70
New York City Police Department 98
New York State 92, 127
Nicholson, Harold J. 173
Nixon, Richard 60–61, 112, 128
Nowak, John 30

Oak Ridge (Tenn.) weapons facility 52–54
O'Brien, John 29, 146–147
Office of Technology As-

sessment (OTA) 137–138
Operations Research Office 55
operator competence 71, 77–78, 79, 96, 107, 123
operator mystification 95–96
operator training 55, 70, 89, 98, 103, 140–141
operators, number of 42, 96, 98, 99, 114, 122, 141, 144
operators' role 25, 42, 69–70, 87, 138, 156, 159–160
ordeals 4–8; faked 8
Orlansky, Jesse 79
Osborne, Tom 150
Oswald, Lee H. 95

Pankin, Peter 166
Papa Gino's of America 146–147
paranoia, collective 51
Park, Robert 172
paternity suits 51
Paterson, Richard 155
Pear, Robert 136
Pentagon 136–137, 157
Personnel Research Inc. 58
Peters, Robert 109
Petersen, Henry E. 129
Phannenstill, Richard 154
pharmacists 118
Philadelphia Police Department 49
Phillips, Michael 162–163
physical measurements 19
pick-a-card gambit 14, 41–42, 159
Pierce, Ralph 51–52
police brutality 18–19
police interrogations 21–22
police officers, as subjects 112
police usage 17–18, 19, 22, 23, 24–29, 39–40, 48–49, 98, 103, 134
political usage 30
Polk County (Florida) school 148–149
polygraph: for police usage 20; home-made 45, 111; non deception

detection 13; sham 22, 31–32; statistics 81
Pontifex, Ed 84
Pope Pius XII 71
Popular Science 45, 111
Possony, Stefan 79–80
pre-employment screening 31, 55, 57, 82, 87, 108, 112–120, 164
Pringle, Henry 41
prisoners of war, U.S. 51–52
privacy, right of 30, 75, 79, 87, 90, 102, 115, 120, 154
psychological stress evaluators (PSEs) 101–110
public school usage 31–32
Publix Supermarkets 146
Puccio, Thomas P. 136
Pugh, Warren E. 19
pulse rates 12

questioning, political/sexual/drug-related/personal 53–57, 68, 77, 80, 86, 112–117, 120, 121–122, 128, 130, 141, 172
Quindlen, Anna 121

racism 145, 161
Ramos, Peter 157
Ramsey, JonBenet 176
Ramspeck, Robert 54
rape cases 26, 50, 134–135
Rappaport, Joseph 30
Raskin, David 164
Reagan, Ronald 136, 137, 139, 140, 165
refusers 25, 58, 74, 76, 87, 121, 127, 136, 152, 173
Reid, John 114, 156–157
reliability 145
religion 4–8
Renzelman, David 175
respiration 14
response time 11
restaurants 83–84
retailing 57, 90, 166
Reuss, Henry 79
Rice, Berkeley 105–107
rice ordeal 6
Richardson, Bill 172
Richardson, Drew 181
Rite-Aid company 118
Rizzo, Frank 130
Robert Half International 146

Robinson, Henry Morton 43–44
Rockefeller, Nelson 91, 93
Rogers, William P. 129
Rollins, Norma 145
Rose, Anton 10, 14–15
Rosenberg, Aaron 108
Rosenfeld, J. Peter 182
Rothman, Howard B. 108
Roy, David 23
Rozelle, Peter 129
Ruby, Jack 95
Ruth, Bud 146

Safire, William 163
Saints Roller Skating Centers 128–129
Samuels, Dorothy 138
Sandacz, Gene 112
Saxe, Leonard 138
Schine, G. David 62
Schneider, Albert 13–14
school usage 148–149
scientific crime investigation 40
scopolamine 37–38
Scott, Orlando, F. 35
Seattle Police Department 112
security risks, number of 56
security testing 77
Segal, Tamir 180
self-incrimination 27, 30, 75
7-Eleven stores 118
Shabecoff, Philip 86–87
Shack, Barbara 132
Shafroth, Will R. 32
Shockley, William 130
showmanship 16–17
Shultz, George 140
Sickler, David 122
Silas, Herman, Jr. 136
Simpson, O. J. 176
Skolnick, Jerome 99, 155–156
Smith, Burke 98
Smith, M. M. 87
Smith, Robert Ellis 158
Smith, William K. 119
Snyder, Lemoyne 51
social control function 31, 45, 66, 86, 96, 153, 155–156, 159–161, 174
Society for Psychophysiological Research 179

sodium amytal 37
Sophocles 6
Spanish Inquisition 7
Speakes, Larry 150
spies 97, 171–172, 173
Stanley, Homer 28
State Department, U.S. 54, 56, 129
Steinburg, Julius 45
Sternbach, Richard 85
Stewart, John 148–149
Sticker, B. 12
Stilwell, Richard 139–140
Stockton, California 56–57
Sullivan, Charles P. 23
Summers, Walter G. 23, 28, 35, 41, 46–47
Sunbeam Corporation 59
Supreme Court, U.S. 169–170
surveys, opinion 158, 179
surveys 118, 123–124, 132, 145, 146, 147
Sutherland, Rob 182
Szucko, Julian 157

Taft, Robert 62
Talley, Lawrence W. 143
Tastet, W. J. 57
Taylor, Roy 81
terrorism 181
testees: class distinctions 95 105, 150, 158; harassment of 56, 98, 141–142, 174; rejection rates 75–76, 88, 90, 116, 118, 132, 143; strategies used by 69, 133, 139–140, 157, 178
tests: costs of 57 87, 116, 121, 142; number given 53, 87, 90, 98, 114, 117, 121, 137–138, 144, 158; paper and pencil 116, 145–146, 153–154; results of failure 147–148; voluntary 53, 55, 90–91, 113, 120–121, 126, 136, 142, 143–144
theatrical usage 16–17, 34–37, 60
Theobald, John 93
third degree 13, 19
Thomas, Clarence 169–170
Tielsch, George 112

Tiffany jewelers 113
Timm, Howard 109–110
Tiner, Mike 142
Tobin, William 27–28
Towle, Max 22
trade unions 59, 90, 91–
  92, 131
Trovillo, Paul 70–71
Truman, Harry 60
truth drugs 37–39

Underwood, Richard 7–
  8, 133
unemployment benefits 74
unionization rates 177
United Kingdom 149–150
United Rubber Workers
  92

Vaira, Peter F. 136
Vance, Cyrus 80
Vickers, Ronald 126
Vietnam War 78, 101

Vinson, Arthur F. 94–94
voice analyzers 101–110
Voikos, Linda 141–142
Vollmer, August 17–18,
  27–28

Walters, C. Glenn 90
Warren Commission 95
Washnis, George 75–76
water ordeals 4–5
Watergate hearings 103
Weinberger, Casper 137
Welch, Joseph N. 62–63
Wendy's Restaurants 178
Weschler, James 61
White, Edward F. 119
Wichita, Kansas, Police
  24–25
Wilder, Douglas 168–169
Willard, Richard K. 138–
  139
Williams, Douglas Gene
  162

Williams, John J. 76
Williams, Pat 163
Wilson, Charles M. 34
Wilson, Jim 175, 181
Wilson, O. W. 24
Winkler, Gus 22
Winter, J. E. 46
witches 5
Wohl, Jerry 123
Woodward, Bob 150
word association 10–11,
  13
workmen's compensation
  30, 123
Wundt, Wilhelm 10

Zale Corporation 116,
  145
Zayre Corporation 145
Zelicoff, Alan P. 174–175
Zonn, Lincoln 87, 116,
  122, 126
Zuckert, Eugene 94–95